AF361357

FILIPINO MIGRANTS AND THE CANADIAN DREAM

Governing Mobility in a Fast-Food Chain

Filipino Migrants and the Canadian Dream explores the power of the Canadian dream and how this social imaginary is leveraged by various institutional actors across transnational networks to govern mobility and work in the bottom tiers of a globalized labour market. The book focuses specifically on the migration management and governance of skilled Filipino workers recruited for entry-level fast-food positions in Western Canada. Drawing on ethnographic fieldwork conducted in both Western Canada and the Philippines, the book examines how migration institutions and social actors shape migrant aspirations, constructing cultural narratives of nations that influence people's decisions to migrate.

Using Tim Hortons – a beloved Canadian institution – as a case study, the book illustrates how the Canadian dream and its implied promises are harnessed (inadvertently) at different stages of the migration process to propel mobility or fulfil profit-driven goals. The analysis highlights how a range of actors – states, corporations, employers, recruiters, diaspora communities, and migrants themselves – contribute to the creation and circulation of these dreams. Ultimately, the book demonstrates that the social imaginary must be unpacked across global circuits, spaces, and scales to fully understand how temporary labour programs operate within the context of a neoliberal economy.

GERALDINA POLANCO is an associate professor of sociology at McMaster University.

Filipino Migrants and the Canadian Dream

Governing Mobility in a Fast-Food Chain

GERALDINA POLANCO

UNIVERSITY OF TORONTO PRESS
Toronto Buffalo London

© University of Toronto Press 2025
Toronto Buffalo London
utppublishing.com
Printed in Canada

ISBN 978-1-4875-0293-5 (cloth)   ISBN 978-1-4875-1632-1 (EPUB)
ISBN 978-1-4875-2220-9 (paper)   ISBN 978-1-4875-1631-4 (PDF)

Library and Archives Canada Cataloguing in Publication

Title: Filipino migrants and the Canadian dream : governing mobility in a
    fast-food chain / Geraldina Polanco.
Names: Polanco, Geraldina, author.
Description: Includes bibliographical references and index.
Identifiers: Canadiana (print) 20250229579 | Canadiana (ebook) 20250229625 |
    ISBN 9781487502935 (cloth) | ISBN 9781487522209 (paper) | ISBN
    9781487516314 (PDF) | ISBN 9781487516321 (EPUB)
Subjects: LCSH: Fast food restaurants – Canada – Employees. | LCSH:
    Filipinos – Employment – Canada. | LCSH: Foreign workers – Canada. |
    LCSH: Immigrants – Canada – Economic conditions.
Classification: LCC HD8039.H82 C3 2025 | DDC 331.7/616479571 – dc23

Cover design: Michel Vrana
Cover image: Broadbent Studio

We wish to acknowledge the land on which the University of Toronto Press
operates. This land is the traditional territory of the Wendat, the Anishnaabeg,
the Haudenosaunee, the Métis, and the Mississaugas of the Credit First
Nation.

This book has been published with the help of a grant from the Federation
for the Humanities and Social Sciences, through the Awards to Scholarly
Publications Program, using funds provided by the Social Sciences and
Humanities Research Council of Canada.

University of Toronto Press acknowledges the financial support of the
Government of Canada, the Canada Council for the Arts, and the Ontario Arts
Council, an agency of the Government of Ontario, for its publishing activities.

Contents

Figures and Tables

Figures

Tables

Abbreviations

AHLA   Alberta Hotel and Lodging Association
AINP   Alberta Immigration Nominee Program
BPO   business process outsourcing
CFIB   Canadian Federation of Independent Business
CFO   Commission on Filipinos Overseas
CLB   Canadian Language Benchmark
CRFA   Canadian Restaurant and Foodservices Association
DOLE   Department of Labor and Employment
E-LMO Expedited Labour Market Opinion Project
ELSS   Entry Level and Semi-Skilled
ESDC   Employment and Social Development Canada
FOI   Freedom of Information
ILAB   International Labor Affairs Bureau
IMP   International Mobility Program
IRCC   Immigration, Refugees and Citizenship Canada
IRPR   Immigration and Refugee Protection Regulations
LCP   Live-In Caregiver Program
LMIA   Labour Market Impact Assessment
LSP   Low-Skilled Pilot
LSS   Low-Skilled Stream
NGOs   non-governmental organizations
PDOS   Pre-Departure Orientation Seminar
PEOS   pre-employment orientation seminars
PLMR   precarious labour migration regime
POEA   Philippine Overseas Employment Administration
POLO   Philippine Overseas Labour Office
PNP   Provincial Nominee Program
OEC   Overseas Employment Certificate
OFW   overseas foreign workers

OWWA	Overseas Workers Welfare Administration
SAWP	Seasonal Agricultural Workers Program
TESDA	Technical Education and Skills Development Authority
TFWP	Temporary Foreign Worker Program
TFWPA	Temporary Foreign Worker Protection Act
TMWs	temporary migrant workers
TMWPs	temporary migrant worker programs

Acknowledgments

The production of this book stems back several years, a duration in which I have accrued too many debts to adequately acknowledge. It began in the Sociology Department at the University of British Columbia (UBC). And since then, it has accompanied me across multiple educational institutions, academic titles, and cities. I am appreciative of and indebted to many individuals throughout this journey.

At UBC, Drs. Jennifer Chun, Gillian Creese, Sylvia Fuller, and Geraldine Pratt were instrumental in shaping the project. They were generous with their feedback and edifying in their guidance, establishing a lasting impact. I owe a special thanks to Dr. Jennifer Chun. The road to academe can be an arduous journey for underrepresented students. Jennifer chose to believe in me – even when I didn't believe in myself – granting me the fortitude to complete this project. This book, and my place in academe, would not have been possible without Dr. Chun's enduring support.

I am grateful to others during my time at UBC whose mentorship and comradery contributed to this monograph. Dr. Amy Hanser introduced me to research at the intersection of culture and work, a line of inquiry that has remained central to my scholarship. Dr. Nora Angeles connected me to relevant actors in the Philippines for field research purposes, while the Liu Institute for Global Issues offered critical research support and a stimulating environment from which to develop the project. Fellow graduate students and comrades from CUPE Local 2278 elevated me through their friendship, including Roger Clarke, Peter Lane, Sharon Lebenkoff, Sanjeev Routary, and Sarah Zell. I am also grateful to Drs. Jamie Peck and Robyn Rodriguez (my internal and external examiners, respectively) for their invaluable advice for converting the dissertation to a monograph. In particular, Dr. Rodriguez's guidance on navigating the academy and publishing were impactful, alongside her rigorous, boundary-pushing scholarship. While years have passed since our last exchange, Robyn's courage to centre social justice beyond the academy inspire me, and she continues to animate me through her work.

At York University, I am indebted to Dr. Luin Goldring for her sustained mentorship. As my SSHRC postdoctoral supervisor, Luin helped me put literature on work and employment more centrally in conversation with scholarship on migration institutions and processes, significantly adding to the robustness of my analysis. Her guiding hand in my research on Mexican fast-food labour migration also added clarity to what is distinct about Filipino migrants, labour flows, and migration institutions. I am also grateful to the Centre for Research on Latin America and the Caribbean for hosting my fellowship and for facilitating stimulating interactions across the university. This includes the opportunity to connect with scholars like Drs. Philip Kelly, Mark Thomas, Stephanie Ross, and Leah Vosko, and well as my then-writing group friends Drs. Ethel Tungohan, Carla Suarez, Stephanie Silverman, Julie Young, and Roza Tchoukaleyska. The stimulating conversations and feedback that these interactions afforded (personal and scholarly) have carried me through to the final production of this book.

I am indebted to colleagues and students throughout the writing process, including at California State University Northridge, the University of Waterloo, and McMaster University. Parental leaves and the COVID-19 pandemic challenged my productivity. Despite this, my colleagues were supportive of the monograph and my development as a scholar. I am especially indebted to Drs. Judy Fudge, Suzanne Mills, and Stephanie Ross from McMaster's School of Labour Studies, and Tina Fetner from the Department of Sociology. I am also grateful to Dean Jeremiah Hurley for his willingness to create and correct the conditions from which my progress became viable.

Closer to home, I owe the most profound thanks to my life partner, Senay Haile, for his unwavering support in what has sometimes been an arduous journey. The road to author and tenure is hard to sustain, especially when balancing academic job markets, dual careers, young children, long commutes, and other life demands. In encouraging me to pursue my dreams, we've experienced precarity, including relocations, stress, and exhaustion. I am grateful that you believed in me and the value of my work, while providing much needed perspective and insight. I am also grateful to our children, Jacob and Simon, who have forced me to take pause and relish life's simple joys. Watching them develop has been the most gratifying experience, and I look forward to our future adventures. I am also thankful to my friends who have cheered me on along the way including Maria Panis, Laura Spencer, and Tram Tam.

My deepest gratitude goes to my mother, Hortensia Sorto de Polanco, and my father, Julio Cesar Polanco Flores, for their unwavering love and support. Leaving El Salvador in the late 1980s, they dared to dream the Canadian Dream, despite the many obstacles associated with migrating. My memories of my childhood are happy ones. They are full of laughter, joy, books, and extra-curriculars despite the many challenges they faced as newcomers to Canada. Only now as a mother and sociologist can I truly comprehend what an amazing feat they accomplished, including learning a new language, integrating into a new culture, and facing labour markets that devalue foreign credentials while raising children. They made my sister and me believe we could amount to anything despite our initial refugee status. To this day, they remain my foundation. Most of my life's accomplishments I owe to my parent's support, especially my mother's willingness to forego her own dreams for those of her children. She is the real trailblazer, thinker, and unsung hero in my story. My sister, Gabriela Margarita Polanco Sorto, has been my constant companion, and I cannot imagine life without her sense of humour and friendship. I am also grateful Gaby has enriched our lives with Jeff, Julien, and Daniel, the world's best brother-in-law and nephews (respectively).

Lastly, I am deeply indebted and grateful to the men and women who participated in this study. As a book on migration governance, my participant pool was diverse, including recruiters, employers, government officials, front-line support staff, and migrant workers. For those involved in labour brokering, their willingness to afford me (partial) entry into their professional worlds provided useful knowledge regarding the intricacies of migration management. Employers shared their motivations for recruiting labour from overseas, while front-line support staff relayed the hardships they faced supporting migrants. For workers, sharing their migration experiences was emotionally taxing, and my most heartfelt thanks goes to them for trusting me with their stories. Not everyone will likely agree with my analysis, but I sincerely hope I have done justice in being balanced in my representation.

I wrote this book from a place of love. It is not meant to be interpreted as a mere critique of the Canadian Dream, but rather a reminder of what's a stake in immigration and labour policy. In an era of fortifying borders and anti-immigrant sentiment, Canadians and their institutions have important decisions to make about the values and integrity of border drawing and labour market regulation. My hope is that in tracing the moral economies that shape our policies and practices, I might encourage readers to evaluate what's at stake and decide on a more just Canada.

FILIPINO MIGRANTS AND THE CANADIAN DREAM

Chapter 1

The Institutions and Governance of Labour Migration

Migration institutions do more than manage and govern the mobility of migrants – they also produce cultural narratives of migration that underpin people's mobility decisions to a range of global destinations. The dreams, imaginaries, and institutions that regulate these flows operate in concert with a host of social actors that draw on moral economies to entice highly skilled migrants to engage in transnational migration.

In October 2011, I interviewed Maya[1] about her experience migrating to Canada as a global fast-food worker. We sipped coffees and ate muffins as she recalled the ups and downs of being recruited from the Philippines to work in a Tim Hortons restaurant. Her account of what drew her to Canada and how these motivations contrasted with her actual experiences helped inform my research on the institutions and (cultural) governance of migration.

Maya's participation in fast-food labour migration followed her aunt's chance encounter with Felix, a Filipino-based recruiter. Maya's aunt, Jane, met Felix in Edmonton, Alberta, while dining at a local Filipino restaurant. Felix was on a business trip to formalize a relationship with the Alberta Hotel and Lodging Association (AHLA), an industry association that advocates for and supports hospitality employers in the province. He was competing with other recruitment agencies to supply migrant workers to the AHLA's affiliated hotels. Spotting an opportunity for her niece to migrate to Canada as a migrant worker like she had, Jane boasted about Maya's exceptional qualities and potential as a service worker. Felix provided his business card and encouraged Jane to tell Maya to connect with him upon his return to the Philippines; apparently, Maya sounded like an excellent candidate. Jane told Maya about her encounter with Felix over Skype the following day, but Maya was in her final semester of graduate studies in business economics and was not looking to go abroad to work. She saved Felix's contact information but reportedly gave the conversation little thought.

Following graduation, Maya secured a job as a trade industry specialist with the Filipino government. Beyond the stability and decent salary that the job afforded, she also found it personally meaningful: "That's my way of helping the government. Helping the Philippines." But after two years in the position, she thought, "maybe it's time to go on a different adventure ... try and see what my options are aside from the Philippines ... I feel like I've done my part helping my country, so I feel like I want to move on." With a host of potential destinations Maya could migrate to given her human capital and social networks, I asked her to reflect on why she chose Canada. After contemplating for a few moments, she responded: "It's English-speaking. It's nice. It's clean. They pay a good wage. There are people from all over the world ... They celebrate difference. Yeah, it's like that. It's a nicer country ... I also have this feeling like Canada ... I can become a citizen. So that's why I feel like, OK, for a better, nicer place, for a better future, I'll choose Canada." Having decided that Canada was her preferred destination, she found Felix's contact information in an email from her aunt.

Felix had been successful in his bid to become one of the Filipino recruitment agencies to supply workers to the Alberta Hotel and Lodging Association's members. He told Maya that all potential workers had to take a six-month training course for room attendants, housekeepers, and food servers. The course consisted of three months of classroom training in the evenings and then unpaid on-the-job training in a hotel in the Philippines. Once completed, Maya explained, "You have a certificate. And then once you have a certificate, then they can add you to their manpower pool. To apply for hotels and restaurants here in Canada." Intent on pursuing this possibility despite the deskilling it entailed, she worked by day at her government job and at night she took her classroom training and then did her "internship" at a Manila-based hotel. After her first Canadian job offer fell through, Maya planned to stay in the Philippines, but when she received another offer, Felix managed to persuade her to pursue it. After all, she had already invested time and money in the six-month training program. He also insinuated that by going to Canada she could eventually become a Canadian citizen. This latter point pushed her beyond the threshold of ambivalence. In 2009, she was on a plane to Alberta to work for Canada's leading fast-food corporation, Tim Hortons.

While I heard many accounts like Maya's throughout the course of my research, I was nevertheless puzzled by her actions. Maya did not resemble the impoverished third-world subject that Western, colloquial discourse suggests would engage in temporary low-waged labour migration. Indeed, her relatively high earning capacity and social status in the Philippines as a working professional with a master's-level degree should have shielded her from such a practice. But Maya was attracted to the possibility of "making dollars," and when describing her motivations to me, she went on at length about Canada's healthcare system, its "free" education and social insurance programs, and the joy of belonging to a multicultural society where "everyone is equal." She even suggested that it sounded like a "dream land." While economic factors incited her desire to pursue "greener pastures" through overseas work, money was not the sole or even central pull factor drawing her to Canada. Maya was motivated by the desire to access the promises that she had come to associate with migration and belonging to Canada. But where do these ideas – including the belief that low-waged labour migration is a pathway to permanent settlement – come from?

Maya's account reveals both what she believed to be the value systems in Canada as well as her understanding of the cultural and legal frameworks that mediate the fabric of Canadian belonging. She saw membership in Canada as including access to generous social services, opportunities for mass consumption, and general sentiments of belonging to a multicultural society where everyone is "equal" – features I will later highlight as central elements of the Canadian Dream. Like the American Dream, the Canadian Dream is a powerful social imaginary, drawing immigrants and migrant workers alike to North America.

While I begin this book with Maya's account of migrating to Canada and the aspirations that incited her mobility, the central theme of this study is not the transnational lived experiences of low-waged service workers. These experiences are important and ultimately animated this study, but my focus is on the migration institutions and social actors that regulate this mobility (including state agencies and the corporations, employers, and recruiters empowered to stimulate, manage, patrol, and oversee cross-border migration) and on the policies and (cultural) forces involved in the governance of this mobility. I focus on a global fast-food chain to analyse how migrant dreams are assembled by migration institutions and social actors across transnational circuits, and to examine how a range of social actors and institutions produce cultural narratives of nations that underpin people's mobility decisions. Understanding the social imaginaries that drive these flows and how these cultural forces are connected to institutions, policies, and actors is paramount for elucidating the actions and experiences of subjects like Maya.

Desire and Global Economic Practices

Desire, and its production, lies at the heart of global processes (Rofel, 2007, p. 1), including processes underlying labour migration. Maya sought to migrate because she yearned for the promises she associated with Canada, not just because of a generic desire for material gain. This observation does not negate the primacy of economic forces involved in shaping international flows; rather, it acknowledges that economic practices are culturally and institutionally informed. (Labour) migration is both an economic and a cultural practice.

Scholars have advanced cultural theories of economic action that examine how sentiments incite capitalist actions (e.g., Bandelj, 2020; Faier, 2009; Healy, 2006; Rofel, 2007; Yanagisako, 2002). Within this tradition, social action is deemed to be constituted by rational calculation *and* by sentiment and desires, which together inform cultural and economic practice. Desires include a wide range of aspirations, needs, and longings that are relationally the product of corporate practices and state policies (Rofel, 2007, p. 3). Subjects assess options, make decisions, and reformulate goals, meanings, and practices through sentiments and desires that are institutionally informed. In the context of (labour) migration, we must both examine how sentiments and imagined worlds incite mobility and study the governance of these aspirations, imaginaries, and practices (e.g., Czaika et al., 2021; Hagen-Zanker et al., 2023; Salazar, 2020).

The "imagined world" that "propels people into the migratory stream" (Mahler, 1995, p. 89) involves specific desires and dreams that migrants associate with specific places, including expectations about what said place will afford them if they can access it. This has been described elsewhere as "cognitive migration," wherein migrants imagine what a future time and place will afford them prior to making a move – a kind of prospective thinking informed by the imagination that shapes the migratory decision-making process (Koikkalainen & Kyle, 2016, pp. 759–60). This prospective thinking goes beyond managing one's political-economic marginality; potential migrants also base their decisions about labour migration upon "the imaginative dreams and pleasures that can be found abroad" (Faier, 2009, p. 82). These imagined worlds that propel migrants onto migratory flows are uneven, relational, and complex, and mediated by institutions and infrastructures.

Research on cognitive migration reveals that Filipina/o subjects perceive global destinations along a hierarchy of desirability. Faier (2009, p. 97) found that America was at the top of her participants' geographic imaginings of desired place; it was a point of orientation around which her participants organized their dreams of a better life. Another study similarly documented that the United States and other Western regions, including Canada and Western Europe, were at the top of Filipina/o migrants' desired destinations (Paul, 2011). While structural forces are no doubt at play, we should still ask: Why these places? Or more precisely, what relational geographic imaginings do Filipina/o migrants attribute to Canada, and what are the historical and institutional origins of these ideas and dreams? In turn, how do these imaginings shape the governance of migration?

In this book, I describe how, in the case of temporary labour schemes, a host of social actors (including states, corporations, employers, and recruiters) are involved in the assemblage of migrant dreams, including shaping expectations of and desires for global destinations. Dreams (like the Canadian Dream) operate as productive sentiments that can be (sometimes inadvertently) leveraged at different moments in the migration process to propel mobility and/or to meet other (usually profit-driven) ends. We must therefore unpack the social imaginary across global circuits and across a range of spaces and scales to understand how it shapes temporary labour programs. While it is subjects who are at the centre of these forces, it is institutions and other stakeholders that govern how these forces operate.

The "Heart" of Canada and the Philippines

To explore the institutional dynamics and production of national imaginaries like the Canadian Dream described above, this book focuses specifically on the migration management and governance of skilled Filipina/o workers recruited transnationally into unskilled fast-food positions in Western Canada. To grasp why Maya desires this paradigmatic version of Canada and to unearth the institutional and cultural roots of her aspiration, we turn first to the state and its role in migration management.

It is difficult to provide a precise definition of the state given its elusive and porous nature. On a basic level, states are political organizations that govern territories or populations, though this definition provides little insight into the specificities of states, including their socio-cultural dimensions. It misrepresents their complexity – the multiple actors that constitute them, the range of scales and localities at which they operate, and the values and affects (read: culture) that underlie their policies and practices. Moreover, while there is often an impetus to view states as "rationalized, administrative forms of politic organization" (Das & Poole, 2004, p. 3), states are not abstract, disembodied, or ahistorical. There are also national and temporal specificities to their development. This section focuses on the sociocultural and moral dimensions of states to establish a theoretical framework for understanding the institutional origins of Maya's longing to leave the Philippines in pursuit of the Canadian Dream.

I refer to the "heart" of Canada and the Philippines in an attempt to ground the Canadian and Filipino states and examine their cultural and moral dimensions. I draw on Fassin's theorizing on the "heart of the state" and his assertion that to "capture" states we need to explore their moral dimensions. To get at the "heart" of a state, we must "penetrate the ordinary functioning of public institutions, but … [we must also] examine the values and affects underlying policies and practices" (Fassin, 2015, p. 2). Specifically with respect to immigration, "What values and hierarchies are mobilized within states to decide how to manage transnational human flows and how can we account publicly for these decisions?" (Fassin, 2005, p. 366). Fassin contends that in pursuing this line of inquiry, one casts a light on the "ethos" or "guiding spirit" of an institution or system. Moreover, by unpacking the moral-political investments that inform state policies like those related to immigration and labour markets, we can shed light on how states are implicated in shaping their nations through values and norms and in giving rise to the national longings that then underlie cognitive migration.

As I will demonstrate, the moral economy of Canadian immigration oscillates between multicultural inclusivity and social (neoliberal) exclusion, while for the Philippines, the moral economy of migration oscillates between a caring, responsible state and one informed by colonial and neoliberal values. These sociocultural and moral dimensions are evident by Maya's yearning for the (multicultural) Canadian Dream on the one hand and, on the other hand, the ease with which she pursued transnational, fast-food employment, and the normalization of this pursuit, despite being a highly educated person being institutionally deskilled.

Privileging values and morals provide the analytical tools for examining the sociocultural organization of (nation-)states and societies. To tease out moral economies, Fassin (2015) proposes that empirical analyses of institutions can illuminate the values and affects that crystallize through policies like immigration. We can unpack the ideological and regulatory forces (including the values and affects) that operate to engender states through institutional policies, as well as map how state agents working within institutions similarly uphold dominant morals, values, and affects (Fassin, 2015, p. 6). He similarly suggests that the heart of the state is best discerned by homing in on the margins: on the policies applied toward the disenfranchised and oppressed.

Accordingly, examining institutions (like migration institutions) at the margins (such as with regard to temporary migrant workers and governing migration policies) positions us well to illuminate the various cultural and moral rationalities at work in how societies operate.[2]

Fassin's theorizing on the "heart of the state" and his call to focus on policies and institutions to understand societies inform my analysis of the "heart" of Canada and the Philippines. To elucidate the values and morals underlying the Canadian and Filipino states and how these bleed into the social imaginary, I focus my analysis on their respective labour and migration institutions, including the values and morals (including tensions and contradictions) that have informed immigration and emigration policies and the institutional responses to labour-market pressures and unemployment in Canada and the Philippines, respectively. While chapters 2 and 4 take on this task in depth, here I provide a brief account of the principal values upheld by relevant Filipino and Canadian policies to illuminate the cultural rationalities at work in informing Maya's mobility to Canada.

Moral Economies at Play

The Filipino state is unmatched in the degree to which it legally deploys workers across the globe. State-sponsored labour migration began with the 1974 introduction of the Labour Code, aimed at mitigating unemployment and systematizing a program of labour export. While intended to operate as a stopgap to ease unemployment and a looming economic crisis, the effectiveness of remittances in offsetting the country's economic challenges led to the expansion of labour export rather than its termination or phasing out.

The moral economy underlying the Philippines' labour export policy is market driven and, aside from concerted attempts to appear and be responsible and caring regarding migrant vulnerabilities, is shaped primarily by colonial and neoliberal values. While state-sanctioned labour export has been systematized for fifty years, it has received a series of different types of criticism and undergone several waves of crisis. Following the 1995 execution of Flor Contemplacion (a Filipina domestic helper in Singapore),[3] outrage erupted across the Philippines regarding the perils faced by overseas foreign workers (OFWs). Protesters organized fierce campaigns and demonstrations, demanding that the state afford protections to workers while overseas. In response, the state instituted reforms geared at protecting migrants and supporting their families, leading to the caring, responsible veneer the Philippines projects. OFWs were also elevated by the state to the status of "modern-day heroes" to overshadow and offset fears regarding the underlying dangers of labour export.

While the state has instituted regulations over mobility and promoted improved labour standards that attend to migrant vulnerabilities (e.g., Parreñas, 2021), critics argue that these shifts have done little to address the conditions that led migrants onto global circuits of labour in the first place or the inherent vulnerabilities they face vis-à-vis labour brokers and employers. Moreover, though the state claimed to make migrants "skilled," "empowering them" through a host of highly regulated practices, "the ultimate goal of this Philippine capitalist state is to produce responsible [read: neoliberal] economic citizens" (Guevarra, 2010, p. 85). Essentially, the labour export policy encourages Filipina/os to seek temporary international work and to regard these global contracts as valuable opportunities, even when they entail deskilling, placing highly educated individuals in low-waged service jobs. As I will demonstrate, Filipina/os' desire for mobility and their tendency to view the West as the promised land reflect a Filipino moral economy firmly embedded within colonial and neoliberal values balanced by institutions and processes reflecting the mandate of a caring and responsible state.

Like in the Philippines, the moral dimensions shaping Canada's immigration policies are market driven, but their dynamics reflect different tensions: multicultural inclusivity and social (neoliberal) exclusion. While Canada and the polity pride themselves as a socially just nation, closer inspection of Canada's moral economy concerning immigration (including in the contemporary period) reveals that it is not, in fact, as welcoming or as progressive as it projects. In chapter 2, I trace the long-enshrined colonial, racist, sexist, and classist immigration policies Canada has enacted to patrol its physical borders and, metaphorically, the nation. Canada's past is an exclusionary one, marked by policies developed to curb racialized flows, and it has only reluctantly accepted racialized migrants, primarily out of economic necessity. In recent years, Canada has also moved from being a country of permanent migrant settlement toward a nation of temporary and circular flows, and the prospects for integration for the growing number of "low-skilled" subjects are precarious at best.

The state has downloaded significant risks and insecurities onto the swelling ranks of newcomers who help staff worksites and boost the economy, all while denying them settlement opportunities and related citizenship rights previously extended to most newcomers to Canada. Despite these policies and practices, which reflect a highly exclusionary moral economy committed to a White settler-colonial nation-state and, more recently, a neoliberal knowledge-based economy, Canada is deeply invested in the idea that it is inclusive and socially just. This contradiction in the country's narrative of its identity plagues Canada and Canadians at multiple scales, from official immigration policies to the workings of state agents, employers, recruiters, and the polity. Oscillating between these two poles – inclusive and exclusionary – the state has sought to resolve this tension through favourable narrations of the nation via the social imaginary.

Canada's Idyllic Nation

Starting in the 1960s, the Canadian state initiated a nation-building project that sought to liberate it from its colonial and racist past by promoting a more favourable image of the country. With civil rights agendas and decolonization movements gaining ground, explicitly racist immigration policies and colonial values became politically untenable. Canada thus sought to project a more cosmopolitan image of itself onto the global stage, reframing Canada's settler-colonial history in an idyllic, romanticized manner and establishing multiculturalism as the basis for national unity and identity (Mann, 2012). However, for these values and presumed ethos to bleed from state policies into a communal sense of identity (a nation) and to consolidate an erasure of the country's colonial and racist past, a new shared Canadian identity was needed.

While Canada's federal institutions have propagated multicultural values and other favourable narrations of its identity, both to unite the country and to launch these same ideas into global circulation (detailed in chapter 2), Canada has struggled to establish an imagined community, particularly given its immigrant composition, ethnic diversity, and its proximity to its powerful neighbour to the south. A constant feature in Canada's articulation of its culture and identity has thus become its difference from the United States and the purportedly contrasting characteristics and values of Canadians and Americans. Canada's regional geographical and related diversity and size have similarly proven a formidable challenge for establishing a shared identity, both domestically and globally. Despite Canada's best efforts to fashion a nation that would readily be "in the hearts and minds of its citizens" and keenly invoked by the membership (and beyond), Canadians are plagued by an enduring search for identity (Cormack and Cosgrave, 2013, p. 12). This has afforded room for another player to intervene in the manufacturing of Canada's nation. Interestingly, it is a fast-food corporation that has swept in to advance this project.

Desiring Canada and the Tim Hortons Nation

Canada's most esteemed and iconic corporation, Tim Hortons, works in concert with the state to develop the dominant Canadian identity and social imaginary. Beyond its role as Canada's leading fast-food corporation and a leading employer of migrant workers (recall that Maya migrated to work in a Tim Hortons restaurant), Tim Hortons is an important institutional source of Canada's reputation domestically and globally, contributing to Canada's imagining as a just and multicultural nation. It builds this image through its iconic brand, including sentimental advertisements that present a romanticized version of Canada's values and norms and produce a commercialized nationalism that even the state and state actors try to draw from to establish legitimacy in their projects. In short, Tim Hortons has become a critical part of Canada's nation-building project (Foster et al., 2011, p. 113) and a key promoter of the social imaginary.

Tim Hortons was founded in 1964 in Hamilton, Ontario, by Tim Horton, a professional Canadian hockey player. Originating as a small coffee and donut shop catering primarily to "male, blue-collar workers" (Buist, 2003, p. 117), by the turn of the twenty-first century it had surpassed chains like Dairy Queen and McDonald's to become Canada's leading fast-food corporation, controlling 22 per cent of the fast-food sector (Bryan & Barber, 2021, p. 75). In addition to its market ascendancy and commercial strength across demographics in Canada, it currently boasts stores in the United States, Mexico, Western Europe, the Middle East, and parts of Asia, including the Philippines. It has reached such heights that, for many, Tim Hortons is more than a fast-food corporation; it is an embodiment of Canada.

Tim Hortons' success in Canada is widely attributed to its iconic brand, proffering a romanticized identity and impression of Canada's moral economy. Tim Hortons advertisers have skilfully connected the company to prevailing Canadian values and norms in a highly flattering and sentimental manner. Marketing campaigns tie symbols of Canada and everyday experiences (such as small towns, hockey games, and quotidian moments among family, friends, and community) back to the corporation. Foster and colleagues (2011) describe this as the use of social memory assets: firms "appropriate the collective memory of a society or culture and convert it to the firm's reputation, identity, or brand" (106). "Specific narratives" (such as accounts of past events) are retold with "schematic narratives" (associating the significance of these events with relevant social institutions) to "co-identify the firm's history and values with those of the broader community within which it is embedded" (106). Using social memory assets, Tim Hortons draws on the symbolic resources that exist in the broader society (such as multiculturalism) and ties these attributes and values back to itself.[4] Tim Hortons thus reinforces the utopian vision of Canada's moral economy and uses the same vision to reinforce its own brand.

Patricia Cormack has written extensively on the role of Tim Hortons in authorizing and legitimizing itself as a site and source of Canadian identity. The identity the corporation promotes is a highly sentimental one – beaming with national pride and dripping with flattering, clichéd symbols of Canada and its moral economy. Moreover, in contrast to the state, Tim Hortons advertisers are skilled at bringing its customers (read: citizens) together around a shared vision and proffering an idyllic and captivating Canadian identity. They do so by approaching the citizenry through market models of communication – a "commercialized nationalism" established along lines of pleasure and consumption rather than dated notions like submission to community and service to others (Cormack, 2012, p. 215). They accomplish this so effectively that the state and state employees such as (aspiring) politicians even look to Tim Hortons for their own continued visibility and legitimacy (Cormack & Cosgrave, 2013, p. 14). Indeed, Tim Hortons has branded itself so successfully as an embodiment of Canada using social memory assets that it has "become a public site in which politics and politicians appear" (Cormack, 2012, p. 213). State personnel regularly make public announcements at Tim Hortons restaurants or flock to the site to benefit from the images, symbols, and values that the restaurant chain purportedly represents.[5] Tim Hortons has grown to such prominence that it has arguably taken over as the unofficial storyteller of Canadian identity, reputation, and political enactment (Cormack, 2013, p. 91).

With the help of Tim Hortons, then, the state proffers a narrative of identity that is readily desired and invoked by its citizens, and this social imaginary of Canada also flows beyond its borders and becomes a desired entity globally. Prospective migrant subjects engage in cognitive migration and come to believe in and desire this glowing vision of Canada and its moral economy: what I propose we treat as Canada's national dream.

National dreams are core myths about nations – "consensual hallucinations" informed by national cultural values (Francis, 1997, p. 10). Migrants' preferences for different destinations are shaped by national dreams. Most countries exhibit some version of a national dream, but these social imaginaries are varied and uneven. Northern and wealthy countries boast favourable qualities and implied social contracts that, in turn, operate as powerful cultural forces that stimulate flows. The most widely circulated national dream in the Philippines and globally is the American Dream.

The American Dream is unparalleled in its ability to stimulate the desire for and the practices of international migration. As I describe in chapters 4 and 5, it is founded on the ideals of material gain and mass consumption: the promise of a "good life," even for immigrant and working-class masses (Hochschild, 1995). As the trope goes, wealth and power are within reach for those industrious enough to go the extra mile to attain it, despite their embodied social qualities (e.g., race), the historical atrocities they may have endured (e.g., slavery), and their social location. The American Dream persists among immigrants and the working masses despite sustained evidence to the contrary and even though only few actually attain it (e.g., Thai, 2014; Louie, 2012; Schmalzbauer, 2005).

In contrast, very little has been written about the substance and origin of the Canadian Dream and its ability to draw migrants to Canada. Unlike the American Dream, the Canadian Dream is premised largely on the ideal of a government that takes care of its people. This ideal includes access to a universal education and medical system, social insurance programs like unemployment insurance and parental leave, and equality and belonging within a multicultural society. Moreover, both within and beyond its borders, Canada is imagined as a country of permanent migrant settlement, where even racialized immigrants of colour and contract workers can (eventually) belong to the social fabric of the nation. These real and imagined qualities (particularly the incorrect perception of the right to settle permanently) stimulate a desire among Filipina/o nationals like Maya to pursue the Canadian Dream. They do so in part because of the dual workings of the Canadian state and Tim Hortons corporation, which romanticize Canada's moral economy, and in part because of the workings of the Filipino state. In the case of temporary labour schemes, the desire to pursue the Canadian Dream is also the product of labour brokers who entice migrants to engage in labour migration.

Recruiters and the Outsourcing of the Canadian Nation

Recruiters are key social actors in the organization of flows; they participate in the selection, training, and deployment of migrants to global destinations. Like states and corporations, they generate and leverage national dreams to entice migrants onto global circuits of labour and are central social actors in the governance of flows. While my discussion on how states regulate mobility has thus far focused primarily on the cultural domain, my analysis of states in this book is two-fold. The first, cultural, dimension explores how states like Canada and the Philippines generate an idyllic and promising notion of immigration and emigration, respectively, as briefly introduced above. The second dimension analyses the bureaucratic processes, including policies and institutional practices, that sending and receiving states use to govern mobility. Both dimensions involve a host of social actors who work in concert with the state to (culturally) regulate migration.

The global revival and expansion of temporary migrant worker programs (TMWPs) has been accompanied by a devolution of power from states to profit-driven actors. Prior to migration becoming a "global business" (Salt & Stein, 1997; Lindquist, 2010), receiving states used to retain more decision-making power with regards to cross-border migration. As sovereigns patrolling the border, they would fashion immigration policies to best suit their needs and regulate the physical and metaphorical border of the territory and nation. Along with the globalization of worksites associated with TMWPs, however, an industry of labour brokers has emerged to help employers engage flexible migrant labour from overseas (McCollum & Findlay, 2018, p. 565). These "agents of the state" (Zell, 2018, p. 193) play a range of roles in selecting, training, and supplying workers, particularly in the front-end processes of the migration chain. They do so in concert with employers, who request and define their ideal workers, and alongside sending and receiving states, which generate policies and retain final say with regard to flows. To understand how temporary labour programs operate, we must interrogate the relationship *between* these social actors and their discourses and practices in the management of migration.

A primary feature of this book is its examination of how recruiters entice migrants to pursue overseas work by exploiting the social imaginary embedded in the colonial mentality[6] and the Canadian Dream. As Maya's story suggests and as I will outline in more detail, recruiters play a role in shaping migrants' preferences and expectations regarding the futures that await them in different destinations. An important function of recruiters is to entice migrants to pursue overseas work (Spaan & van Naerssen, 2018, p. 684), and dreams featuring prominently in these persuasions. Recruiters and sending states endorse the benefits of overseas work by manufacturing expectations about different destinations while minimizing the risks associated with migration. In the case of the Philippines, they also disparage the sending context by harnessing the colonial mentality to cast the Philippines as inferior and even hopeless.

Centuries of colonization by Spaniards and Americans in the Philippines led to widespread "internalized colonialism" (David, 2013, p. 62). This colonial mentality exalts anything associated with the colonizer as superior while rendering inferior the culture, society, and political systems of the colonized. Life and employment in the Philippines are thus cast as comparatively undesirable (Espiritu, 1996). The colonial mentality is not specific to Filipina/o subjects. Research has documented degrees of internalized colonization among other historically colonized groups, including African American (Jackson & Cothran, 2003; Traore, 2004) and Latino populations (Miranda, 2011; Padilla, 1999; Sanchez et al., 2025). But Filipina/os must also contend with a new "migrant citizenship" established by the Filipino state, whereby being a "good Filipino" increasingly means engaging in overseas work (Rodriguez, 2010). Alongside migrant social networks and other sources that promote ideas about the superiority of life and work in the West, the collective fabrication of the social imaginary operates as a leading cultural force stimulating the desire for and practices of South-North migration.

What the above discussion suggests is that there are both cultural pull forces and cultural push forces at work, and that sending and receiving states, recruiters, employers, and corporations are central actors in their deployment. The cultural pull forces include the national dreams associated with foreign destinations that invoke desires and practices of (labour) migration. The cultural push factors include prevailing social imaginaries like the colonial mentality that make departing the sending context more enticing. These cultural pull and push forces downplay the risks of migration and play up the advantages of deskilling, often associated with South-North migration. Together, they operate as strong cultural forces that work in concert with structural forces and social networks to sustain the out-migration of qualified subjects to Canada.

Though I present here a fairly "tidy" account of the social relations and transnational practices that govern temporary migration schemes and corporate employment strategies, I do not consider the production of social imaginaries that drive flows or the various actions of those involved to be following any kind of master plan or coherent project. Indeed, as I document empirically throughout this book and explicitly examine in chapter 7, the social imaginary is often the outcome of messy, fragmented discourses and bureaucratic practices – ideas and processes that often contradict each other and are rarely motivated by monolithic ends, especially across different stakeholders. Together, however, they form a seemingly coherent narrative of nations, including the narrative of nations that helps us understand migrant flows.

Canada's Fast-Food Labour Program and the Contours of Canadian Citizenship

In recent years, Canada has augmented its temporary and circular migration programs, including expanding its Temporary Foreign Worker Program (TFWP) both in scale and the range of occupations it covers. This expansion has produced one of the most significant changes to Canadian migration patterns in the twenty-first century. These shifts in flows also point to profound changes in the contours and practices of regulating membership and belonging in Canada.

Historically, Canada has relied sparingly on guest worker programs. Introduced in 1973, Canada's TFWP was designed to ease labour-market pressures for employers and sectors experiencing shortages. In the higher tiers, this included fast-tracking the recruitment of professionals into sectors like academia, medicine, and engineering. For occupations considered "low-skilled," migrant workers were recruited exclusively into the agricultural and domestic caregiving sectors. Similar programs include the Seasonal Agricultural Workers Program (SAWP), operational in Canada since 1966, and the Live-in Caregiver Program and its subsequent renditions, including the Caregiver Program,[7] which has been operational in Canada since 1992. Predecessors of these programs (like the Caribbean Domestic Scheme) date back to the 1950s (Hsiung & Nichol, 2010, p. 767). In 2002, though, Canada introduced the Low-Skilled Pilot project (LSP), now widely referred to as the Low-Skilled Stream (LSS). Under the LSS, low-waged employers can recruit workers transnationally for occupations classified by the Canadian federal government as "low-skilled." Initially slow to take off, the construction, food services, and manufacturing sectors have since latched on to the program. As described chapter 2, the fast-food sector in general and Tim Hortons more specifically have in fact built a business model around the TFWP.

The LSS allowed a new set of young, eager, educated workers to enter Canada as temporary migrant workers (TMWs) on the bottom rungs of Canada's labour markets. Maya, for example, was willing to be deployed for employment in a Canadian fast-food restaurant because of the ideas and dreams she associated with Canada. She believed that a temporary work contract – even in a fast-food restaurant – would ultimately lead to permanent residency for her and a better life for her family, even though her education and experience made her better suited to higher-skilled work. She believed in the possibility of permanent residency because Canada's long-standing and reconfigured Live-in Caregiver Program (LCP) facilitates the transition from temporary to permanent status for domestic workers, and she thought the same conditions would also apply to her (as they had for her Aunt Jane, who migrated to Canada years earlier under the LCP). What Maya did not know was that the Low-Skilled Stream does not offer the same prospects. She was also unaware that the immigration system and cultural context of reception in Canada had changed. Once a country of permanent migrant settlement, Canada has progressively moved toward a model of temporary status migration.

In 2010, the number of individuals entering Canada on temporary visas surpassed those selected for permanent migrant settlement, undermining Canada's tradition of being a country of permanent – rather than temporary or circular – migration. With the expansion of the TFWP to include lower-skilled occupations beyond agriculture and domestic caregiving, the number of (low-waged) migrants recruited to Canada surged. By 2011, there were already triple the number of migrants in Canada on temporary worker permits compared to a decade earlier in 2000, with most of the growth occurring in Western Canada (Polanco & Zell, 2017, p. 269). This upward trend of recruiting temporary contract labour remains steady. In 2023, the number of temporary foreign work permits that became effective was 182,820 – an 88 per cent increase from 2019 – with employers granted permission to hire almost 240,000 temporary foreign workers for that year (Alsharif, 2024a). Filipina/o citizens were the number one citizen group with work permits under the TFWP between 2007 and 2014 (IRCC Facts and Figures, 2016).

In the fast-food sector, the practice of recruiting migrant fast-food workers is now widespread and continuously ballooning, with employment in the food service sector increasing by 4000 per cent nationally between 2016 and 2023 (Alsharif, 2024b). Canadian employers were approved for 8,333 food counter attendants and kitchen helpers' positions in 2023, nearly double those approved for 2022. From 2002 to 2019, a total of 54,885 food-counter attendant[8] work visas were approved under the LSS. The majority streamed to the provinces of Alberta and British Columbia. In Alberta, 80 per cent of these workers were recruited from the Philippines, and in British Columbia, 77 per cent (IRCC, 2020).

A growing number of Filipina/os are recruited on temporary work visas and channelled into segmented labour markets, confined like Maya to low-skilled and low-status occupations with limited opportunities for upward mobility. Unbeknown to many of these workers, they face a system in which they have minimal control and few options for transitioning from temporary to permanent status. The

LSS is highly ambiguous with regard to the prospects of attaining permanent residency, as I describe in chapter 5. It doesn't directly preclude permanent settlement (as does Canada's long-standing Seasonal Agricultural Workers Program, SAWP), nor does it provide a two-step (Hennebry, 2010) institutionalized path toward permanent residency, like the LCP and its later renditions do. Instead, under the policy framework of the LSS, employers have the power to select which migrant workers (if any) they will help nominate for permanent residency through a Provincial Nominee Program (PNP), essentially pitting migrant workers against one another in a competition for the coveted path to citizenship. The percentage of migrants who transition from temporary to permanent status through a PNP in the case of food-counter attendants is low. Migrants may also transition to permanent residency while technically under Canada's International Mobility Program (IMP), though this process, too, is precarious and uncertain (and covered in more detail in chapter 2). Migrants like Maya thus enter Canada lacking the legal right to settle permanently, but they are not formally denied the possibility, a situation that introduced a new precarious and institutionalized form of mediating belonging and integration into Canada.

If citizenship represents the epitome of social and political membership, as Bosniak (2006) argues, the trend toward precarity and uncertainty regarding citizenship means that the possibilities for social and political membership in Canada are declining. Rather than selecting people to work and live as full members of society, the expanded TFWP excludes a growing number of newcomers while elevating the importance of immigrant status in the regulation of belonging.

Scholars like Goldring and Landolt (2012, 2013) have widely documented the negative and long-term socio-economic impacts on migrants who enter Canada with precarious legal status. That the majority of those who enter Canada as low-waged migrants are racialized people from the global South also raises questions about the variables of race and nationality in shaping conditions of inequality and poverty. Moreover, the move toward employer-dependent processes for citizenship, forcing migrants to depend on the benevolence of their employer and granting employers the power to dash or fulfil migrants' hopes for settlement, raises questions about the neoliberal precarity that underlies both the labour programs themselves and the social conditions mediating the contours of membership and belonging. Membership is increasingly being commodified and outsourced (transnationally, via sending states and labour brokers), with implications for the social fabric of belonging in Canada.

Ethnography of a Global Fast-Food Chain

This book describes the results of an inductive, transnational, and multi-sited ethnographic case study of a Canadian Filipino fast-food labour chain. Heeding Fassin's (2015) call to conduct ethnographic analyses of institutions and drawing on the insights of global ethnography, which promotes taking a situated and grounded approach to examine processes of globalization (e.g., Burawoy et al., 2000; Burawoy, 2001; Paerregaard, 2009), I elected to "follow the connections" (Marcus, 1995, p. 102) of this global fast-food chain – including the social relations that constitute it – to gain a better understanding of the relationship between temporary labour programs, institutions, the social imaginary, and globalization. Moving beyond a methodological nationalism that has characterized much Canadian literature on temporary labour programs, I visited multiple sites for shorter periods of time[9] (Hendry, 2003, p. 499), both in Western Canada and the Philippines, and I connected with social actors and spaces institutionally relevant to the organization of temporary migration flows. My goal was to take what can be seen as an "abstract" global process (i.e., global labour flows) and offer a situated, grounded, and embodied account of how transnational labour migration operates, including an examination of the central actors, activities, moral economies, and discursive frameworks involved in organizing global labour flows both pre-departure in the Philippines and upon arrival in Canada. Moreover, I trace the "global forces, connections and imaginations" (Gille & O'Riain, 2002, p. 280) that constitute a transnational labour chain, taking the Tim Hortons corporation as my case study for analysis.

This approach was informed by the notion that although the global is often imagined as an unsituated space and the local is often imagined as being situated in the grounded and every day, the global economy and economic globalization (like any other element of global flows) take form in concrete, physical spaces (Sassen, 1998, p. xix). While *local* and *global* are useful analytical abstractions, they are not "real" in a tangible sense. Rather, it is in the everyday and in situated spaces that we must examine and make sense of globalization (and the forces that promote it) through what Burawoy and colleagues (2000, p. 26) refer to as "grounded globalization."

To "ground" globalization in this specific study, I began with an inductive design that sought to make visible the emerging flows of temporary service sector workers to Canada. I had heard rumours that hospitality employers were beginning to recruit migrant workers to Western Canada to work in occupations like hotel cleaning and fast-food service roles, but during the planning stages of this project (which date back to 2008), these accounts remained largely unresearched and unsubstantiated. As global recruitment for low-skilled occupations in Canada had historically been limited to the agriculture and domestic caregiving sectors, my first task was to make sense of what was happening. Because Canada's leading fast-food corporation, Tim Hortons, was identified in news reports as a noteworthy receiver of migrant workers, I decided to limit my focus to said corporation. I filed multiple Freedom of Information (FOI) requests with the labour and immigration arms of the Canadian federal government to ascertain if TMWs were being recruited to work in Western Canadian Tim Hortons restaurants, and if so, from which countries. I thus obtained information about the sending countries, where in Canada the workers were being requested from, the gender of the workers sought, and whether a Canadian-based labour-market intermediary (i.e., labour recruiter) was involved in the recruitment (and if so, which one). I discovered that more than three-quarters of the workers solicited by employers in Alberta and British Columbia were from the Philippines; thus, I chose to focus on the Philippines as the source country. I also learned that the Tim Hortons corporation was increasingly performing the third-party recruitment for their franchise restaurants (i.e., centralizing recruitment internally) and that there appeared to be a growing preference for soliciting women over men (features of these flows are taken up in chapter 5).

Once I confirmed that fast-food employers had indeed "gone global" in their recruitment practices and that Tim Hortons was at the forefront of advocating for and recruiting migrant workers, I decided to use a three-pronged design for this study. The first prong involved the FOI data described above. The second and third prongs consisted of semi-structured interviews and ethnographic field research through the method of participant observation.

Between 2009 and 2011, I conducted sixty-two semi-structured interviews as well as ethnographic research in Alberta and British Columbia and in the Philippines. The Filipino component of the study took place in the summer of 2011. I conducted expert interviews with the range of social actors involved in organizing these fast-food flows, including Canadian and Filipino government employees; Tim Hortons franchise owners in Western Canada; labour consultants and recruiters for fast-food restaurants in Canada and the Philippines; frontline settlement workers and supporters of migrant workers in Canada (including grassroots organizers, church-affiliated supporters, and union staff); and Tim Hortons food-counter attendants (i.e., migrant workers). Ethnographic research included participant observation in government and industry conferences; in grassroots organizing spaces in both Canada and the Philippines; and, in the Philippines, through community visits to "migrant communities,"[10] recruitment fairs, and government-mandated and -operated Pre-Departure Orientation Seminars (PDOS). Data was also gathered through numerous formal and informal conversations with similarly positioned key informants. All relevant information was digitally recorded and transcribed or documented as ethnographic fieldnotes. The data was later coded and analysed using the software program NVivo.

In a follow-up study I conducted in 2015, I added Mexico as a third field site to provide a comparative lens on how the shift from local to global recruitment practices in Western Canada was altering work and employment conditions in the fast-food industry. This follow-up study included data obtained from FOI requests to the labour and immigration arms of the Canadian federal government, secondary data secured from the Mexican and Canadian governments; forty-three expert interviews; and ethnographic research conducted in places and with actors parallel to my Philippines–Canada study. While the Mexico–Canada project is distinct from the study described in this book, the interviews with recruiters, employers, government bureaucrats, and those who interact regularly with migrant workers in their defence (e.g., NGO workers, union staff, and grassroots organizers) provided useful, up-to-date data. On a few occasions, I even met Filipina/o migrants who had entered Canada as fast-food migrant workers but who were of interest within the scope of my Mexico-Canada study. In these cases, I allowed our interviews to touch on the Filipino Canadian context and obtained useful additional data to bolster my analysis. By exploring a Canadian-Mexican fast-food labour chain, what was distinct about the Filipino context, Filipina/o migrant workers, and the Philippine migration apparatus became clearer. When relevant, I draw from these data to enrich my descriptions and analysis. To further contextualize hospitality migration to Canada, I also updated my FOI requests to obtain more recent statistics on fast-food flows to Western Canada and other fast-food corporations that have gone "global."

The Organization of This Book

Studies have shown the power of the American Dream to draw workers to the United States in pursuit of material gain (e.g., Guevarra, 2010; Mahler, 1995; Thai, 2014). Little is known, however, about the draw factor of Canada as a dream destination or how the Canadian Dream is manufactured across stakeholders within transnational contexts. There is also a lacuna of knowledge on low-waged food services labour migration, despite the growing trend in regions like Asia, the Middle East, Western Europe, and now North America. With this transnational analysis of a Filipino Canadian Tim Hortons labour chain, I show how a constellation of social actors generate and exchange ideas about the benefits of migration, including dreams associated with potential host destinations like Canada. Governed by a host of institutions and actors, these ideas in turn stimulate desires and mediate flows. Accordingly, I claim that migration institutions must be systematically unpacked across global circuits and across spaces and scales to grasp the multitude of cultural and economic forces shaping migration in what is increasingly a global market for (temporary) labour. This is the task we undertake in this book.

In chapter 2 – "Tim Hortons and the Low-Skilled Stream" – I show how Tim Hortons, in concert with employment agencies and industry associations, successfully lobbied the state to expand Canada's TFWP. The LSS brought a new set of young, eager, and educated workers into Canada as TMWs on the bottom rungs of the Canadian labour market and without a clear path to permanent settlement. The LSS has thus contributed to an ongoing trend of declining opportunities for formal citizenship and belonging and an increase in precarious pathways to membership. It is also a market-driven and employer-dependent means of regulating legal belonging, moving away from Canada's multicultural version of belonging. This market-driven version has implications for the substance and meaning of Canadian citizenship and Canada's moral economy and points to the shifting boundaries of the Canadian nation-state.

In chapters 3 and 4, "Beguiling and Brokering the 'Great Filipino Worker'" and "Migrant Dreams and the Colonial Mentality," I provide an overview of the Filipino migration apparatus, empirically showing how the Filipino state in concert with the migration industry attempts to cultivate and supply a "superior" workforce to global employers while also actively drawing on and perpetuating a colonial mentality framework to encourage higher-status migrants to engage in precarious, overseas labour migration. I build on previous research on the Philippines as a "labour brokerage state" (e.g., Guevarra, 2010; Rodriguez, 2010) and on the promotion of Filipina/o nationals as having a "comparative advantage" (Guevarra, 2014) by focusing both on the promises and dreams associated with overseas work (the cultural pull factors) as well as the cultural push factors that make migrants willing to engage in transnational deskilling and segmentation into the bottom tiers of global labour markets. In the Filipino case, the colonial mentality (David, 2013) – actively produced by the state – is a powerful push force, informed by a colonial and neoliberal moral economy. It operates in concert with the pull forces of the Canadian Dream. Together, these forces constitute the institutional and cultural drivers of migration.

In chapter 5, "Harnessing Dreams to Manufacture Consent," I turn back to Canada to look behind the counter at fast-food worksites and examine how employers secure a compliant, "ideal" workforce through an immigration program that capitalizes on the exploitation of migrant dreams. Due to the low-status, low-waged, and demanding nature of the fast-food labour process, high turnover rates and human resource challenges have long plagued the sector. Changes in Canadian immigration programming have resolved this problem. Through the LSS and PNPs, a precarious immigration scheme has emerged that has workers competing with other migrant workers at the scale of the worksite for employer-nominated citizenship. The odds of securing citizenship in this way are long, but neither workers or employers are always aware of this shortcoming. Similarly, some migrants spend time working under Canada's International Mobility Program in their path toward incorporation. Their hopes of nomination facilitate employers' access to a pool of migrant workers who are willing to work hard and even accept outright abuse, as they view the worksite as the space where they can secure a ticket to permanent residency and, in turn, the Canadian Dream and a better life. This arrangement marks a new migration-employer regime in Canada that I have coined a "precarious labour migration regime" (Polanco, 2016). This labour regime is transnational in nature and involves a host of social actors, with cultural forces operating as a primary force in shaping worksite and industry dynamics.

In chapter 6, "The Institutional Resilience of National Dreams," I explore why the Canadian Dream, much like other national dreams, continues to thrive despite a global landscape of broken dreams. National dreams like the Canadian and American Dreams continue to operate as powerful cultural forces that propel (labour) migration despite so much evidence to the contrary, including marginalization, labour exploitation, and a deep level of disillusionment as migrants come to terms with the realities of working and living on the bottom rungs of receiving labour markets and societies. With racialized, low-waged migrants facing such harsh realities, how and why does the Canadian Dream continue to thrive? I draw on the literature and on empirical data to explain the dream's apparent resiliency: I focus on migrant transnational social fields, the prestige and social status associated with migration to Canada, and the elasticity of national dreams.

Moreover, unlike Western-born workers who can only compare their work and lives to their local realities, migrants have a "transnational social optic" that provides a "dual frame of reference" from which they comparatively assess their lives and are assessed. Migrants attain status from their migration, work, and earnings in Canada, but they also accrue status from their social networks and home countries. Rather than sharing the realities and pain of the structural shortcomings of Canada's new immigration regime with their social networks in the Philippines, migrants often take their lack of transition from temporary to permanent status as their own personal "failing" and conceal their hardships. By keeping silent about these experiences and by returning home with gifts and other symbols that serve as signs of success in Canada, migrants and the diaspora (unwittingly) maintain the illusion of the promises associated with the Canadian Dream. I also analyse the Canadian Dream more specifically as it is conceived in the Philippine context. Scholars have noted that perceptions of a place and national dreams vary by communities and nations (Park, 1997), and this is a book about the Filipino Canadian Dream.

In chapter 7, "A Global Infrastructure of Migrant Dreams," I consider the interactions *across* the different social actors and institutions that manage fast-food labour migration to Canada. I denote the tensions, contradictions, and fragmented nature of these processes, while illustrating that institutions do not operate either in tandem or isolation. Moreover, while the moral economies shaping the regulation of flows may appear neat and tidy (including in chapters 2 through 6), in fact it is often the incidental interplay of a host of interests, values, and operations. Social actors and institutions are not informed by monolithic goals, though they often uphold dominant morals, values, and affects through their policies and practices.

In chapter 8, "Reimagining a World beyond Labour Migration," I consider the implications of national dreams in shaping life trajectories, and the institutional governance of migration in an age of proliferating TMWPs, restrictive immigration programs, and globalization. I also consider how the difficulties that migrants face securing these national dreams shape migrant subjectivities, including internalized perceptions of being winners and failures. Beyond Tim Hortons and fast food, this case study points to broader questions about the meaning and substance of citizenship in an age of neoliberal economic agendas and contracting borders. I describe a shifting landscape in which institutions and intermediaries patrol membership and belonging through temporary labour schemes, and call attention to the increasingly exclusionary ways in which race and class are shaping processes of inclusion and exclusion, while theorizing what it would take to get us beyond this trajectory.

In the appendix, I provide a Filipino Canadian Infrastructure of Migration Map for the Low-Skilled Stream that illustrates the different stages of migration from the perspective of workers, employers, labour market intermediaries, and states. The map traces the different institutional actors regulating mobility across the transnational circuit, and the lengths to which aspiring migrants must go through to secure a low-waged, fast-food contract in Canada. Besides elucidating the governance structures regulating migrant mobility, the map draws attention to dependency and vulnerability institutionally experienced by migrants as they pursue the Canadian Dream.

Throughout this book, you'll meet more migrants like Maya: Filipina/o nationals recruited to perform low-waged, service work often incongruent with their credentials, under a migration program with precarious pathways to membership. I highlight their desires, dreams, and experiences to illuminate the lived realities of neoliberal labour and migration policies, and to denote that globalization is embodied and grounded. The sweeping changes that Western nation-states often enact to immigration policies have long-term, cascading effects. They are thus structural yet highly personal and consequential. Stated differently: migrants have desires and dreams, yet infrastructures enable and constrain these dreams.

Chapter 2

Tim Hortons and the Low-Skilled Stream

Get me a Filipino. I want a Filipino.

In 2011, I sat in a coffee shop in Calgary, Alberta, with Rachel, an in-house human resource specialist for a fast-food corporation. I'd met Rachel at a two-day industry event for personnel who recruit migrant workers. She agreed to join me for an interview, during which she recounted the many things she found unsettling about the fast-food sector's turn to migrant labour. She was new to her job. She had worked in the human resources field for years but never in fast food, so she self-identified as someone still becoming accustomed to the sector. Her perspective was refreshing, as she had not yet been normalized to the cultural landscape of the quick-service restaurant industry and seemed eager to unload her insights and frustrations.

She described at length her dismay that the Canadian government was making migrant workers available to fast-food employers, given that, in her opinion, much of the labour shortage in this sector was due to conditions that many would contend should not be sustained with a new class of vulnerable workers but rather improved and made more palatable to the existing labour pool. After describing the challenges faced by franchisees in different regions across Alberta, she sat back, put her coffee down, and started shaking her head. Inching slowly toward me she whispered, "But you know what I really can't stand? What really gets to me? It's how these franchisees call me, leave me a message, 'Get me a Filipino. I want a Filipino.'" I smiled back, hoping she would not misread my body as Filipina or racialize me as "of colour," which might deter honest reflections. "Why do you find that disturbing?" I asked. She looked a bit taken aback by my question (perhaps unaccustomed to the seemingly obvious queries researchers tend to pose) and took a moment to reflect. Finally, she responded, "I guess [*long pause*], whatever happened to just hiring teenagers? I mean, do you think it's okay that [name of corporation] gets to hire these young college grads? You know, so many of them even think they're coming to immigrate, bring their families ... I don't know, it just feels wrong."

Rachel's sentiment that "it just feels wrong" to recruit low-wage migrants on temporary work visas derives in part from a cultural sensibility among Canadians that qualified newcomers should be granted the right to settle permanently in Canada. The denial of settlement violates Rachel's perception of Canada's moral economy and her moral subjectivity regarding immigration. Indeed, she repeatedly expressed her astonishment that the Canadian government is facilitating employers' ability to request and recruit "a Filipino," considering this transnational employment practice rather "un-Canadian." Rachel's idea of Canada as a welcoming country where newcomers are granted rights to permanent settlement and to sponsor the migration of their families is not, by her account, the sociolegal landscape that many newcomers now face when entering Canada. Instead, a growing number enter Canada as guest workers, are segmented into the bottom tiers of the labour market, and face barriers to belonging and integration. These conditions stem from larger shifts in the organization of migratory flows and changes to the rights and responsibilities extended to newcomers to Canada.

The expansion of the Temporary Foreign Worker Program (TFWP) is altering the substance and meaning of citizenship in Canada. Unlike a previous version of belonging – multicultural belonging – wherein most newcomers could reasonably expect to be integrated into Canada and enjoy a corresponding set of entitlements (albeit with some marginalization), a growing number now face a market-driven version in which exclusion prevails. This market orientation has introduced new profit-driven actors to the management of flows – actors who, with only minimal accountability, seek specific qualities in their ideal candidates for Canada. This development is having far-reaching consequences for Canada's social fabric and its integrity as an immigrant nation.

Fast-Food Flows and the Globalization of Canadian Worksites

As described in chapter 1, while Canada is well versed in the use of "high-skilled" migrant workers to address purported labour-market pressures, "low-skilled" migrant workers tended to be confined to the agricultural and domestic caregiving sectors.[1] This changed, however, in 2002, when Canada introduced the Low-Skill Pilot Project (LSP) – now known as the Low-Skilled Stream (LSS) – which dramatically expanded Canada's guest worker program in both scale and scope. Under the LSS, employers who can establish a "need" can recruit foreign workers for employment in any occupation classified as TEER[2] category 4 or 5 under the federal government's skill-level classification system (previously the National Occupational Classification [NOC] system levels C and D). This expansion of Canada's TFWP has affected migration patterns to Canada, populated worksites with workers with different citizenship status and introduced new subjects with a limited set of rights and entitlements.

All Canadian provinces and territories have seen the recruitment of fast-food temporary migrant workers (TMWs): 54,885 work permits were granted for food-counter attendants under the LSS between 2002 and 2019. An additional 8,390 work permits have also been issued to TMWs for employment as food-counter attendants under the International Mobility Program (IMP), totalling 63,275 work permits for noncitizen/nonpermanent residents working as food-counter attendants during that period. Contract workers labouring under the IMP are technically TMWs, but the IMP does not include migrant subjects like Maya, introduced in chapter 1. Instead, it covers TMWs awaiting decisions on permanent residency applications, postgraduates awaiting work permits, the spouses and common-law partners of skilled workers, and those in Canada on humanitarian grounds (e.g., refugees). The IMP also encompasses exchange programs like International Experience Canada, which permits youth from specified countries to live and work in Canada for a maximum of two years (colloquially known as working holidays). The IMP statistics suggest, then, that beyond the LSS, fast-food employers are turning more generally to workers with limited citizenship rights and entitlements to address purported labour-market pressures.

Table 2.1 shows the total number of food-counter-attendant work permits granted in Canada under both the LSS and IMP by province and territory from 2002 to 2019. As I describe in chapter 5, the number of TMWs labouring under the IMP in Alberta and British Columbia (the region covered in this study) is small relative to the LSS, with the bulk likely consisting of TMWs previously employed under the LSS and awaiting a decision on their permanent residency applications. This is not, however, likely to be the case for all provinces and territories in Canada. Indeed, the total number of work permits granted under the IMP in Yukon, Manitoba, Saskatchewan, Quebec, and Newfoundland and Labrador outpaces those granted under the LSS. Because it is impossible to ascertain whether these permits were for workers

Table 2.1. Total work permits granted to food-counter attendants under LSS and IMP, by province or territory, 2002–19.

Province	Total	Percentage
Alberta	36,220	56.72%
British Columbia	17,475	27.37%
Saskatchewan	4,609	7.22%
Ontario	1,365	2.14%
Quebec	761	1.19%
Manitoba	743	1.16%
Newfoundland and Labrador	719	1.13%
Yukon	584	0.91%
Nova Scotia	537	0.84%
New Brunswick	486	0.76%
Northwest Territories	275	0.43%
Prince Edward Island	70	0.11%
Nunavut	12	0.02%
Total	63,856	100.00%

Source: IRCC, 2020.

previously under the LSS now awaiting a decision on a permanent residency application or for other migrant subjects altogether (e.g., refugees or spouses of skilled workers), table 2.2 shows the number of work permits granted across Canada under the LSS for food-counter attendants.

As tables 2.1 and 2.2 show, the provinces with the largest number of food-counter attendants working on temporary visas (both LSS and IMP) were Alberta, British Columbia, and Saskatchewan. Limiting the analysis to LSS workers, Alberta boasted the highest number of TMW food-counter attendants at 35,085, followed by British Columbia at 14,650, and Saskatchewan at 2,280. The majority were Filipina/o nationals: 80 per cent in Alberta, 77 per cent in British Columbia, and 75 per cent in Saskatchewan. Workers have also been recruited from other countries, including El Salvador, Greece, Poland, China, and Myanmar (to name a few).

Table 2.3 illustrates the total number of work permits granted for food-counter attendants per year from 2002 to 2019 under the LSS. At its height in 2013, Canada saw a peak of 9,525 work permits granted for food-counter attendants. There was then a steady decline in fast-food flows; by 2018, there were only 125 work permits granted for food-counter attendants under the LSS. This downward trend reflected policy shifts and government responses to public controversies surrounding the TFWP, as described below, as opposed to employers

Table 2.2. Total work permits granted to food-counter attendants under LSS, by province and territory, 2002–19.

Province	Total	Percentage
Alberta	35,086	63.38%
British Columbia	14,649	26.46%
Saskatchewan	2,279	4.12%
Ontario	1,206	2.18%
Nova Scotia	477	0.86%
New Brunswick	468	0.85%
Newfoundland and Labrador	376	0.68%
Quebec	369	0.67%
Manitoba	178	0.32%
Northwest Territories	174	0.31%
Prince Edward Island	45	0.08%
Yukon	39	0.07%
Nunavut	10	0.02%
Total	55,356	100.00%

Source: IRCC, 2020

Table 2.3. Total work permits granted to food-counter attendants across Canada under LSS, 2002–19.

Year	Total
2002	25
2003	60
2004	25
2005	55
2006	345
2007	2,440
2008	6,415
2009	6,125
2010	5,190
2011	7,890
2012	8,715
2013	9,525
2014	5,630
2015	1,120
2016	665
2017	140
2018	125
2019	395
Total	54,885

Source: IRCC, 2020.

losing interest in recruiting workers transnationally. Indeed, by 2023 employers received approval for 8,333 food counter attendants and kitchen helpers work permits (Alsharif, 2024b), reaching almost peak recruitment levels in the sector. Thus, while there have been ebbs and flows in the policy domain including restrictions that have emerged for employers recruiting migrant workers, many sectors remain committed to the use of "foreign" labour and continue to lobby to maintain said access with employer-favourable results, including in hospitality and fast food (chapter 7). While this case study of fast food and Tim Hortons focuses on a specific industry and corporation at a particular moment in time, it is likely quite representative of other industries and corporate practices. The LSS and similar policies expanding temporary labour migration have culturally and legally institutionalized barriers to inclusion for many newcomers in fast food and beyond. As Rachel alludes, they have altered the conditions and meaning of belonging in Canada.

Canadian Immigration Policies and the Rationing of Membership

Citizenship is the principal goal driving Filipina/o migration to Canada; thus, its meaning and regulation is central to this study. Although citizenship is diffuse, here, I'm concerned with rights and belonging specifically within Canada.[3] I seek to contribute to scholarship that treats citizenship as a form of membership and belonging, examining how the globalization of worksites is altering how rights and membership are rationed and regulated by a host of actors under guest worker schemes in Canada and other Western nations.

Citizenship is often theorized as "a form of membership in a political and geographic community" (Bloemraad et al., 2008, p. 154); it is a concept that reflects a community's boundaries and facilitates their analysis. Citizenship asserts idealized norms of the qualities that should facilitate or deny membership within a nation (Anderson et al., 2011, p. 548). In other words, citizenship reflects imagined communities and narratives of belonging; it is the "signifier par excellence of membership in the nation-state" (Thobani, 2007, p. 69).

Within a nation-state system where large and diverse flows of international migration are increasingly the norm, citizenship marks a tension between those who "belong" and those who are viewed as beyond the nation-state's boundaries; it determines the substantive rights and responsibilities that are extended (or denied) to a nation's newcomers. Furthermore, citizenship involves a set of practices that "shape the flow of resources to people and social groups" (Fudge, 2005, p. 634). It is therefore an institution that is both unifying and divisive; for a "we" to exist and for resources to be funnelled to this "we," some must fall outside of the community's boundaries (Bloemraad et al., 2008, p. 156). Citizenship thus denotes inclusions in and exclusions from a national community along the lines of legal status, rights, participation, and a sense of belonging (Bosniak, 2006; Bloemraad et al., 2008). It tells us about a nation's moral economy regarding membership. Those deemed outside the purview of the national community through designations like "illegal" and "migrant worker" are often denied important rights and protections that are extended to citizens.[4]

Citizenship and immigration policies have shaped Canada's nation-building project. In the postwar era, assimilationist policies gave way to a multicultural version of belonging, and then recent changes to temporary migration policies laid the foundations for the current period of market-driven precarity and exclusion for many migrant workers. Tracing these shifts in Canada's nation-building project by looking at immigration policy and institutions aligns with Fassin's (2015) directive to focus on institutions to illuminate the values and effects of the state – in this case, I look at Canadian immigration institutions to foreground Canada's moral economy concerning migration. This historical perspective allows us to appreciate that although there were many shortcomings associated with the Canadian state's assimilationist and even multicultural immigration policies, these previous immigration regimes nevertheless eventually offered most newcomers permanent settlement, a core Canadian value. Indeed, this is why many Filipina/o TMWs, among others, believe they will eventually be granted formal legal membership in Canada. However, as shown above for fast-food workers, in recent years the number of temporary-status migrants recruited to Canada has increased sharply, and many of these individuals are confined to insecure and ambiguous systems for transitioning from temporary to permanent status. This removal of a clear path to permanent settlement for some migrants marks an important shift in Canada's moral economy, informed by and aligned with regressive exclusionary, austerity, and individualist neoliberal values.

Canada's immigration institutions have always focused on labour, as a central directive of Canadian immigration policy has been addressing labour market pressures. The federal institutions mandated with this task are Employment and Social Development Canada (ESDC) and Immigration, Refugees and Citizenship Canada (IRCC). ESDC addresses labour market issues, including labour shortages, through a range of programs, and IRCC makes policy documents and decisions and regulates migration flows to Canada. Together, they collaborate to address labour shortages through programs like the TFWP. Provincial governments also play an increasingly active role in shaping migration to their regions through Provincial Nominee Programs (PNPs) – immigration programs jointly administered by IRCC and provincial governments that aim to fast-track employer-nominated temporary foreign workers applying for permanent residency into occupations and regions identified as under pressure. The significance of PNP programs in relation to fast-food labour flows is briefly described below, though taken up in more detail in chapters 5 and 7.

Canada has seen several distinct temporal periods of migration flows (Boyd & Vickers, 2000; Li, 2003). These periods mark discrete economic, political, and geographical conditions that have informed how newcomer belonging is (racially) managed and shaped by the prevailing values of the time. During Canada's earlier years, from 1867 to 1895, immigration policies were geared toward domestic and infrastructure development in central Canada (Li, 2003). A laissez-faire philosophy toward immigration sought to attract people of European descent and encourage production in factories, mines, and other non-agricultural sectors. While this is widely described as an "open-door" period, there were already signs of racial exclusion. For instance, in 1885, the Chinese Head Tax was introduced to exclude those of Chinese descent from entering and settling in Canada. Still, the bulk of those looking to enter Canada during this period were individuals racialized as "White" from the European continent, and they – along with Chinese subjects who managed to enter the country – were granted the right to settle permanently in Canada.

The second period, from 1896 to 1914, featured the biggest wave of immigration in Canadian history (Li, 2003). This period was characterized by acute labour shortages across regions and sectors, and immigration policies were geared toward promoting migration and settlement, especially in the Prairie provinces. Indeed, "the building of the transcontinental railway, the settlement of the prairies and expanding industrial production intensified demand for labour" (Boyd & Vickers, 2000, p. 3). Accordingly, the Canadian government launched aggressive recruitment campaigns to address labour market pressures. Despite this need for labour, however, and notwithstanding the large volume of immigrants that arrived in Canada, not everyone was considered desirable for entry. The Chinese Head Tax of 1885 had increased from $50 to $500 by 1903, and in 1908 the Continuous Passage Act was introduced to exclude nationals from India from setting foot on Canadian soil. Those who did set foot, however, had the right to settle permanently in Canada (Simons, 2010, p. 56).

The 1915–46 period was shaped largely by economic and geopolitical relations, namely, the First and Second World Wars and the Great Depression (Boyd & Vickers, 2000). The First World War brought migration flows to Canada almost to a standstill, and although the 1920s saw a return of migration to the region, the Great Depression and the Second World War soon curtailed it. The leading source country of immigrants during this period was still Britain, although migrants also came from other countries, primarily in Western and Eastern Europe, with only a small proportion (less than 6 per cent) arriving from non-European countries (Boyd & Vickers, 2000, p. 7). Continuing with its program of racial exclusion, with the onset of the Second World War Canada introduced discriminatory policies against Japanese Canadians, this time as war-related measures. In 1942, Japanese Canadians living within a 100-mile radius of the Pacific Ocean were interned in detention camps and their citizenship rights were suspended, as they were considered an "enemy race" (Thobani, 2007, p. 94). Their detention continued to the end of the Second World War, at which point the Canadian government encouraged Japanese Canadians (more than half of whom were born in Canada) to "repatriate" back to Japan. More than four thousand left (Canadian Council for Refugees, 2000).

Post-war immigration policies and the introduction of the points system in 1967 marked important qualitative shifts in Canadian immigration policies, reflecting the changing values of the Canadian state and society. From the mid-1940s to the early 1960s, Canada's model continued to privilege Whiteness and gave preference to immigrants applying from preferred countries, namely the United Kingdom, the United States, France, and various Commonwealth countries. However, beginning in 1962, Canada began selecting newcomers based on assessments of their individual attributes, including personal characteristics like age, education, official language skills, and regional employment prospects for their skills, and it formally removed national origin as a factor in evaluating prospects for admission. In an era of broad-scale decolonization movements and civil rights agendas, employing race-based criteria to select migrants became indefensible (Thobani, 2007, p. 146). Instead, Canada sought to project a cosmopolitan image of itself onto the global stage – one that would identify Canada as a leader in human rights and as a socially just country.

The stated objective of the new points system was to implement "tools for controlling the occupational composition of immigration" (Green & Green, 1995, p. 1007). The new system also favoured sponsored dependants and nominated relatives, who could enter with fewer points than those required for independent applicants. Overall, the implementation of the universal points system was aimed at selecting newcomers based on their perceived suitability to integrate into Canadian society, their ability to receive financial support, and, most important, their capacity to fulfil identified labour-market needs (Green & Green, 1995; Ongley & Pearson, 1995).[5]

In 1971, Canada became the first country in the world to implement a policy of "multiculturalism within a bilingual framework" (Joppke, 2001, p. 438). Multiculturalism differs radically from assimilationist policy in that it places some of the onus of incorporating immigrants onto the state. It imagines the essence of the Canadian nation as tolerant and welcoming, as a nation that formally embraces and celebrates difference. It "departs from the perception of all citizens as individuals who are merely members of a larger dominant political community. Instead, it views them as having equal rights as individuals while simultaneously meriting differentiated rights as members of identity groups" (Shachar, 2000, p. 66). The result has been the inception of an imagined nation that welcomes multicultural and multiracial immigrants – a departure from its foundational colonial and racist moral economy.

The prevailing sociolegal and economic context shaped the development of multiculturalism; it was a product of the "golden years of industrial citizenship in Canada" (Fudge, 2005, p. 640). The industrial citizenship regime was tied to the growth of the welfare state and the expansion of social rights designed to offset the jarring inequalities produced by capitalist markets. Citizenship rights were closely tied to redistributive policies, a strong social safety net, and improved labour conditions. A new state-citizenship relationship developed wherein the state assumed greater responsibility for the social welfare and integration of its members, and members could benefit from increased entitlements. Unions played a central role in advancing these conditions. Social rights were secured largely by workers through collective bargaining and improvements to the employment relationship, including more worker-friendly conditions of employment (such as minimum wages and paid vacation), anti-discrimination policies, rights to representation, improved employment standards, and broader claims for social justice. In sum, though the shortcomings associated with industrial citizenship are widely documented, including its male bias (e.g., Fudge, 2005; Vosko, 2000), industrial citizenship was intimately tied to improved social entitlements and greater stability, including a strong economy, the growth of the welfare state, and related civil, political, and social rights (Fudge, 2005). Access to permanent residency and, in turn, citizenship rights were not distinguished between high- and low-skilled migrants beyond limited streams like the Seasonal Agricultural Workers Program (SAWP) and LCP; the latter which still facilitated viable prospects for incorporation.

As an official policy of belonging, the multicultural framework presented Canada as a humanitarian and welcoming country, to which diverse subjects could migrate primarily with the intent of settling and participating as equal members of society. Newcomers enjoyed the right to public settlement services such as language courses and legal aid, the right to work under favourable employment conditions, and the right to benefit from a generous welfare state, including access to medical services and educational institutions. They also benefited from the rights to employment insurance during difficult times and to sponsor the immigration of family members. Given the values this model of citizenship promotes, it is unsurprising that Maya and others like her expected a favourable reception in Canada.

The problem is that this model of citizenship and the multicultural version of belonging no longer prevails. Industrial citizenship began to unravel in the 1980s with the advance of globalization and neoliberal restructuring (Fudge, 2005). The 2001 Immigration and Refugee Protection Act institutionalized a framework for selecting entrants that rewarded human capital instead of identified skill sets that would (in theory) resolve specific labour-market pressures (Li, 1998, 2003; Reitz, 2004; Simons, 2010). In its current form, Canada's economic development model – and in turn, its immigration program – prioritizes building a knowledge-based economy, with a corresponding emphasis on human and economic capital. Prospects for immigrant selection are increasingly tied to favourable assessments of skill, and citizenship rights are differentiated between those classified as skilled (included) and low-skilled (denied).

As Sassen (1998) notes, socially undervalued, low-wage workers are an integral component of the engine that drives a knowledge-based economy. While Canada seeks to offer direct permanent entry only to those it defines as skilled and/or with financial resources to invest through initiatives like the Business Immigration Program, it still needs cleaners, restaurant staff, and manual labourers to function. The existence of the LSS and PNPs is evidence of this reality. The revamped points system is (purportedly) not satisfying regional demands for labour; thus, the federal government, in concert with provincial governments, permits temporary labour migration through these alternative (and precarious) streams.

While Canada continues to organize its immigration program to align with economic and labour-market needs, the state no longer extends formal citizenship status or the reasonable prospect of permanent residency to a growing number of those who participate in the economic development of the country. In other words, though Canada has long sought to patrol the boundaries of its nation-state and limit the entry of those it deems "undesirable" along a host of social lines (such as nationality and "race"), it has only recently begun denying permanent migrant settlement or attainable pathways to secure formal citizenship to certain labour-market participants. Beyond the individual hardships this poses for many newcomers at work and in the labour market (chapter 5), the expansion of a guest worker scheme in the bottom tiers of the economy marks an important shift in the substance and meaning of Canadian citizenship and in the values upheld by the state. The "heart of Canada" is now precarious and neoliberal.

Social Exclusion and Precarious Belonging in Canada

Analyses of precarity – in employment and in immigration status – are key to understanding the intersecting exclusionary forces temporary migrants currently face. Beginning in the 1970s, the manufacturing sector in North America began to decline, and labour regulations and the power of unions were weakened, leading to an erosion of the standard employment relationship.[6] Precarious employment has since become widespread.

Vosko (2010, p. 2) describes employment precarity as "work for remuneration characterized by uncertainty, low income, and limited social benefits and statutory entitlements." This new dominant social relation between employers and workers has contributed to dramatic transformations in societies, including greater economic inequality, higher rates of poverty, the physical, psychological, and moral dislocation of people, and a decline in the middle class (Kalleberg, 2009). Risk and uncertainty have been downloaded from employers to workers, creating favourable conditions for capital accumulation at great cost to workers.

Studies have shown that women (Vosko, 2000, 2008), millennials entering the labour market (Martin & Lewchuck, 2018), and racialized immigrant women in Canada (Premji et al., 2014) are more susceptible to precarious employment conditions than others. Among newcomers, legal status is particularly important in shaping conditions of precarious employment. Goldring and Landolt (2012, 2013) found that initial entry into the Canadian labour market with precarious legal status is linked to long-term negative economic outcomes, even after transition to more permanent status. They also show that the labour market is segmented along lines of legal status and that precarious legal status increases the probability of labour market and employment insecurity.

In Canada, as elsewhere, employment insecurity has become widespread, especially among the most vulnerable populations in an increasingly segmented labour market. Fast-food TMWs, for example, are migrants lacking formal citizenship status, segmented into low-wage worksites in the bottom tiers of the Canadian labour market. Their employment insecurity limits their opportunities to become upwardly mobile. Even if the labour market afforded newcomers security through access to well-compensated employment (which it generally does not), migrant workers would be denied such access as they are not legally allowed to circulate in the labour market. In contrast to the economic security and large middle class that characterizes the standard employment relationship, then, low-wage TMWs now enter Canada in a context of polarized labour markets and the growth of below-the-poverty-line wages. These new conditions create significant barriers to the multicultural version of belonging, precisely because the conditions in which belonging was previously facilitated no longer exist. Market-driven citizenship now prevails. The power of employers and industry associations to promote market-driven immigration policies that disenfranchise segments of the precariat has helped usher in a new version of cultural and legal exclusion in Canada, alongside a new moral economy that turns a blind eye to precarious belonging.

Industry Lobbying for Migrant Workers: "It Took a Lot of Convincing"

Precarity in worksites and migratory flows is a product of the commercialization of citizenship in Canada brought about by the offloading of migration management to profit-driven actors. In Western Canada, the tourism and hospitality sector (including food and beverage employers like Tim Hortons) was instrumental in lobbying for the recruitment of flexible labour and for the expansion of the TFWP. Insisting that growth was imminent but that local workforces were unable to accommodate it, the sector was successful in institutionalizing these changes. My interviews with industry representatives and government staff, along with a number of government and industry reports, suggest that the relationship between state agents and corporate entities was key to the success of these reforms – along with propitious timing.

On 2 July 2003, the International Olympic Committee announced that Vancouver – and by extension, British Columbia – would host the 2010 Winter Olympic Games, seen as an opportunity for British Columbia to achieve short- and long-term economic gains through investments and tourism revenue. Leading up to the announcement, the province doubled its marketing budget from $25 to $50 million (Grant Thornton, 2006, p. 2) and created a task force in 2001 to determine projected human resource needs. Funded by key tourism groups and the labour arms of the provincial and federal governments, industry representatives formed a working group and hired a labour market economist to determine likely demand for tourism-related jobs, identifying "Food Service Counter Attendant" as one of the occupations that would face a labour shortage. They generated a five-year "human resource development strategy" and formed go2 (now go2HR) – an industry association that would lobby for their interests. The provincial government suggested that if the sector could provide proof of projected labour market shortages in tourism and hospitality, it would be receptive to proposals for new immigration and labour programs (BC Tourism HRD Task Force, 2003, p. 8).

In late 2002, representatives of the BC and federal governments (including ESDC and the BC Ministry of Skills Development and Labour) formed a multistakeholder committee called the 2010 Human Resources Planning Committee. The committee's report, "Planning for Gold," suggested that between 2003 and 2015, the highest employment growth would be in "Accommodation/Food/Recreation" and that "food counter attendants & helpers" was the eleventh occupation most under pressure (HRPC, 2003, p. 6). Industry, including fast-food stakeholders, latched on to these findings to lobby the government for changes to the TFWP, yet government representatives were initially resistant, arguing that "major policy shifts [to immigration programming] were not necessary to ensure an adequate supply of skilled immigrants to help meet labour demands" (HRPC, 2003, p. 33). There was tension regarding whether a labour shortage actually existed; industry insisted it did, while government representatives were sceptical, and the report was equivocal on the matter. In response, industry advocates concluded that they needed to direct their attention to promoting amendments to the TFWP.

Other industry reports during this period presented similar findings and reflect the tourism and hospitality sector's shift toward lobbying the government for amendments to immigration programming, to secure temporary, low-skilled labour migration. A discussion paper produced for go2HR, for example, described the housekeeping labour shortage in BC's Kootenay region and the purported shortcomings of existing temporary migrant worker streams for addressing this shortage (Grant Thornton, 2006). The report identified the TFWP's "lengthy application and review process" as a significant obstacle for employers and suggested that BC's PNP program needed to adapt to cover other relevant occupations such as that of food counter attendant (Grant Thornton, 2006, pp. 6–7). The same report noted that at that critical juncture, government was becoming more responsive to addressing tourism and hospitality labour "needs" by considering amendments to immigration programming, including the "Minimal Skills Pilot Project" (the Low-Skill Pilot) and a Mexican bilateral labour program, both of which later came to fruition. Establishing the existence of labour shortages was seen as key: "Government buy-in that labour shortages in the accommodation industry is a serious and legitimate issue is critical to the establishment of a program that will adequately address this issue" (Grant Thornton, 2006, p. 16).

Industry employers in Alberta, while not operating within the Olympics context, also sought to lobby the government for pathways to global recruitment during a similar historical period marked by a pending oil and gas boom. Concerns that labour shortages would impact the province's "economic growth and prosperity" drove the creation of a "Workforce Strategy for Alberta's Tourism and Hospitality Industry," consisting of government representatives and key stakeholders from the tourism and hospitality sector, including the Alberta Hotel and Lodging Association (AHLA), the Canadian Federation of Independent Business (CFIB), the Canadian Restaurant and Foodservices Association (CRFA), and corporations like Tim Hortons and McDonald's (Alberta, Employment, Immigration & Industry, 2007, p. 1). These corporations and industry associations stressed the need for amendments to immigration policies, faulted the TFWP and PNPs for favouring more highly skilled workers despite supposedly greater "needs" in lower-skilled occupations, and called for streamlining the TFWP to make it more employer-friendly and responsive to industry. Like in BC, they specifically identified "food counter attendants and kitchen helpers" as occupations under pressure. The AHLA, CFIB, and CRFA agreed to take the lead in proposing "changes to temporary foreign worker policies to better meet the needs of tourism and hospitality industry and workers, along with removing remaining barriers for lower skilled workers" in addition to proposing a "further expansion of the Provincial Nominee Program, allocating more spaces for less-skilled immigrants to fill jobs in the tourism and hospitality industry" (Alberta, Employment, Immigration & Industry, 2007, p. 10).

My empirical data is entirely consistent with these accounts, including the reported ideological tensions, networks, and deliberations between government representatives and industry associations involved in shaping and expanding the TFWP. Throughout the course of my research, labour recruiters, immigration lawyers, and labour consultants identified the early to mid-2000s as a period of government reluctance to acknowledge a labour shortage in the bottom tiers of the labour market. A labour consultant explained that for TMW recruitment to really "take off," officials needed convincing that there was indeed a labour shortage. In his words, "the attitude was, 'we understand the need for temporary foreign workers for nurses or for engineers,' but the culture, the mindset in that department [ESDC regarding low-skilled workers] … was, 'just go out and hire one.' That was sort of the milieu that we operated in." An immigration lawyer in Vancouver explained that "there was an ideological opposition on the part of this government to the foreign worker program … They weren't anti-immigration at all. But they were anti-temporary immigration. And I'm not sure why the federal government was so scared of it … it took a lot of convincing."

In an interview in 2010, a senior employee at go2HR told me about his organization's role in initiating the expansion of the TFWP. There had been a Low-Skill Pilot project in place since 2002, yet he noted that "there were virtually no occupations in the tourism industry that were being granted labour market opinions [the first step in the process of recruiting TMWs]." He described the government attitude as: "It's low-skilled, you should just go out and find somebody. You don't have to bring someone over from the Philippines or whatever." Given this perception, go2HR oversaw a series of labour market studies to gather empirical data to lobby the government for access to TMWs. The go2HR employee explained, "Part of the reasons we were doing the labour market study was to quantify what industry already knew … So we strategically looked at the Whistler area … we were using that for support on why the TFWP should expand … we made our point. And the government finally said okay, we'll start approving labour market opinions." This employee's account clearly captures how profit-driven actors used state/corporate social networks and deliberations to facilitate precarious labour migration.

In line with this version of events, a senior-level government bureaucrat at Service Canada told me that while the TFWP had a long-standing history in Canada, there had been no viable program for employers of low-skilled workers to recruit TMWs outside of domestic caregiving or agricultural work. "It was because employers had repeatedly come to government saying they were unable to identify workers …, we brought in, based on industry feedback, the Low-Skill Pilot." He further explained that with the economic boom, "when things skyrocketed," the Alberta, British Columbia, and federal governments created the Expedited Labour Market Opinion Project (E-LMO) in September 2007 to expedite access to TMWs for occupations identified as experiencing acute labour shortages. Initially, the project included only twelve occupations, largely in the construction, healthcare, and hospitality industries, but by early 2008, in consultation with industry, this number had almost tripled to include thirty-three occupations, including food counter attendant. Industry lobbying appears to have played an important role, as the Service Canada official noted: "If I look at the tourism and hospitality sector, we have long-standing, positive relationships with some of the key representative groups, and that's something that helps us on a regular basis in terms of identifying projected labour market needs like the E-LMO and gaps in policy issues." His account aptly describes how employers, corporate entities, and states work in concert – as well in tension – to manage the border.

The E-LMO was in operation until April 15, 2010, just over a month after the closing of the 2010 Winter Olympic Games. In my research interviews, employers, labour consultants, immigration lawyers, and industry association representatives repeatedly identified the termination of the program as a setback and expressed their frustration with the lack of expedited flows of flexible workers to Canada. Indeed, the E-LMO had reduced wait times for labour market opinions in relevant industries, sometimes from months to just five days, and the end of the program brought a return to longer wait times, though nowhere near those of the pre-E-LMO era. Furthermore, two-year work visas issued via the E-LMO were shortened to just one year when the program ended, requiring employers to recruit workers more frequently and expend more energy and resources on the recruitment process. While profit-driven actors appear to have considerable sway to exert influence on migration flows, they ultimately do not have the final say; the state retains final control over the territory.

While my interview participants were aware of the economic downturn and rising domestic unemployment levels in Canada at the time, many were nevertheless openly critical of these policy changes, especially ruing the loss of the E-LMO. Some mentioned quite candidly that the growing unemployment rate did not make it easier for employers to recruit food-counter attendants, contending that the labour shortage was not due to a lack of workers but rather due to a limited availability of *preferred* workers. For instance, a fast-food labour consultant explained that the LSS existed to recruit workers into occupations that were "unattractive to Canadians" and that the only people otherwise available for such jobs were "people that you would not want to employ to serve food in the restaurant because you'll lose your restaurant." While some such workers might be looking for work, he remarked, "they have to be able to handle customers, handle health regulations, and do things in a reasonably methodical time manner [*sic*], make change, and there's lots of people out there that are not capable of that." He later identified Aboriginal peoples, recent immigrants, and aging populations as belonging to this group of undesirable workers, and suggested, "Maybe with a lot of coaching, but when you're running a Tim Hortons or a Subway, you are not running an employment repatriation course [*laughs*], you know?"

The impressive power of Tim Hortons to direct policy agendas and patrol the border merits special mention, particularly with respect to shifts in immigration programming. Tim Hortons was an active member on the "Workforce Strategy for Alberta's Tourism and Hospitality Industry" and the "Labour Mobility Working Group." The latter group eventually resulted in the "Canada–Mexico Labour Mobility Mechanism," through which chains like Tim Hortons and McDonald's have recruited Mexican food-counter attendants to Western Canada (see Polanco, 2019). While bureaucrats and tourism stakeholders were often reluctant in my interviews to name Tim Hortons or the corporation's human resource specialists by name, many identified Tim Hortons' labour strategies manager as instrumental in expanding the TFWP and in tirelessly defining and promoting the interests of fast food, including lobbying the government for access to migrant workers.

In 2011, I attended an industry conference on the TFWP in Calgary, Alberta. In attendance were more than sixty delegates – primarily employers, immigration lawyers, third-party labour recruiters, human resource specialists, and government bureaucrats involved with the TFWP portfolio. Also present was a senior human resource specialist for the Tim Hortons Corporation. While observing his interactions with government bureaucrats, I initially thought that he, too, was a government bureaucrat, as he appeared well acquainted with the others and their exchanges were jovial and friendly. Those he did not know (especially human resource specialists) swarmed around him, eager to make his acquaintance. On more than one occasion I witnessed government bureaucrats direct both employers and human resource personnel to him when they were unable to answer questions regarding the TFWP low-skilled stream. At one point during the conference, a high-ranking government bureaucrat stood at the podium and referred to him as "our [the government's] resident expert on the NOC-C/D Program," the title many in government used to refer to the LSS. Over the years I have even heard government bureaucrats at conferences jokingly refer to the LSS as "the Tim Hortons Program."

The tourism and hospitality sector saw largely favourable policy shifts in immigration programming through their efforts until, ultimately, a moratorium derailed these advances. On April 24, 2014, following allegations that a McDonald's franchise owner in British Columbia was overlooking Canadian job applicants in favour of migrant workers, the government instituted an immediate suspension of all transnational recruitment of food service workers. This highly publicized announcement instigated a watershed of further media reporting on similar cases, intensifying the controversy and public pressure surrounding the already controversial TFWP. Major amendments to the LSS followed, including more stringent requirements for advertising job vacancies, caps on the percentage of TMWs per worksite, a "'four-in, four-out" rule that dictated a cumulative maximum stay of four years in Canada (since retracted), and a general shift away from approving requests for food service TMWs. While the moratorium was eventually lifted on June 20, 2014, recruitment levels for years remained stagnant.

In that context, the tourism and hospitality sector revived its lobbying efforts to focus on temporary migration flows that continue to the present. In response to a review of the TFWP following the moratorium, the Tourism Industry Association of Canada authored a letter to government stressing the sector's "need" for TMWs and advocating for a "TFW Tourism Stream" on a national scale that would resemble Canada's long-standing program for seasonal agricultural workers (Tourism Industry Association of Canada, 2015, p. 3). "Like the Agriculture Stream of the TFWP," it argues, "tourism needs a dedicated program … Sub streams could include seasonal (winter or summer), low-skilled (housekeepers, cleaners, some food service positions) and specific higher skilled (ski instructors, hunting guides) streams" (Tourism Industry Association of Canada, 2014, p. 22).

Provincial lobbying efforts related to the TFWP also persist. Go2HR developed a new labour market strategy for 2020, including providing "tourism industry input to government to help formulate/revise policies and programs on foreign workers and immigration" and "ensuring the tourism sector is represented at and participates in government labour market initiatives" (BC Tourism Labour Market Strategy, 2012, pp. 16–17). Alberta industry associations like the AHLA are likewise organizing at the provincial and federal levels for renewed access to the TFWP, including advocating for reduced costs for Labour Market Impact Assessments (LMIAs, the first step in recruiting migrant workers under the Low-Skilled Stream), extending the duration of work permits to a minimum of two years (rather than the current one-year norm), making additional occupations eligible for TMW recruitment, and – actively promoting precarity – organizing against the proposal for occupation-specific work permits under the TFWP that would permit precarious migrant workers some limited mobility in the labour market. The Canadian Federation of Independent Businesses is calling for the introduction of a worker visa that would "give foreign workers in entry-level categories in areas with labour shortages an opportunity to work with an employer for two years as a defined step toward permanent residency" (Goodman, 2014), in effect expanding immigration programming geared at employers while indenturing the worker to the specific employer for a duration of two years. Restaurants Canada (formally the Canadian Restaurant and Foodservices Association) is lobbying against increases to minimum wages, with public campaigns claiming that despite the sector's efforts to recruit from underrepresented groups, it still faces shortages and needs to look abroad. Restaurants Canada also opposes government plans to publicly expose and penalize employers who violate rules under the TFWP.

Considering the cumulative and concerted nature of these industry lobbying efforts, the drop in labour flows of food-counter attendants proved to be a momentary setback to recruiting generations of precarious hospitality workers to Canada under the TFWP, as suggested in chapter 7. From a capricious terrain of controversies, profit-driven actors continue to lobby immigration institutions by shaping policies, while state agents facilitate this process.

**Legislated Nonbelonging: The Lived Realities
of Fast-Food Denizens**

An employer seeking to recruit a TMW under the LSS must apply for a LMIA from Service Canada, the servicing arm of ESDC. A LMIA evaluates the impact that hiring a migrant worker would have on the local labour market. In theory, domestic workers should not be negatively impacted by the recruitment of migrant workers,[7] thus part of the LMIA includes verifying that employers have made appropriate efforts to draw labour from local labour pools and that they are seeking to hire migrant workers as a last resort.

Once an employer has received a positive LMIA from Service Canada, the recruitment process can begin. For Filipina/o workers, this involves a Canadian employer (or its designated third-party labour representative) contracting a recruiter in the Philippines.[8] The employer specifies the type of workers needed, and the recruiter goes about finding them.

Once a worker has been selected (often a joint initiative between the recruiter and the employer or its representative), the Canadian embassy in Manila assesses the suitability of the applicant for temporary employment in Canada. This assessment includes a criminal record check, an evaluation of past work experience in the occupation in question, and ensuring adequate language capital, sufficient education (usually a minimum of a college degree in the case of food-counter attendants), and recent ties to the Philippines (the latter presumably ensuring the worker will not try to overstay their contract by going "underground"). The worker's contract must specify a wage consistent with the prevailing median wage identified in the National Occupational Classification (NOC) system, which is the median hourly wage paid to Canadians working in an occupation in a specific geographical area. In the case of unionized workers, the wage is determined by the collective bargaining agreement. Regulations stipulate that TMWs must be extended the same benefits as those offered to domestic workers, including medical coverage and registration in compensation and workplace safety insurance plans. Employers must also cover the transportation costs to and from Canada and assist migrant workers in finding suitable and affordable accommodations, though it is not uncommon for employers to violate both requirements.

In theory, TMWs enjoy the same employment rights as other workers in Canada. However, precarious migrant workers are disproportionately vulnerable to exploitative working conditions, in part because their "temporary" citizenship status disempowers them from accessing their employment rights (Parreñas et al., 2021; Preibisch, 2010; Preibisch and Encalada Grez, 2010; Sharma, 2002, 2006). I found settlement workers to be especially informative regarding the kinds of challenges faced by the fast-food migrant workers they assist. A constant challenge settlement workers identified was a desire to leave an abusive employer. A worker's legal right to stay in Canada is tied to their employment contract, meaning that despite maltreatment, workers are unlikely to exit the employment relationship without first securing another LMIA and work contract (which require lengthy, costly, and bureaucratic processes and a willingness on the part of another employer, and are therefore not always obtained). As one settlement worker explained, "We see problems between employers and employees. That's the main issue. The worker is so upset and wants to leave the job but they also want to stay in Canada, so they want us to help them get another employer. We sometimes try to help, but how can we? We are not in the employment industry, you know?" Another settlement worker in Vancouver said many workers ask, "'Well, if I want to be a whistle-blower and talk about the issues, what is the protection that you can give me?' And unfortunately," the settlement worker explained, "I don't have that."

Despite their entitlement to employment rights, workers recruited under the LSS are formally denied other rights granted to (would-be) citizens, including the right to settlement services. This is a challenge for migrant workers not only because they are excluded from services like English-language training courses but also because they do not technically have the right to access most publicly funded advocacy support systems such as legal aid, which could potentially help them resolve employment or related issues. As one settlement worker said, "Where can we refer these people? Who is the advocate that can help them? So at the level of advocacy there is really not much that can be done." Another settlement worker recounted, "Many of them would come desperately and panicky looking for assistance ... They would need legal representation, [but] we don't have the capacity ... of doing that ... We cannot meet these demands."

I also heard from fast-food workers themselves about the difficulties they face in the worksite and beyond. Most migrant workers in my study told me at length about how their employers would speak to them rudely or disproportionately assign them the most difficult tasks, which they attributed to their "non-Canadian" migrant worker status. Unpaid wages and overtime were also a point of stress for many workers. Nonetheless, the majority were reluctant to confront their employers about these conditions because of their vulnerable positions in Canada. Indeed, these challenges are widespread and have been featured in media reporting. For instance, four former Tim Hortons workers in British Columbia filed a human rights complaint against a franchise owner in Dawson Creek. According to their allegations, the owner referred to these TMWs as "Mexican idiots," assigned them the most menial jobs in the restaurant and punished them for speaking Spanish while on the job. Two of the workers were fired and sent back to Mexico (Carman, 2012).

Beyond the worksite, migrant workers have also reported problems related to accommodations and the reimbursement of travel costs. Under the LSS, employers are responsible for helping workers to find suitable accommodations. Some employers capitalize on this policy by buying homes and charging TMWs above-market rent or making it possible for their friends to do the same. A worker in Alberta told me that she and her roommates, all of whom were Tim Hortons TMWs, would take turns sleeping because there were five of them in the two-bedroom apartment they rented from their employer. They each paid

$700 a month for this accommodation – a rate well above market value. In Edmonton, Alberta, a group of migrant workers from Belize recruited to work in McDonald's restaurants were housed in a penthouse suite one and a half hours away from their place of employment by bus. The five workers were charged $280 biweekly for the rent (exceeding the advertised rental price for the penthouse by more than $600 a month), which was automatically deducted from their pay cheques. When the workers approached the franchise owner about moving, the employer reportedly threatened to continue deducting the rent from their pay cheques even if they moved out. One of the workers was reportedly fired after publicly complaining online about the situation. Moreover, the workers had been told that the employer would reimburse them for their visa and travel costs (a stipulation under the TFWP regulation), yet the workers say they were never reimbursed (Tomlinson, 2014).

The disposability experienced by migrant workers is arguably the most pronounced expression of their precarity and of the legislated production of nonbelonging generated by the TFWP. Employers are under no obligation to support or protect TMWs and can merely replace them when they are no longer seen as useful. The case of Maria Victoria Venancio (Vicky), a TMW from the Philippines, captures this extreme form of precarity. In 2012 in Edmonton, Alberta, Vicky was riding her bike to the McDonald's restaurant where she worked when she was struck by a car. The accident left her quadriplegic. Because she could no longer work as a food counter attendant, her employer dismissed her, and the government sought to deport her. In the process, she lost her provincial health care benefits. Community activists (most notably Migrante Alberta) rallied around her to resist her deportation. They engaged in a host of activities, including public shaming campaigns against the Canadian government to urge the state to grant Vicky permanent residency status. In 2017, after five years of lobbying and living with uncertainty, she was eventually granted permanent residence in Canada. Had Vicky not garnered the attention and support of relevant actors, the Canadian government would certainly have deported her back to the Philippines.

As these examples show, low-wage migrant workers live in conditions of pronounced precarity, rendered possible through the regulatory framework of the LSS developed by state agents in concert with profit-driven actors. These workers are streamed into segments of the labour market with the most unfavourable work and employment conditions and are highly susceptible to maltreatment, including verbal abuse, being assigned the most difficult and unappealing job tasks, unpaid wages, overpriced living conditions, disposability, and (threats of) repatriation. Such insecurity under the LSS is the norm, not the exception.

Employer-Mediated Prospects for Belonging

The precarity described above is further exacerbated for Filipino TMWs, whose expectations are based on the long history of Filipinos migrating to Canada, both as immigrants and migrant workers. This history and Canada's reputation of being welcoming have created the (inaccurate) perception in the Philippines that a temporary work contract in Canada is a step toward securing Canadian citizenship status, as was indeed the case under previous migration regimes. Nurses immigrating to Canada in the 1960s and 1970s were followed in the mid-1970s by garment workers and by family members benefiting from family reunification policies. By the mid-1980s, Filipinas were being recruited primarily as live-in domestics, first under the Foreign Domestic Movement (Pratt in Collaboration with the Filipino-Canadian Youth Alliance, 2003), then under the Live-in Caregiver and Caregiver Programs, respectively, and currently through the Home Child Care Provider Pilot and Home Support Worker Pilot. These programs all have a direct and institutionalized (though imperfect) process for transitioning to permanent residency status. In contrast, under the Low-Skilled Stream, the prospect of attaining permanent residency is both indirect (it requires the nomination of the employer at their discretion with the state retaining final decision-making power) and numerically improbable (see the statistical analysis in chapter 5). Yet the perception persists in the Philippines that a temporary work contract in Canada can lead to Canadian citizenship, and this belief leads many workers to endure conditions they might otherwise resist or refuse. As one research participant stated, "Because the nannies, or the women caregivers, after two years they get nominated … So I thought for sure, me too." The prospect of being nominated for permanent residency and the presumed benefits associated with Canadian citizenship exert a strong disciplinary force on workers.

Some PNP programs do fast-track permanent residency applications for food-counter attendants through employer-initiated and/or employer-sponsored nomination processes, as described in chapter 5. Significantly, though, and unbeknown to most workers, nomination under a PNP is not the same as attaining permanent residency status under the domestic caregiving streams, where workers themselves can initiate the immigration process after meeting a set of criteria. Under PNPs, employers alone have the power to decide whether to support the nomination of a worker. Employers are also limited in how many workers they can support per worksite, and whether their region is even open to nominations. The LSP and PNPs therefore create fierce competition among workers to be the "chosen ones" selected for nomination. These policies have introduced a new labour regime in Canada (described in detail in chapter 5) – one that disciplines and motivates workers with the (improbable) promise of attaining Canadian citizenship while providing employers with a relatively permanent and compliant workforce in a sector that has long had to contend with staffing challenges and high turnover rates.

Employers are now directly inserted in the immigration process, both shaping immigration policies and regulating migrants' opportunities for migration and permanent residency. And the workers coming to Canada through these new programs are significantly more disenfranchised than those who came through previous immigration programs. They receive limited opportunities to belong – culturally and legally – in "multicultural" Canada.

Multiculturalism, Temporary Labour Schemes, and Nonbelonging in Neoliberal Canada

Canada has an exclusionary history when it comes to addressing labour market needs in concert with its nation-building agendas. Historically, it has sought to preserve "Whiteness" in the service of the nation and has only reluctantly accepted flows of those previously deemed "undesirable" – along a host of social lines – to address labour market pressures. When changing social values made it indefensible to employ criteria based on national origin or race to select migrants, Canada shifted gears and officially embraced a policy of multiculturalism in 1971, shortly following the 1967 introduction of the point-system to regulate migration. Both policies would allow Canada to be identified as a socially just, cosmopolitan country, marking the beginning of a new moral economy in Canada – one of multicultural inclusivity – that rejected (at least in theory) colonial and racist values. Together, multiculturalism and a reconfigured immigration program positioned Canada as a human rights leader on the global stage and obscured Canada's history of past wrongdoings, including Canada's (mal)treatment of centuries of racialized migration flows. Multiculturalism also clouded the country's violent history of colonization and genocidal acts against Indigenous peoples in Canada, instead casting the Canadian state in a highly favourable light.

But multiculturalism is more than just a policy geared at accommodating difference; in the case of Canada, it has a symbolic value that is unmatched in any other Western country. Indeed, "we [Canada] are unusual in the extent to which we have built these practices into our symbols and narratives of nationhood. We tell each other that accommodating diversity is an important part of the Canadian identity; it is a defining feature of the country" (Kymlicka, 2003, p. 4). This narrative of nationhood bleeds into migrants' hopes and dreams of what can be expected of Canada. Yet as I have shown in this chapter, multicultural Canada is more myth than reality. Canada (like many Western nations) is not as progressive or welcoming as official policy implies, especially with the advent of recent neoliberal policies. This discord is evident in the disillusionment of the in-house human resource specialist with whom I began this chapter – Rachel – and her pronounced discomfort with the LSS. Rachel appears to believe in the myth that Canada is a country that is welcoming and accommodating, thus she is troubled by the lived realities of low-wage migrants and by how employers explicitly seek their flexible, precarious labour. She is dismayed with the global recruitment of fast-food workers because of what it seems to imply about Canada, supplanting her positive vision of Canada's moral economy characterized by multicultural inclusivity with one marked by neoliberalism and social exclusion.

As an official policy of belonging, the multicultural framework materialized at the tail end of the golden period of industrial citizenship, when migrating to Canada had come to symbolize benefiting from a government that takes care of its people. The framework implies that Canada is a prosperous country where diverse subjects can migrate with the intent of settling and where, upon arrival, they are encouraged to participate as equal members of society – with rights to access public settlement services like language courses and legal aid, to work under favourable employment conditions, and to benefit from a generous welfare state, including access to medical services, educational institutions, and employment insurance during difficult times. Immigration into multicultural Canada has also involved the right to sponsor the immigration of family members.

My account of the lived realities of Filipina/o fast-food migrants shows, however, that this is not the reception that most newcomers recruited under the LSS receive. Their precarity stands in stark contrast to their hopes and dreams of belonging to a multicultural country that is generous and welcoming and champions human rights. And profit-driven actors have been instrumental in advancing their disenfranchisement and minimizing the integrity of Canada as an immigration nation. Market-driven citizenship now prevails precisely because Canada moved away from the economic and political policies that maintained the SER to embrace a neoliberal, market-driven model of development, effectively "implementing the transformation of (welfare) citizenship into denizenship" (Lea, 2013, p. 5).

These changes were not the product of abstract and disembodied forces. Situated actors and processes have produced these results. As I have documented in this chapter, industry stakeholders were instrumental in lobbying for and gaining access to flexible labour through the expansion of the TFWP. They successfully convinced state agents to amend immigration policies in their favour, heralding capital's new role in managing migration. Further, industry associations and corporations like Tim Hortons are building a business model out of these new immigration streams, and in the process, they are altering the substance and meaning of belonging in Canada. While guest worker schemes are not the sole cause of the shift toward market-driven citizenship, and temporary migrant workers are not the only ones to feel the brunt, temporary migrant worker programs are an emblematic part of this reconfiguration of citizenship and belonging.

Schierup and Lund (2011) have documented a similar process in Sweden, where, in their words, despite a "liberal multiculturalism that offered an extended and substantial body of citizenship rights … to 'newcomers,' … the last two decades have, step by step, led towards neoliberal disciplinary strategies" (56). This "business-friendly 'guest worker' system," they contend, has resulted in "new labour migrants, excluded from the edifice of citizenship, the most important bulwark of Swedish exceptionalism" (60–1). Like Sweden, Canada is moving away from its "exceptionalism" (if it ever existed), largely through the expansion of its TFWP. In response to profit-driven actors, the state has altered dominant perceptions of immigration to reflect neoliberal values, in effect altering Canada's moral economy. On a global scale, fierce competition by migrant-sending countries to supply workers around the world, coupled with subjects' eagerness to pursue the promises they associate with settlement in countries like Canada, facilitate these cultural and legal exclusions in host destinations.

In the next chapter, we turn to the Philippines to explore how Filipina/o labour recruiters and the labour brokerage state promote the temporary labour migration of fast-food workers to Western Canada and help fashion these transnationally mediated conditions of non-belonging.

Chapter 3

Beguiling and Brokering the "Great Filipino Worker"

In Vancouver, British Columbia, I met with Manuel, a Filipino bureaucrat, at the Philippine Consulate General office, known elsewhere as the Philippine Overseas Labour Office (POLO). I was excited about the meeting, eager to gain a more nuanced and Canada-based account of the Philippine migration apparatus and its transnational regulation. POLO offices are the operating arm of the Philippine government's Department of Labor and Employment (DOLE) in receiving countries. They exist primarily to administer and enforce the Philippine government's policies and programs related to Overseas Foreign Workers (OFWs) and are one component of the highly celebrated Philippine "labour brokerage state" that manages migration through mobilizing, exporting, and regulating the flows of migrants from and to the Philippines (Rodriguez, 2010).

Upon commencing the interview, I realized how fortunate I was to be meeting with Manuel. He had a wealth of first-hand experience working in POLO offices across the world and spoke freely of the situation of OFWs in comparative perspective. Manuel began by describing the role of the Philippine Consulate General office in Canada and elsewhere, its diplomatic and marketing practices, and his views on the benefits of temporary labour migration. He also relayed his insights into why countries like Canada require Filipina/o OFWs:

> My labour market analysis of Canada is that this is a country which really needs immigrants and foreign workers ... It [Canada] cannot close its doors ... First, if you talk about the area, it's so huge. You really need people. Second, it's an aging society. The birth rate is so low. Most of the people are in senior homes already you know? ... You need immigrants, foreign workers to run the society. And in the Philippines, we have so many workers!

Manuel's account offers a glimpse into key dynamics underlying Filipina/o labour migration to Canada. While most Filipina/o temporary migrant workers (TMWs) in Canada are college-educated (Bonifacio, 2014), many are nonetheless segmented into low-waged occupations that domestic workforces are generally unmotivated to work in; cleaning toilets, washing cars, caring for the elderly, and serving food behind the counter of fast-food restaurants are tasks that do not appeal to many local job seekers. Manuel's comment also acknowledges the discrepancies between Canadian and Philippine labour markets. Canada is a country with an aging population and a low birth rate. In contrast, the Philippines is perceived as boasting a reserve army of young workers eager to be selected for employment abroad. Manuel seemed to view global labour migration as a result of complementary shortcomings between these transnationally connected regions.

Over the course of my research in both Canada and the Philippines, other social actors offered similar descriptions to explain the labour flows linking the Philippines with Western Canada. Lao, a Manila-based Filipino bureaucrat employed at the Philippines' Overseas Workers Welfare Administration (OWWA), said, "The unique situation that Canada finds itself in with its acute labour shortages was a good match for the Philippines' overabundance of labour. It's an aging population … You couldn't find people to flip your burgers [locally so] … you've got these people [Filipina/o TMWs] to help you out."

Like Lao and Manuel, many studies explain the global movement of workers from developing to developed regions by emphasizing northern countries' economic growth and severe demographic decline and the so-called reserve armies of young, eager, and available workers in the Global South (e.g., Borjas, 1990; Piore, 1979). The shift in northern countries toward temporary labour migration and away from permanent migrant settlement is generally considered to be the product of this supply-and-demand combination (as well as other similar combinations, such as skill discrepancies) serendipitously linking different countries' strengths and weaknesses. Alongside a politics of contracting borders, this logic has led Lao and Manuel, agents of the Philippine migration apparatus, to view the global movement of workers as a win-win-win arrangement for migrants and sending and receiving countries. While persuasive, these macrostructural accounts – and the moral-political investments that inform them – imply that "humans are more or less atomistic individuals that operate in an institutional, social, and cultural void" (Haas, 2008, p. 9). The cultural and institutional contexts in which the global workforce migrates are absent from these structural accounts.

In the following two chapters, I focus on the sociocultural and institutional dimensions in the sending context that organize migrant labour flows. I analyse the social imaginary of the "great Filipino worker" (Guevarra, 2010) and how the Canadian Dream and associations tied to a colonial mentality operate as cultural pull and push forces. To establish a theoretical framework that captures the role of (values within) institutions and the social imaginary in mediating sending-context dynamics, I employ a four-pronged analysis that explores (1) the migration institutions, including the values governing sending-context flows; (2) the representation of Filipina/o migrants and how their image is constructed by profit-driven actors during marketing, selection, and training, shaping Canadian employers' migrant worker selection; (3) the national dreams ascribed to receiving countries that stimulate individual desires to engage in overseas work; and (4) the disparaging social imaginaries imputed to the sending context. Cumulatively, these institutional processes and social imaginaries – which are manufactured in large part through the transnational workings of state migration institutions, agents, and labour brokers – constitute the socio-cultural and moral dimensions that regulate mobility and mediate sending-context dynamics.

To begin this analysis, I examine how Filipina/o migrant workers are marketed and branded through key migration institutions of the Philippine state. In an increasingly globalized world wherein more countries want to supply workers than receive them (Stalker, 2000), competition to "supply the best" informs labour brokering practices (Polanco, 2019). This "best" is established through an image construction and commodification process that is built into labour-recruitment practices. Compared to other sending states, the Philippines has a "comparative advantage" in its delivery of flexible and esteemed workers. In addition to supplying "ideal" workers – docile, hardworking, English-speaking, and loyal – Philippine migration institutions, in tandem with recruiters and recruitment agencies, aim to deliver workers with knowledge of the cultural norms in their host destinations. This cultural knowledge is another dimension through which the Philippines maintains and promotes the social imaginary of the "great Filipino worker" (Guevarra, 2010), who is purportedly better equipped than other foreign nationals to navigate the cultural landscape of the receiving destination. As I demonstrate empirically, the efforts of the Philippine migration apparatus have proven successful: Tim Hortons employers have opted to select most of their overseas workers from the Philippines, even though they are free to recruit workers from any country.

Marketing "Ideal" Migrant Workers

Prevailing values and norms within institutions, alongside structural forces, establish the cultural terrain in which transnational employers can be hyper-choosy and select an "ideal," "tailored" worker for employment in their restaurants. This certainly holds true for Tim Hortons employers who recruit Filipina/o migrants under Canada's Low-Skilled Stream (LSS) program.

The Philippines institutionally organizes its migration apparatus to outpace other labour-sending states by establishing and delivering the social imaginary of the Philippines as home of the "great Filipino worker" (Guevarra, 2010). Indeed, the Philippines has received considerable scholarly attention for its unmatched role in brokering labour and exporting workers across the globe (e.g., Gonzalez, 1998; Lorente, 2011; Parreñas, 2001, 2015). Scholars like Guevarra (2010) and Rodriguez (2010) have paved the way for understanding how the Philippine migration apparatus operates, documenting how migration institutions and recruitment agencies produce "superior" Filipina/o workers for export through their institutional and discursive practices. This production involves constructing and commodifying the ideal image of Filipina/o workers and projecting this image onto migrants. Rodriguez (2010) provides a detailed account of how the Philippine labour brokerage state accomplishes this task through a three-pronged strategy of researching and marketing, training workers, and documenting mobility.

The Philippines researches global labour markets to identify (anticipated) shortages of workers in foreign labour markets. The institutional bodies involved in labour market research are the Philippine Overseas Employment Administration (POEA) through its Marketing Branch and the International Labor Affairs Bureau (ILAB) through consular and POLO offices in host destinations.[1] Researching labour markets is a mutltiactor, transnational, and diplomatic process. In the Philippines, the POEA's Marketing Branch researches countries expected to face labour shortages by region (like Europe, the Americas, and the Middle East). In the receiving context, employees of ILAB (who work as bureaucrats in consular and POLO offices) conduct complementary research on the ground through activities like networking with employers and business associations and liaising with local government officials. Together, they coordinate this two-part strategy to first identify labour shortages and then market Filipina/o workers on the ground in potential host destinations.

Through his job at the consulate office in Vancouver, Manuel was involved in identifying labour demands in Western Canada, relaying this information to the POEA's Marketing Branch in Manila, and marketing Filipina/o workers on the ground in Western Canada. Manuel explained, "Marketing is part of my diplomatic work. I go and try to convince them [local employers] to recruit Filipino workers over other foreign workers … To impress upon them that we have the necessary skills to do the job. 'Very good workers, we're all over the world. Most of our employers are satisfied with their performance.'"

Similarly, Jose from the POEA's Marketing Branch in Manila explained:

The Philippine Overseas Labour Office [in receiving countries] … is providing us with information … They are our eyes, ears, and soul in the foreign land. That's the biggest part of their work, aside from the documentation of the Filipino workers' jobs. So, they are there to look after opportunities. Where are they, and what are they? Can the Philippines come into the picture? … Tell the [recruitment] agencies … that these occupations exist in Canada.

Jose's framing of overseas labour offices as the state's "soul" in the foreign land is indicative of the Philippine moral economy concerning migration. The soul is the essence of a person, the nature of their identity. Identifying POLO offices as the "soul" of the Philippines in "foreign lands" suggests that the dominant values and affects of the Philippine state – its essence – is to facilitate migration. His comment also reveals how state institutions and recruitment agencies work in concert to promote migration.[2] Recruitment agencies are informed by state agents of possible job openings in select destinations and, with the support of POEA and ILAB agents, organize marketing missions. They are salient actors in the institutional marketing process. As Manuel noted, he markets Filipina/o workers in cities like Vancouver as part of his diplomatic work (for ILAB). I later learned from Jose that agents like Manuel provide employers with marketing booklets (such as "Hiring Filipino Workers: Employers' Guide") and videos (like "World's No. 1").[3]

Upon request, I was provided with a copy of "World's No. 1" by a POEA employee during my field research in the Philippines. The fifteen-minute video aims to convince local employers like Tim Hortons that the "great Filipino worker is the world's number 1." The message is relayed repeatedly by showcasing young, attractive workers, emphasizing the rigorous educational systems that workers must go through to be considered for overseas work, and featuring glowing recommendations from past employers. Viewers are told that because of their hard-working, adaptable, loyal, fun-loving, caring, and daring spirits, "the Filipino [is] the preferred choice in the international labour market." Indeed, "aside from the natural traits that set him apart from the rest, the Filipino worker has the competitive advantage over other nationals of labour-sending countries. His education, training, and work values give him the distinct edge." Moreover, "The Filipino worker has a passion for excellence in every work he does. The Filipino worker embodies hard work and dedication. The Filipino worker is a global worker, a competent and dependable worker … Foreign employers are guaranteed only the best. Truly, the Filipino worker has made his global mark as the world's number one" (DOLE, 2009).

State marketing materials like this video and the promises that migration agents like Manuel make about Filipina/o migrant workers help to construct the image and social imaginaries associated with these workers. State institutions, agents, and recruiters promise high-quality, cheap workers, but they also promote their workforce's comparative advantage. Their added export value as labour commodities derives from racialized global tropes, including the trope of productive femininity (Guevarra, 2010): the belief that female (or feminized) workers are better equipped to meet objectives of capital accumulation. Filipina/o workers are often gendered and racialized as possessing qualities that are highly feminized (Tyner, 2004, p. 67). The dimensions constituting this comparative advantage include the qualities featured in the video "World's No. 1," like being cheap, docile, and obedient (see Salzinger, 2003). In the case of food-counter attendants, these, and other qualities (like language abilities and education) permeate the marketing efforts directed at Canadian employers.

The second prong through which the state migration apparatus establishes its superiority is through worker training. Training workers with the skill sets needed to meet global demands is a focal point of the Philippine migration apparatus. To this end, the state relies on the transnational marketing research of ILAB and POEA officers. They ascertain projected needs for workers (such as for nurses, construction workers, and welders) and work toward preparing workers in the Philippines with these specific skill sets. The range of program offerings is meant to align with global demands, and programs are provided through institutions like the Technical Education and Skills Development Authority (TESDA). As a government agency, TESDA's mandate is to train Filipina/o workers for national and international labour market(s), though preference is arguably given to the latter. The state licenses private facilities to offer courses and certification for a range of globally in-demand occupations such as domestic work and welding (Rodriguez, 2010, p. 35). For many occupations, prospective OFWs must receive certification through a TESDA course to be approved for deployment abroad. The Philippines emphasizes its certification of workers when marketing its comparative advantage over other sending states, claiming Filipina/o workers are *certifiably* skilled for the occupation in question.

The third prong through which the Philippine state brokers workers to the world is through documentation. The goal of documentation is to promote the orderly and efficient movement of workers from and to the Philippines, with workers *returning* to the Philippines post-contract being an important component. After all, the raison d'être of temporary migrant worker programs (TMWPs) is the temporariness of contract labour-receiving states want workers, not citizens. Indeed, this is why some schemes, like Canada's Seasonal Agricultural Workers Program, are celebrated as "model programs": They boast high rates of migrant returns (Hennebry & Preibisch, 2012). Prior to departure, migrants must obtain an Overseas Employment Certificate from the POEA as part of documentation, certifying that the state has validated the host country requirements (like visas and medical exams), and that the migrant has participated in state-mandated workshops aimed at their empowerment. Cumulatively, documentation (for a fee)[4] bestows confidence in employers and receiving states that the worker is ready for deployment and that they have been thoroughly vetted.

The Filipino state does not act alone to produce and market its workers for export. Labour recruiters are key social actors involved in commodifying labour migrants and promoting ideas and perceptions of the "ideal worker." In concert with the state's migration apparatus, recruiters draw on gendered and racialized logics to manufacture the trope of the "great Filipino worker" (Guevarra, 2010) and leverage these essentialist cultural traits to produce ideal subjects for export. (Would-be) employers are then influenced by these qualities and practices. Just like other products in the consumer market, the transnational delivery of workers involves an image-construction and commodification process.

A growing body of literature examines the representation of migrant workers and the role of recruiters in marketing and preparing contract workers for export. Constable (2007), Loveband (2004), Tyner (1996a, 1996b, 2004), Liang (2011) and Barber (2008a), for example, have analysed the national, ethnic, gender, and corporate elements of how migrant workers are commodified and positioned in competitive markets. The "ideal migrant" (read: Filipina/o) is reliable, docile, competent, loyal, disciplined, and low-cost – qualities that are highly feminized (Tyner, 2004, p. 67). These "processes of ethnicization" condition workers' experiences as contract labour in receiving destinations while channelling workers and hierarchically ordering them in the labour market (Loveband, 2004, p. 339). While recruiters play a central role in shaping "ideal migrant" archetypes, employer preferences influence the traits that recruiters seek and emphasize. For instance, Liang (2011) found that many Taiwanese employers had preferences for "light-skinned" women, which in turn influenced recruitment practices. Moreover, the (im)migrants considered "ideal" for select occupations and the qualities associated with different migrants varies temporally and spatially and lends itself to racial and cultural stereotyping (Barber, 2008a).

While systems of supplying TMWs vary across regimes, they are all geared toward satisfying employer demands and guaranteeing the delivery of the socially imagined ideal migrant subject. Rodriguez and Schwenken compare the Philippine and Indian systems of managing migration, noting that a broad range of social actors have investments and interests in producing ideal subjects, including recruiters and the migration arms of the state. This is more than just an image construction leveraged toward facilitating labour export under saturated conditions; it is an entire process of subjectification geared toward producing "market-based subjectivities" (Rodriguez & Schwenken, 2013, p. 378). Migrants are inscribed with desirable traits and are encouraged to *become* subjects who are able and willing to adjust to (often) harsh working conditions (Rodriguez & Schwenken, 2013, p. 383) through locally amplified tropes like "modern-day heroes" in the case of the Philippines (Guevarra, 2010).

Ultimately, the state and labour brokers seek to mobilize the exportation of "ideal subjects" to generate remittances that can be leveraged to alleviate a failing economy. Analyses must therefore focus not only on receiving countries' policies and practices but also on the policies and practices of sending countries. The importance of cultural preferences and beliefs in recruitment and marketing drives home Findlay et al's (2013, p. 147) point that "the economy cannot and should not be perceived as a rational sphere that is separate from the social realm ... recruiting and hiring decisions are social and cultural as much as they are economic."

While the state's migration apparatus and recruitment agencies selectively market Filipina/o workers to the world, choices about migration are also driven by workers' cultural sensibilities and preferences. These sensibilities, too, are produced largely through the Filipino migration infrastructure. In the next section, I draw on interview, ethnographic, and Freedom of Information (FOI) data to show how a host of transnational social actors produce subjects capable of navigating the cultural landscape of Canada to work in Tim Hortons restaurants.

Preparing and Training Subjects for Export

One way the Philippine migration apparatus produces and maintains the social imaginary of the "great Filipino worker" (Guevarra, 2010) is through Pre-Departure Orientation Seminars (PDOS). PDOS are mandatory workshops for all emigrants and OFWs, officially meant to prepare migrants for employment and settlement abroad. The sessions are organized by immigrant status, skill, and country designation, and migrants must attend the session that corresponds to their personal situation. Different divisions of the Philippine migration apparatus conduct these sessions. For emigrants (those migrating to another country permanently), sessions are conducted by the Commission on Filipinos Overseas (CFO), whose mandate includes strengthening emigrant ties with the Philippines. For OFWs, some PDOS sessions are organized by the Overseas Workers Welfare Administration, whose mandate is to protect and promote the welfare of OFWs and their families, and some are led by accredited recruitment agencies or non-governmental organizations (NGOs) subcontracted to conduct orientations. OWWA conducts PDOS for a limited number of countries, including Canada. For most countries, though, NGOs conduct sessions primarily for those classified as "unskilled," including domestic and construction workers bound for Asia and the Middle East,[5] while recruitment agencies are usually accredited to conduct sessions for those defined as "skilled." The distribution of the institutional actors leading the various PDOS and the range of mandates they cover reveal the various motivations of the state, a theme I return to in detail in the conclusion.

PDOS range from half-day to full-day seminars and cover topics like travel regulations, immigration procedures, and settlement processes. In the six seminars I attended, I identified several consistent themes across the different orientations. For instance, the preeminent value of remitting funds was emphasized in each session. In three sessions, bank representatives explained how easily money could be remitted through their institutions, while in the other three sessions workers were given details about places they could visit for relevant information. Travel regulations were discussed, and workers were reminded of the criteria to be cleared for departure, including medical exams and attendance at PDOS sessions. While the general content of orientations was standardized, including the obligations of Filipina/o migrants to their families and nation,[6] cultural differences were also stressed in different ways across the sessions.

The first PDOS I observed was run by an NGO in Manila. There were eight female participants present that day, all contracted as domestic helpers for employment in the Middle East. Two presenters were facilitating the seminar: a Filipino man in his early forties (a former migrant activist) and an older Filipina woman wearing a hijab (herself a former migrant). On the walls were posters with Arabic text and a map of the Middle East, suggesting that the NGO conducted sessions primarily for workers bound for the Middle East – an observation later confirmed by the male facilitator. The presentation emphasized Middle Eastern culture, religion, gendered norms, and strategies for navigating employment.

At the outset, workers were warned that countries like the United Arab Emirates, Kuwait, and Saudi Arabia were a "different world" from the Philippines. Respect for human life (especially for women) was not the same "over there"; it was crucial that OFWs understand these differences and their place within that society. The women were encouraged to wear a headscarf and cautioned to avoid spending unnecessary time in public or making direct eye contact with men. They were discouraged from taking non-Muslim religious items with them and told to avoid religious conversations unless directly questioned by their employer. The importance of establishing an obedient relationship with the female head of the household was stressed, and they were told to avoid unnecessary contact with male household members. If the male head of the household says, "Maria, can you help me to take a bath?" participants were instructed to respond: "I am sorry sir, this is not part of my contract." The facilitator later explained that sexual violence against Filipina domestic workers by male employers and other household members (like sons) is rampant in the Middle East. Other methods for avoiding unwanted sexual advances were also suggested, and participants were reminded of their role as mothers, wives and "good Filipina women."

The session for emigrants bound for Japan was markedly different than that for migrants en route to the Middle East. While the orientation for the Middle East sought to prepare migrants to navigate a landscape fraught with potential dangers, the emphasis for Japan was on motivating migrants to respect hierarchies and Japanese mannerisms and practices. A male employee of OWWA organized the second session I attended and started out by remarking on how different the culture in Japan was. According to the facilitator, Japanese people are a reserved group of individuals with a more closed and serious culture. Hierarchies and demonstrating respect are of utmost importance, unlike the dynamics characterizing relations between Filipinos. It is therefore, the facilitator cautioned, highly inappropriate to treat them as one might treat a fellow Filipino. Attendees were warned not to be too loud and not to make too much physical contact or tell jokes. The facilitator described common practices in the Philippines like touching an acquaintance or commenting on a stranger's baby. When respondents nodded, he explained that one does not do that in Japan. Attendees were encouraged to bow their heads (especially with bosses and other superiors). There was a strong emphasis on appropriate ways to behave with bosses and future husbands (should they marry a Japanese man) and how to earn the respect of one's superiors. These instructions were likely motivated by typical social roles for Filipinas in Japan, which include care, entertainment, and marital work. The facilitator even demonstrated bowing techniques and the lowering of one's head. He warned attendees about the dangers of organ theft by people posing as medical professionals, just as attendees were warned about rape in the Middle East. Attendees were advised to discontinue contact if a doctor informed them that they required surgery; if they were still concerned, they were advised to return to the Philippines for further medical examination. The facilitator later explained there had been an increasing number of migrants returning from Japan with missing organs.

During my time in the Philippines, I also attended two sessions for migrants bound for Canada, one for emigrants and one for OFWs. The way Canada was portrayed by CFO and OWWA agents in these respective sessions (including a recruiter in the session for OFWs bound for Canada) reveals how ideas about Canada's multicultural, orderly, and welcoming nature (further) beguile Filipina/o subjects to migrate to Canada. Migrants were informed they were going to a multicultural society, so they should expect to meet people from all over the world and embrace this opportunity. They were told that while they may be familiar with American cultural products like music, movies, and food, Canada had additional features they should be aware of. For one, Canada is a very big, quiet, and peaceful country; a land of polite and (mostly) accepting individuals. Attendees were told that upon arrival in Canada they would immediately notice that Canada is an orderly place. People walk to their right, respect physical space between each other, and form lines; they do not stand too close or push to get on the bus, apparently in contrast to the Philippines. Canada is also a much more egalitarian society, so they should not expect to be addressed by their official title, nor offended if they are not. They should not, however, misinterpret this as an invitation to address their superiors by their first names. Instead, they should use *Mr.* and *Ms.* unless directed otherwise. Attendees were also assured that making eye contact in Canada is appropriate, though they were highly discouraged from being too loud or overly touchy. "Do not ask to hold someone's baby unless you are invited!" one of the facilitators warned. Also, "If someone falls, you don't grab them! Don't touch! You ask them first, Can I help you? ... Canadians do not like to be touched."

During my attendance at the OWWA session for OFWs heading to Canada, I was embarrassed to find myself being incorporated into the presentation. Participants were asked to guess my ethnic and racial background. Everyone nodded – of Filipino descent, maybe second generation. A few participants guessed I was half Filipina, half American (which I interpreted to mean "White"). They gasped when the facilitator told them I am not Filipina at all, but rather of Latin American origin. He then explained, "She is Canadian," and went on, "but look at Geraldina! Looks Filipina, like us, right? And even someone that looks like her, that looks like us, can be Canadian." This was the moment I realized that these training sessions are also meant to (re)affirm a certain set of desires and expectations. There were nods and smiles across the room. It appeared the participants, many of them contracted for employment in Tim Hortons restaurants, were being invited to imagine their own incorporation into Canada, fomenting their aspirations for citizenship through labour migration.

In the Philippines, the dream associated with Canada is of a country where even racialized immigrants of colour can belong to the social fabric of the nation. By migrating to a multicultural society on a work contract, Canadian-bound OFWs can purportedly expect to become full members of the Canadian polity, with the right to settle permanently, obtain permanent residency and formal citizenship status, sponsor other family members' migration and incorporation, and access an array of rights and social services including a generous healthcare and education system. This promise stimulates and perpetuates a desire among migrants to pursue the Canadian Dream through labour migration. Meanwhile, the messages relayed about the Middle East and Japan stand in stark contrast. The Middle East migrants are warned of a society where human life is generally not respected and a destination OFWs should fear, especially women. The PDOS for Japan invokes less fear than that for the Middle East, but there is no illusion that migrants to Japan might be incorporated into the social or legal fabric of the nation. Canada is clearly portrayed as preferable in this hierarchy of potential destinations.

Recruiters (profit-driven actors) are involved in PDOS sessions either through invitation by agents working on behalf of state intuitions like OWWA (like at the Canada session I attended) or by delivering full sessions in-house. At time of writing, OWWA had forty-six land-based PDOS-accredited providers (as opposed to PDOS for seafarer migrants), most of them private recruitment agencies authorized to conduct PDOS sessions for "skilled" recruits. While some may argue that "skilled" workers require less protection, empowerment, and country-specific information, being classified as a "noncitizen" renders workers vulnerable due to their citizenship status, despite their skill designation. The practice of ascribing skill is also dubious since some occupations designated as "skilled" in the Philippines would not qualify as such in the destination country.

PDOS sessions, partly led by profit-driven actors as we have seen, serve a host of profit-driven objectives. They help the state to legitimize its labour export program by countervailing criticism among the polity about the vulnerability imposed onto OFWs and, in turn, they leave its neoliberal moral economy intact (as discussed in the conclusion). PDOS sessions also prepare different cultural subjects for distinct destinations – an important element in perpetuating the social imaginary and marketable image of the "great Filipino worker." Drawing from its understanding of the values and norms of receiving contexts, the Philippines – through the workings of multiple institutions and agents – equips workers with relevant knowledge, preparing subjects with a "comparative advantage" for export. Indeed, sharing this knowledge with migrants may empower them with useful information (such as warnings about rape and organ theft), which migrant advocates have long pressured the state to include in country-specific briefings. It may well equip them toward becoming self-advocating subjects (Parreñas, 2021). At the same time, though, sessions tailor workers for saturated markets, by socializing them with cultural aptitudes to give them a comparative advantage. The state and other elements of the local migration apparatus strive to produce and deliver "superior" subjects that can "fit" anywhere in the world.

Selecting "Ideal" Migrants for Canadian Fast Food

Though Tim Hortons employers (like other low-waged employers) are free to recruit migrant workers from any source country under Canada's LSS, they nonetheless seek to recruit most workers from the same country. The following data was gathered through FOI requests to Employment and Social Development Canada (ESDC) and Immigration, Refugees and Citizenship Canada (IRCC), the labour and migration arms of the Canadian federal government.

Figures from the former describe the number of positive labour market impact assessments (LMIAs) that ESDC granted to Tim Hortons employers (or intermediaries working on their behalf) applying to recruit migrant workers to Alberta and British Columbia between 2004 and 2014. As mentioned in chapter 2, LMIAs assess the potential effect hiring a migrant worker will have on the labour market in question; LMIAs must be positive or neutral (i.e., they must not have a "negative" impact on the local labour market) for ESDC to approve the request.[7] Employers can either "name" the worker in the application or submit an "Unnamed LMIA," indicating that the candidate(s) will be selected later. If the LMIA comes back positive, however, the employer must name the worker on the official positive LMIA letter. This is useful for research purposes as it tracks the gender and country/ies from which they plan to source the worker(s). During LMIA assessment, only the projected impact on the labour market is under consideration, not the source country or candidate. However, once approved, the migrant must also secure a work visa from IRCC, at which point the candidate is evaluated before they can legally work in Canada.

In total, Tim Hortons in Alberta and British Columbia submitted LMIA requests with positive results for 15,577 food counter attendant positions between 2004 and 2014. Of these, the top source country was the Philippines at 78 per cent, followed far behind by Mexico at 4.3 per cent, Jamaica at 2.3 per cent, and India at 1.4 per cent, indicating an intent to hire and preference for Filipina/o workers.[8] In Western Canada, across fast-food chains, most migrant staff working as food-counter attendants were also Filipina/o nationals between 2003 and 2019.[9] In Alberta, 80 per cent of TMWs with work visas as food-counter attendants were from the Philippines during this period, while in British Columbia, Filipina/os constituted 77 per cent (IRCC, 2020). Overall, both Tim Hortons and the fast-food sector more broadly have demonstrated a strong preference for recruiting and employing Filipina/o TMWs in their Western Canadian restaurants.

In the earlier years of the LSS (starting in 2004), franchisees either conducted the recruitment process on their own (filing the LMIA paperwork and visa applications themselves while establishing the relevant networks in the Philippines), or they relied on intermediaries in Canada to begin the process of locating offshore labour. Due to the employer-led and industry-led nature of Canada's LSS, a host of actors have since emerged to assist Canadian employers in selecting and recruiting workers. Some franchise employers oversee this recruitment process themselves, while others have opted to hire labour consultants or other specialists to help them navigate the bureaucratic and legal processes. At the corporate level, some corporations have moved this process in-house and hired or assigned internal human resource specialists to help franchisees locate and recruit offshore labour. In 2004, 25 per cent of Tim Hortons' recruitment was conducted by the franchisee and 75 per cent by an outside recruitment agency or other intermediary (e.g., law firms) – none by the Tim Hortons corporation. By 2009, 47 per cent of recruitment was conducted by the franchisee, 13 per cent was conducted by a recruitment agency, and 40 per cent by the Tim Hortons corporation, indicating that the practice of contracting out to private agencies was on the decline and being centralized at the level of the franchisee or the corporation. By 2014, the Tim Hortons corporation had taken over most of the recruitment of TMWs for their Alberta and British Columbia franchisees, filing 67 per cent of positive LMIA applications.

Like with nationality, the gendered composition of the workforce sought by Tim Hortons franchise restaurants has become more uniform – in this case, feminized. Interestingly, in 2005 Tim Hortons received positive LMIAs for more male than female workers (81 per cent and 19 per cent, respectively), but by 2008 this had shifted, with women accounting for 67 per cent of approved LMIAs. Since then, this gendered employment trend has remained consistent; in 2014, approved LMIAs were granted for 64 per cent female and 36 per cent male workers. Over the ten-year period between 2004 to 2014, Tim Hortons restaurants in Western Canada requested a temporary migrant workforce that was 61 per cent female and 35 per cent male as indicated by positive LMIAs, with 4 per cent gender unspecified.[10]

Other quick-service restaurant chains, like McDonald's, have also demonstrated a strong preference for Filipina/o workers. Between 2004 and 2014, McDonald's restaurants in Alberta received positive LMIAs for 9,395 food counter attendant positions, 78 per cent of whom were from the Philippines, 3.3 per cent from Jamaica, 1.8 per cent from Belize, and just under 8 per cent nationality unspecified. In British Columbia, the nationality of workers is slightly different in composition, though 70 per cent of solicited workers were still from the Philippines. Interestingly, the gendered breakdown of workers requested by McDonald's is more even than for Tim Hortons. In Alberta, 49.6 per cent of applicants receiving positive LMIAs were male and 50.4 per cent female, and for Filipina/o applicants specifically, the figure was evenly split at 50 per cent. British Columbia shows a similar trend, with 53 per cent female and 47 per cent male overall, while in the case of Filipina/o applicants specifically, 52 per cent were female and 48 per cent were male. This analysis of positive LMIAs by Tim Hortons and McDonald's shows that both chains have a strong preference for Filipino labour, with Tim Hortons having a moderate preference for female workers over male.

A range of selection criteria guide recruitment practices for (Western Canadian) fast-food work, and these preferences are often subjective and linked to industry goals alongside essentialist branding of national workforces. When a transnational employer or its designated third-party representative makes a "manpower request" through the Philippines migration apparatus, they are encouraged to specify preferences and "skills needed, and other qualifications and personal characteristics" (Tyner, 1996b, p. 81) such as age, gender, education, physical build, and religious orientation (when relevant). Although selecting workers along some of these lines is in direct conflict with Canadian provincial and federal human rights legislation (Preibisch, 2010, p. 416), my field research documents that recruiters contracted by Canadian corporations widely use criteria like age, nationality, and marital status to inform fast-food worker selection. Moreover, transnational employers (or those working on their behalf) can request qualities and gain access to applicant information they would not have access to in Canada, enabling and arguably encouraging employers to be highly selective (read: discriminating) along a range of dimensions. They are also being encouraged to make essentialist calls in their request for desired workers, including along lines of language competence.

For jobs requiring customer-service interactions like in the fast-food sector, English-language capital features prominently in defining the "ideal worker," with Filipina/o workers often preferred over other foreign nationals, like Mexicans (Polanco, 2019). As Zell and I have documented elsewhere (Polanco & Zell, 2017), language capital is often treated as a form of human capital that brings opportunities and rewards in labour markets. Interestingly, while language competence is often perceived as objective and fixed, research has shown that assessments of language competence are in fact highly subjective and racialized. Language competence and perceived accents are *ascribed* onto bodies through racialization processes and are "fluidly tied to other individual attributes, including gender, race, ethnicity, and national origin" (Polanco & Zell, 2017, p. 271). Moreover, language competence is an embodied form of capital that, in concert with other markers of status, operates as a marker of social differentiation in international labour markets. Worker "suitability" and "preferability," then, are not shaped solely by an assessment of who can objectively speak a language; their determination is a result of a subjective and racialized comparative assessment. Compared to other racialized migrant workers, Filipina/o migrants are often preferably assessed as possessing stronger English-language skills, (partly) because of marketing efforts by the Philippines migration apparatus. English-language competence was emphasized in the marketing video "World's No. 1" and was repeatedly highlighted when describing the comparative advantage of Filipina/os labour by government agents and recruiters.

In contrasting the Mexican and Philippine migration apparatuses, I have also shown that due to the distinct workings of sending-state migration institutions and recruitment agencies, national subjects are uniquely "branded" (Polanco, 2019). Guevarra (2014) applies the concept of "nation branding" – the attempt by states to establish a competitive identity for their country in the global economy – to explain how sending states brand their national subjects. Moving from the scale of the nation onto the body, she shows how in the case of TMWPs, sending states promote the "added value" and "comparative advantage" of their national workforces over other countries through discursive and institutional practices. Specifically, "essentialist traits are 'reproduced and repackaged' onto workers by both labour brokers and the state to secure global contracts" (Polanco, 2019). Becoming the "ideal labour resource, [one] with a comparative advantage" (Guevarra, 2014, p. 131) requires actively ascribing unique traits and a higher value onto a country's nationals through social imaginings that take form in discursive and institutional terrains and practices. The perception of Filipina/os as docile, educated, English-speaking, and low-cost involves an active branding of Filipina/os as embodying these qualities. In being branded with these qualities, they *become* (or at least, are perceived to become) subjects with these qualities. This branding, alongside worker conditioning such as through PDOS sessions, produces the social imagination of Filipina/os as the "ideal labour resource" in the international market for temporary labour.

Employers' cultural perceptions of global workers also influence who they prefer for transnational employment, arguably the result of essentialist branding on the part of profit-driven actors. As a Tim Hortons franchise owner explained:

There are foreign workers that come from many different countries ... Turkish foreign workers, Moroccan foreign workers have been recruited into Canada ... [But] Filipinos speak English from a relatively young age ... Culturally, it's an easy fit for North America ... There has been a North American influence in the Philippines so that is one of the reasons why Filipinos find it easier culturally to transition ... That's what I've been made to understand. So certainly, I make that comparison to my Indian foreign workers ... the Filipino foreign workers were more easier to acclimate than the Indian foreign workers ... Not that they're not good workers, they are, but there certainly was a difference.

This employer further explained that his Filipina/o TMWs were better equipped to "understand" Canadians and Canadian culture, particularly when compared with Indian foreign workers. While he stressed that British Columbia is "very multicultural" and as such it is "great" to have workers from across the world, he still found that, culturally, Filipina/os were better equipped with the knowledge to "acclimate" to Canada. Clearly, these are highly stereotypical and subjective assessments – ideas that he has been "made to understand" by a host of social actors. His comment also lends support to my assertion that culturally apt subjects are prepared in the Philippines by a host of actors. This employer desired workers who were young, able-bodied, and English-speaking, but he also sought a workforce that could navigate the cultural landscape of Canada. Until he was marketed the "North American influence" advantage, the employer was unaware of the historical relations between the United States and the Philippines that made Filipina/o workers better as they were comparatively "easier to acclimate." Ironically, the video "World's No. 1" describes this as the Philippine's "rich colonial history" (DOLE, 2009). Profit-driven intermediaries shaped his perceptions regarding the comparative merits – and shortcomings – of different global workers.

Thus, branding efforts by state and profit-driven actors clearly impact employer preferences. When describing why Mexican TMWs are "less desirable" for fast-food employment, a Canadian recruiter explained that the problem with Mexicans was that, culturally, they were unwilling to "appease" [read: accede] to customers, coworkers, or management. Moreover, they were "easy to offend" and show their anger, a cultural characteristic he regarded as more common among Latinos than Asians. In contrast, he found that Filipina/o workers make better food-counter attendants because they hide their feelings. He also claimed that in contrast to Mexicans they were very eager to please: "[Employers] like the Filipinos because they ... work hard, they kind of keep their problems in their back pocket, or if they are angry, they very rarely show it to outsiders. And they have a very ... gracious way of talking and presenting themselves."

He later compared Filipina/os to Indian workers. Apparently, the relative shortcoming of Indians is their language skills (including perceived accents) – despite English being among India's official languages, just like in the Philippines – and an inability to integrate easily into Western culture. He also observed that Filipina/os generally get less homesick than Indians, which he attributed to their culture of mobility, familiarity with American lifestyle, and long histories of overseas employment.

While these assessments are highly subjective and draw heavily on stereotypes along dimensions like ethnicity and "race," they become "real" and take on significance under managed migration programs, as evidenced through the social composition of flows. Labour is socially valued and differentiated, with different workers considered ideal for distinct occupations (McDowell, 2008). This differentiation is especially true for interactive jobs where there are exchanges between customers and workers, making it difficult to distinguish the product being sold from the interaction itself (Hanser, 2008).

Interestingly, employer preferences and recruiter practices are not the only determinants of preferred worker qualities and of which workers are inserted into different circuits of labour. A running joke among recruiters in the Philippines was whether there is something "different" or "special" about fast-food work in Canada. I did not grasp the significance of the joke until a recruiter elaborated. When he first began recruiting Filipina/o migrant workers for the Canadian fast-food sector, he did not place much value on an applicant's education; it seemed irrelevant to the work and was not identified as a requirement in "manpower" requests. However, he quickly realized that he needed to recruit migrant workers with at least a college education, as (according to his observation) the Canadian embassy in Manila was denying visas to migrants with less than a college degree. Other recruiters recounted similar experiences, perhaps explaining in part why the work then became defined as "skilled." Visa determinations by Canadian government bureaucrats in Manila thus influenced recruiter selection processes in the Philippines, which in turn shaped who was defined as "ideal" or even suitable for Canadian fast-food work. This aptly illustrates that under managed migration schemes, the social construction of the "ideal worker" is a multi-actor, multi-institution, transnational social production, involving a host of institutional actors, including government bureaucrats, recruiters, language schools, and visa personnel, to name a few.

Institutions, Social Imaginaries, and Migration

The social imagination plays a prominent role in organizing labour flows under TMWPs. While much scholarship has focused on the economic and structural forces underlying flows, sociocultural and moral dimensions shape these dynamics too. By examining how these values affect the organization of temporary labour flows – alongside the institutional infrastructures and actors that enable them – we gain greater insight into the dynamics of the sending context, including, in this case, the role of the social imaginary in mediating migration from the Philippines to Western Canada. In this chapter, I have homed in on the representation of Filipina/o migrants and on how their image is constructed through researching/marketing, training workers, and documentation.

The Philippine migration apparatus prepares workers for export by matching the worker to the brand. The branding of workers and their conditioning are important elements involved in configuring flows. These qualities shape employment and recruitment practices, determining who is selected for employment, from where, and for what purposes (McCollum & Findlay, 2018, p. 600). Indeed, employer perceptions do not emerge solely from the individual; preference is manufactured, and in the case of Tim Hortons and the Canadian fast-food industry more generally, the Philippine migration apparatus has been successful in creating demand for their labour. People are made into "valuable commodities" – along essentialist dimensions – under managed migration schemes (Lindquist, 2010), however distasteful it is to describe migrants as products of use and exchange. Their branding is largely the product of institutional and discursive workings on the part of recruiters, recruitment agencies, migration institutions and agents engaged in manufacturing racialized, essentialist ideals. Marketing and branding operate as the cultural "pull" forces of migration.

Individual migrants, however, do not necessarily identify with the "market-based subjectivities" (Rodriguez & Schwenken, 2013) ascribed to them, as extensively documented in Barber's work (e.g., 2008a, 2008b, 2013). One worker described her views about having to tolerate verbal abuse in a Tim Hortons restaurant: "It's different here, different situation … I am not in my country." Were it not for her temporary status in Canada, she explained, she would say "fuck you" to her employer, but instead she is limited to saying, "Yes, I will do that sir. Yes, I will do." She is not being "obedient" or "docile" given innate gendered and racialized qualities; she is using her agency to *perform* these qualities given the structural nature of the temporary work contract. While this demonstrates that migrants have power and are adaptable, autonomous subjects who make decisions under flexible employment arrangements, it also highlights the deep inequality and structural constraints that limit their options. Indeed, by consenting to her employer, she retains her job and her employer's positive perceptions of her, with the unintended consequence of upholding the trope of the Philippines as home of the "great Filipino worker" (Guevarra, 2010).

Beyond this marketing, we must also unpack the moral-political investments of the Philippine migration apparatus and how this shapes the dynamics of flows. Philippine labour is mobilized to generate remittances that can be leveraged to alleviate a failing economy and address exorbitant levels of national debt, given the moral economy of the state. This occurs irrespective of the vulnerability it exposes Filipina/o workers to or efforts to address migrant vulnerabilities, including the dependent position it places workers in vis-à-vis employers, labour recruiters, and other labour market intermediaries. The Philippines is widely regarded as having the world's most sophisticated labour migration apparatus, with well-tuned migration institutions and recruitment agencies operating transnationally to market, train, deliver, and return workers post contract. This migration apparatus consists of multiple institutions and actors, driven at times by competing interests and mandates. For instance, while OWWA may be tasked with advancing and protecting the well-being of OFWs and their families, recruitment agencies (in concert with ILAB agents and the POEA) compete to churn out "docile" workers to global employers. These efforts and interests seem contradictory at best. However, the labour brokerage state is not a uniform entity. It is a complex set of institutions and networks embodied by multiple actors driven by a host of motivations.

While this complexity is surely true and worthy of recognition, the overarching moral economy of migration in the Philippines is also evident: It is informed by a soft aim to be responsible and caring of its citizenry but dominated by a neoliberal rationality that crystallizes throughout the entire marketing and brokering process. Stated differently, the current dominant moral framework in the Philippines with respect to migration is marked by neoliberal values; it seeks to download the risks and responsibilities of reproducing the next generation from the state onto individual workers and the polity via migration and remittances from temporary migrants. Moreover, its goal is to "produce responsible [read: neoliberal] economic citizens" (Guevarra, 2010, p. 85) who willingly take charge of their well-being. This includes their economic welfare and that of their family, arguably a role that the state should be performing by creating viable employment options domestically, or at least paying for the fees required to pursue mobility, like training and documentation (which it does not).

Accordingly, while different state institutions may defend divergent interests and agendas (such as "empowering" workers while also rendering them "docile"), they ultimately operate to facilitate migration and compete in saturated markets. Given that institutions "are the site where the state is produced" (Fassin, 2015, p. 6), one might logically conclude that at the "heart" of the Philippine state is its labour export program and the neoliberal values that foment it.

Chapter 4

Migrant Dreams and the Colonial Mentality

I met Rosamie in an upscale coffee shop near her place of employment in Makati, Philippines. At the time, she was working in the accounting department of a business process outsourcing (BPO) company in central Manila. BPOs provide outsourced services to (mostly overseas) clients for a range of business operations, including accounting services, software development, and call centre work. By local standards, jobs in BPOs are well paid and prestigious – especially those in Makati, the financial centre of the Philippines. BPOs draw workers primarily from young, educated, and English-speaking segments of the Filipino labour market. Rosamie fit this profile perfectly.

As we settled into the interview, it became clear that Rosamie was an articulate and well-educated working professional. She holds a degree from a well-respected university in the Philippines, yet from 2009 to 2011 she worked as a temporary migrant worker in a Tim Hortons restaurant in British Columbia. Her account of what drew her to Canada – despite the deskilling it entailed and her perception that a brighter future lay overseas – illuminates both the cultural pull *and* the cultural push forces of migration: the social imaginaries that inform perceptions of receiving and home contexts (respectively), and that influence evaluations to migrate and the decisions to do so.

In the mid-2000s, while working toward her accounting degree, Rosamie heard anecdotes that Filipina/o nationals were migrating to Canada to work as service workers. Unlike other occupations and regions that Rosamie considered undesirable (such as domestic work and relocating to Hong Kong or the Middle East), service work in Canada appealed to her: "Middle East, Saudi – no way, I don't like it. Canada to me sounds different. It is my dreamland. Since I was a kid, I was, like, 'I want to go to the US … I want to go to Canada or America. If I migrate, I want to go there.'" To attain the required experience, she worked at a Jollibee restaurant. Managing both her studies and a part-time job was "a nightmare," she told me and laughed, but she was committed to both her studies and her long-term plans. And labouring in a low-status job below her social location in the Philippines to secure a temporary work contract as a fast-food worker in Canada paid off. She eventually secured one of these coveted positions while also being employed as an accountant for an international organization. Six months following her initial application, she was on a plane headed to Canada.

While I heard many accounts like Rosamie's over the course of my research, her belief that life and employment in Canada were undoubtedly superior to life and employment in the Philippines was still jarring. How could she see temporary work in the bottom tiers of the Canadian labour market as an inherently better prospect than employment commensurate with her professional training in the Philippines? What about the costs associated with this migration? When I asked her why she would leave her job and boyfriend for a temporary contract in Canada, I expected her to reply as others had: to tell me about the superiority of the promises of the Canadian or American Dream (or, as she called it, "my dreamland"), including prospects for material gains and, in the case of Canada, perceived opportunities for permanent settlement. But after acknowledging how hard it would be to leave her family and boyfriend, her conclusion was stark: "There's nothing in the Philippines."

This comment was as uncomfortable as it was illuminating. Reflecting on this interview, I went back to other interviews to code for parallel responses on the framing of the Philippines. Unanimously, all my participants who were fast-food workers had articulated some version of this sentiment. The Philippines had little to offer by way of a brighter future (even for skilled, working professionals), while "greener pastures" (through low-waged work) lay overseas. They were indirectly describing the role of cultural pull and push forces in their decision to migrate.

Maya, introduced in chapter 1, echoed Rosamie's account. Both women had college educations with professional work experience in domestically well-respected occupations. Yet both seemed willing – if not eager – to work in the bottom rungs of the Canadian labour market despite the loss of their professional jobs and cost to their professional identities. While this eagerness is not unique, it begs for analysis. Guevarra (2010) asks how Filipina/o citizens can embark upon the "unimaginable": forsake their professional training and jobs for "fast tickets" out of the Philippines, often involving low-wage contracts and deskilling. What is insightful about her query – which she tackles meticulously throughout her monograph – is that what *should* be viewed as "unimaginable" is in fact treated by the state and many citizens as unremarkable. So unremarkable, in fact, that an average of 1.19 million overseas foreign workers (OFWs) were deployed yearly by the Filipino migration aparatus between 2016 and 2019 (Opiniano and Ang, 2024), many of them engaging in transnational deskilling. Guevarra accounts for this willingness by examining the role of the social imaginary in shaping perceptions of the West that fuel nursing flows to the United States.

Within the governance approach adopted here, this willingness to embrace the unimaginable can be interpreted, at least partly, as the result of cultural push factors manufactured by institutions. Moreover, although many researchers have documented the role of migrant dreams in stimulating these flows and inciting the desire for migration (especially concerning the United States and the American Dream), how portrayals of the source country shape perceptions of home and figure into people's desires and decisions to migrate remains undertheorized. These portrayals are the product of institutional arrangements informed by a moral economy. Seeing "nothing" in the Philippines *pushes* people to look abroad, but the "nothing" they perceive is not accidental – it is an imaginary manufactured by institutional forces that are informed by and speak to a deeply embedded colonial mentality and neoliberal ideology. Migration is not simply about the implied promises of countries like Canada and the United States (the *pull*), then; rather, it's about how these contexts are imagined and juxtaposed with the home context, including one's particular situation and social location (the *push*).

The decision to migrate rests first on cognitive migration: "the comparison and weighting of advantages and disadvantages between the place of residence and the possible destination" (Spaan & van Naerssen, 2018, p. 686). In the case of the Philippines, the place of residence is cast as a place of hardship and comes to hold a degraded designation, particularly when weighed in relation to other potential (Western) destinations. This is as an active project produced and reinforced by the Filipino migration apparatus alongside recruiters and other intermediaries to sustain flows of highly qualified citizenry available for deployment onto global circuits of labour.

In this chapter, I explore how migrants perceived and articulated the Philippines – their place of residence. According to my empirical data, there is a strong consensus that the Philippines has little to offer by way of a better future, even among those of a higher social location, and even among those who are fiercely nationalistic and yearn to be in the Philippines when abroad. The pull-force of migrant dreams cannot fully account for this tendency, as this migration entails significant costs. The question then becomes how and why some people perceive the Philippines so negatively that even skilled professionals yearn to migrate only to obtain low-waged jobs. To answer this, I argue that the Philippines has been subjected to processes of colonization and, in turn, it has leveraged colonization as a strategy to shape the social imaginary in a manner that promotes mobility. More precisely, through the dual workings of the Filipino migration apparatus and recruitment agencies – that is, through institutional forces – Filipina/os are bombarded not only with the message that success and brighter futures lie overseas but with the notion that the Philippines is "a place of hardship" (Guevarra, 2010, p. 131). This hardship is the "nothing" that Rosamie saw in her place of residence.

I apply an institutional lens to examine this manufacturing of hardship, in line with Nititham's (2011, p. 189) suggestion that "the decision to move abroad is not merely a personal choice, but one that is situated within larger institutional frameworks." The desire to migrate is institutionally manufactured, and it is further enforced by messages (unintentionally) relayed by the diaspora that migration is a primary means to obtain affluence and individual and familial status. Together, these institutional and sociocultural elements propel – or push – mobility. Of course, structural forces (such as high unemployment levels and differential earning capacities) also propel migrants into the migratory stream, and migrants spoke of these factors, too, when explaining their migration decisions. But institutional forces help explain the cultural-subjective dimensions of labour flows; specifically, they offer insight into why middle- to high-status migrants, such as college instructors and business professionals, would want to work as entry-level staff in Canadian Tim Hortons restaurants, marking the cultural pull and push forces of these flows.

The Colonial Mentality and the Production of Migrant Dreams

Deidre McKay begins her fascinating book *Global Filipinos* by recounting a parade she attended meant to reflect stages of local history and progress. The parade mapped out an epitomized ideal for local and national progress, with (labour) migration presented as the final, optimal state. As she explains, "The parade was intended to discipline … desires" and stimulate a global yearning through government campaigns that aimed "to deliver development and create a global nation through migration" (McKay, 2012, pp. 6, 13). The parade was a vivid and literal expression of a teleological framing of development – an inevitable march toward progress.

Development and its framing have much to do with shaping individual and collective aspirations and identities, both institutionally and culturally. Development is both a series of interventions geared at social and economic "progress" and an entire "metanarrative that structures worldviews" (Bulloch, 2017, p. 2), including teleological notions of progress that operate on subject desires and identities (McKay, 2012). The Philippines – embedded in a hierarchical ordering of progress toward modernity – becomes an "abnormality" in need of reform, an amelioration that rests on emulating and pursuing (literally and figuratively) the West (McKay, 2012). Development metanarratives and a colonial history bleed into people's individual and collective psyches and shape desires and decisions to engage in (labour) migration. These forces have impelled the Philippines in the postcolonial period to transform its economy into a labour-export economy (Tadiar, 2003, p. 7) marked by a "pervasive cultural Americanization of the population" (Espiritu, 1996, p. 40; see also Espiritu, 2003). The United States (and more broadly the West) has come to hold significant ideational value premised on the implied promise of a better life.

The colonial mentality, as a form of internalized oppression, operates to exalt the colonizers' values and beliefs while oppressing those of the colonized (Nadal, 2011, pp. 90–1). It is a form of "auto-racism" pervasive in the Philippines that involves a tendency to negatively compare oneself to "Amerikanos" (Westerners) and conclude with a sense of comparative deficiency (Bulloch, 2013, pp. 221, 229). As a cultural knowledge system, this mentality shapes thoughts, feelings/attitudes, and actions (David, 2013, p. 105), including those related to migration. Indeed, scholars have credited colonization as the initial impetus of Filipina/o immigration to America (e.g., Choy, 2003; Espiritu, 1996, 2003; Lott, 1976; Nititham, 2011), bolstered by a contemporary Filipino culture and media that glorifies American values and lifestyles (David & Nadal, 2013, p. 302).[1] Moreover, the impressions borne from colonization are pervasive and, coupled with neocolonial and neoliberal development metanarratives, fuel desires to migrate to Western destinations – notwithstanding that subjects are impacted by the colonial mentality to various degrees.[2]

Exaltations of the West, particularly following American colonization, shaped the desire to migrate to the United States. It also informed the Philippines' position within a global racial hierarchy, further fuelling the trope of US superiority (Basch et al., 1994, p. 38). Labour migration to Canada is not the same as labour migration to the United States, as Canada and the United States are separate countries with distinct geopolitical relations and histories with the Philippines. The lure of the United States as a global destination and how it activates a desire to engage in migration, then, should not be confused with the impact that Canada has on desiring (Filipina/o) subjects. While the social imaginaries of the two countries are distinct (as are the histories of colonization and oppression borne from them), I discovered that most of my participants considered Canada only slightly less desirable than the United States[3] and in many ways an extension of the West.[4] Though my participants expressed a range of preferences for a host of Western destinations, what was consistent was how these places activated disparaging sentiments regarding the Philippines, which I suggest are moments of a colonial metanarrative at work.

In the next section, I home in on this metanarrative by empirically illustrating that my subjects were impacted by degrees of a colonial mentality that shaped their perceptions of the Philippines, which in turn facilitated their migration. I then turn to the institutional forces implicated in the production and perpetuation of this colonial mentality, examining specifically how state migration institutions and recruitment agencies are centrally involved in its manufacturing.

Desiring a Life Outside of the Philippines, Disparaging the Place of Residence

Without exception, during my interviews, all migrants disparaged the Philippines, even those who were fiercely nationalistic, who appeared to be doing relatively well in the Philippines, and who longed to be back in the Philippines while abroad.

Ernesto's description of what "pushed" him to pursue migration illustrates this disregard for the Philippines. Ernesto held a master's degree and was gainfully employed in his profession when he first learned of the opportunity to go to Canada as a migrant worker. He became interested in Canada when he saw an online job advertisement for a service worker position. When asked why the job posting enticed him, he talked about the perceived limits of the Philippines. First, he discussed how hectic and disorganized traffic was and drew an analogy between traffic and life in the country: "Everything is so disorganized in the Philippines," he proclaimed. "The corruption, the traffic ... You notice that people don't even walk to their right here?" he asked, suggesting that this perceived detail of life in the Philippines was emblematic of its "disorderliness."

He asked me how I was coping with taking jeepneys and buses in the city, but before I could respond, he critiqued the lack of signage for transportation. He then suggested that the Philippines provides no services and that everything is slow and bureaucratic. When asked to describe what he meant by services, he elaborated: "The health care … also education … Those are options which are not available, readily available in this place. You want to ensure education which is good [for your children] … you really have to spend for them if you want them to go to good schools or [the] best schools here in the country. In the Philippines you have to give everything [your wages] for just a decent school." After describing more things he did not like about the Philippines (including the weather: "It's too hot!"), he concluded: "Even in the Philippines, you have a good job, still … the future, you cannot say that you have a good future, right? You cannot say that you have a good future … a chance in the Philippines."

Other working professionals – including a medical representative for a global pharmaceutical company, a manager for a popular international foundation, a nutrition and health specialist, a business professional, and other qualified subjects – echoed dimensions of Ernesto's description. The medical representative said, "Life in our country is bearable if you have simple needs, if you can only do what [*pause*] do what you want to do according to your needs and the very basic things you need, then it is okay. If you want more than basic needs, you are unhappy … If you want greener pastures, you won't find it in the Philippines." This perceived lack of "greener pastures" and the notion that life is only "bearable" if you have "simple needs" was illustrated with a range of supposedly unappealing features associated with the Philippines, including the weather, the lack of social services, the lack of safety, high levels of corruption, traffic congestion and "disorderliness," and a broader sentiment that the Philippines offers no future.

About a third of the migrants I spoke with said it was too hot in the Philippines. Some said they preferred Canada's weather. A few even claimed they liked Canadian winters, not only in mild climates (like Vancouver) but in frigid regions: "It is really hard for me … in the Philippines. It's really hard. 'Cause I am sweating. Really, I am sweating too much. And it is really hard for me to adjust to the weather, 'cause back there in Canada, it is really kinda [*pause*] even in the summer, it's nice. It's warm … I even don't mind the winter. Not like here … it is really hot." While not everyone claimed to not mind Canada's winters, (some even discussed at length how hard winters had been for them in Canada, at first), some appeared to look down on the Philippines' tropical weather, insinuating that excessively hot summers accompanied by rain storms and sometimes flooding were symbolic of the country's "backwardness." An accountant said, "The weather is so much better in Canada … I like wearing sweaters! In *these* countries, it's just *too* hot … And the rain. You see the flooding? … It's too much." While these participants might not have *actually* preferred Canada's frigid winters over heat waves in the Philippines, it is telling how many articulated this sentiment.

Most participants described the low purchasing power of the Filipino peso, even for working professionals: "But comparing Canada to Philippines, I better stay here [in Canada] … If you work hard here, you get money, but if you work hard in the Philippines, you get a different kind of money [*laughs*]. It is, uh, like really hard." A business professional had a similar view: "Here in the Philippines, it is no matter … what kind of work [you perform] or how hard [you work], you are not going to get it. Like for me, for this iPad, I can buy this in my one month or two months' salary [in Canada], but here in the Philippines, even if I work for my lifetime, I cannot buy this. So, it is different. It is hard here." Another respondent suggested that the Philippines was unsafe, especially for her children: "Having the kids in the Philippines is not going to work … you cannot say it is safe here [in the Philippines], right? You never know. Compared to Philippines, I don't think I've ever – I'd ever leave Canada." Another respondent simply explained: "I have good job but not a future in the Philippines … I go for greener pastures."

The theme of "no future" and the need to migrate for "greener pastures" was ubiquitous and can be readily tied to a colonial mentality. This tendency to regard "success" as residing *outside* of the Philippines, along with a prevailing metanarrative that hardship and hopelessness typifies the national context, is pervasive in the Philippines (Guevarra, 2010; McKay, 2012; Nititham, 2011). This view is firmly rooted in (neo) colonial discourses wherein progress involves movement away from "backwardness" (or "underdevelopment") toward modernity. This suggests that progress exists "outside" the national context (especially in the West) (Bulloch, 2017, p. 188) and that a unique form of cultural, economic, and social success can only be obtained beyond the borders of the Philippines (Choy, 2003, p. 7).

Critically, this view includes perceptions of what one can afford in the West, which in turn rest on the belief that the Philippines is a place of hardship, even for those of comparatively higher social location. As part of this imaginary, migration involves a shift from poverty to prosperity that facilitates the formation of a more "cosmopolitan," "sophisticated," and "worldly" identity (McKay, 2012). Indeed, migration is ubiquitously imagined as the path by which success and future goals will be achieved (e.g., Guevarra, 2010; McKay, 2012), including self-actualization and the accrual of cultural capital (Nititham, 2011, pp. 190–192). As we will see, the migration institutions of the Filipino state and local recruitment agencies condition Filipina/os to see this perceived hopelessness, despair, and to glimpse a brighter future outside the Philippines.

Many of my respondents also claimed that Canada was better than the Philippines because in the Philippines there is rampant discrimination. One respondent suggested that it was hard being "fat" in the Philippines because no one would hire her, and people would often remark on her weight. In contrast, she found Canada to be very accepting. Remarkably, most of the migrants I spoke with claimed there was no discrimination in Canada. These statements came even after they'd described a series of work and employment violations, perceived discrimination by "Canadian" (read: "White") coworkers, and (at times) blatant acts of racism perpetrated in the broader society. Many considered enduring multiple forms of discrimination in the Philippines the status quo (including with respect to age, physical features, etc.); in contrast, they perceived Canada as open and accepting. Indeed, they were quick to describe acts of discrimination in the Philippines and label them as such; yet they often refrained from labelling parallel experiences in Canada as acts of discrimination. One respondent, after a lengthy description of blatant racism she had experienced from her employer and customers in Canada, remarked, "I love Canada! … There is no discrimination." Indeed, many celebrated Canada's "multiculturalism" and "openness" (central elements of the Canadian Dream) even in the face of direct experiences to the contrary.

Arguably, many features of life and employment in the Philippines described by my participants reflect structural and physical rather than cultural "push forces" of migration. For instance, Canada *does* provide a stronger social safety net than the Philippines. The purchasing power of the Canadian dollar *is* higher than the Filipino peso. It *can* get really hot in the Philippines, and flooding during my time there *was* pervasive. But the sentiments expressed by my participants went beyond relaying the structural differences between the Global North and the Global South. They reveal a broader celebration of the supposed virtues of the West (Canada) and a widespread disparagement of the sending context (the Philippines), sometimes along contradictory lines. This "logic of the dominant global order" impels and limits subjective and national dreams (Tadiar, 2004, p. 7) and celebrates the virtues of low-waged migration to Canada. Indeed, my participants spoke of the West as "a source of prestige, power, money – a more expanded world when compared to the Philippines" (Espiritu, 2003, pp. 44–5), regardless of difficult experiences and the costs of migration. Despite missing their families while abroad and feeling happier when in the Philippines, many participants claimed that life was inherently better in Canada, downplaying or even disregarding the difficulties associated with their migration due to the pervasive belief that West is best.

Low-waged, migrant workers from Mexico marvel at Filipina/os' apparent disaffection with the Philippines. In a separate study I carried out examining fast-food labour migration from Mexico, some of my Mexican participants recounted how their Filipina/o counterparts talked about life in the Philippines (Polanco, 2019). Those I spoke with suggested that the Philippines must be *so* poor compared to Mexico, because in their experience, Filipina/o nationals appeared so desperate to leave the Philippines for employment abroad. As one Mexican migrant said, "When you don't have a strong economy, you have to look for it. I imagine that that's the way it is in the Philippines. For them, it's a really big need, and for me, no. But for them, no, they're *really* poor." Another Mexican migrant said the following: "Mexico, compared to the Philippines, is an altar. Let me explain … I see how they live in their country [by how they described it], and they're really fucked. More than us [Mexicans]."

These observations by Mexican migrant workers who interact regularly with Filipina/o migrant workers in Canada offer a fascinating glimpse into how some Filipina/os perceived and portrayed their country. Bulloch (2013, 2017) found something similar in her research on the role of the colonial mentality in shaping constructions of self and the Western "Other": not only was "Amerika" (the West) idealized as a land of affluence, but it was imagined in "polar opposition to the Philippines," which became defined in terms of pronounced poverty. Bulloch's (2013, p. 227) participants saw the Philippines as "one of the poorest and least developed countries" even though the World Bank (then as now) ranked it as a middle-income country. This severe and pervasive overestimation of poverty and underdevelopment in the Philippines is reflected in the tendency to see "no future" in the Philippines and to disparage it to such an unwarranted degree.

What makes these and similar accounts so striking is the difference in social location between the Filipina/o and Mexican migrant workers. As I have documented elsewhere (Polanco, 2019), while Tim Hortons employers required Filipina/o migrant workers to have, *at minimum*, a college degree, they insisted that Mexican migrants have, *at maximum*, a high school diploma. I found that 86 per cent of workers deployed by the Mexican state for fast-food work had, at most, a high school diploma. A significant proportion had also spent years living and working undocumented in the United States and had been deported. Thus, even though Mexican fast-food migrant workers had considerably less education than the Filipina/o participants in my study, and even though they had fewer options in their country of origin than their Filipina/o counterparts, it was the Filipina/o migrant workers who most disparaged their country of origin, who saw no future for themselves or their families if they did not migrate, and who perceived low-waged labour migration to the West as the sole path to "greener pastures." Where do these sentiments come from?

The colonial mentality – experienced by several historically colonized groups – has many layers, as each person experiences it in a distinct way, and a minority are liberated from it altogether. Characteristics like class, age, gender, religion, sexuality, and other social dimensions impact how the colonial mentality is experienced, activated, and projected. So, there is no single or obvious pathway for how a history of colonization and metanarratives of development shape people's perceptions of their place of residence to stimulate south–north flows. Nonetheless, as we have seen, the Philippines' history of colonization and its colonial mentality – wherein Filipina/o subjects regard most aspects of the colonizer's world as superior to their own – *do* appear to shape people's dreams of (labour) migration. Migrants may not even be aware of these forces, as individuals are "subjects-in-process, only partially conscious of their motives and actions" (Thobani, 2007, p. 7). As one migrant reflected: "I'm not really like a desperate one [a subject in dire need of global work], but why did it come … to a point where I said to myself that I think I should give it [labour migration] a try?" She appears to be intimating that it *is* remarkable that she and other Filipina/o subjects alike willingly engage in transitional deskilling for temporary work in the West.

If this practice cannot be explained simply through a structural or economic analysis, we must also examine the cultural and subjective domain. Why do so many Filipina/os see only dire prospects if they stay and promises of prosperity and fulfilment if they leave? In the next two sections, I show how institutions of the Filipino migration apparatus – along with labour recruiters and the diaspora – promote a social imaginary of the colonial mentality that produces and facilitates migrant dreams.

The Institutional Production of Colonial Desires and Western Dreams

When we recognize that embracing transnational deskilling is not universal across developing countries, as my Mexican example indicates, we must explore the *specific* historical processes and institutional arrangements that produce the desire for this kind of labour mobility. Tadiar (2004) employs the concept of fantasy production to address how dreams materialize within relations of power and how, in the case of the Philippines, they have placed the country on a particular economic trajectory – toward an industry of labour export. As a kind of hegemony, fantasy shapes our desires and actions. Collectively, colonized nations and people are limited by and subjected to their imperial history. Yet colonized nations and people are also agentic actors. Thus, while the West "owns the codes of fantasy," the non-West is also a willing and active participant in generating imaginaries predicated on these codes: the "postcolonial nation-states of the non-West demonstrate that they have acquired a certain fluency in these codes of fantasy of the West, making full use of them in the pursuit of their elites' desires" (Tadiar, 2004, p. 12).

The Philippines is not a passive victim, then, impelled by the forces of colonization, development, and globalization; its policy decisions and migration apparatus actively promote ideals of the colonial mentality. The state could have chosen other strategies for developing its economy but instead pursued a labour-export policy characterized by Rodriguez (2010) as a peculiar trickle-up economics. Labour brokerage is not only about placing people onto global circuits of labour. It also requires a careful program of enticing citizens to go abroad and to consider this migration an opportunity (Guevarra, 2010).

While the Filipino state claims it merely "manages" an inherent desire among Filipina/os to migrate abroad and credits recruiters with promoting the promises of foreign jobs and destinations, both the state and recruitment agencies are active partners in advancing the belief that the Philippines is a place of hardship. Indeed, negative comparisons with external contexts must be generated through a host of institutional discourses and practices. In the case of temporary labour schemes, this conditioning involves promising people that "brighter futures" lie abroad and bemoaning the limits of the Philippines. The state relies on a pervasive media presence through which it indoctrinates the polity on the "normalcy" (read: inevitability) of labour migration, and it bolstered this idea with campaigns that configure migrants as modern-day "heroes."

These media messages are reinforced and institutionalized through concrete government policies. Historically, the Philippine Overseas Employment Administration's (POEA's) migrant worker education program has been an exemplar of "early learning indoctrination" (Guevarra, 2010, p. 62) that "pushes" Filipina/os to migrate abroad. The program includes pre-employment orientation seminars (PEOS) that offer practical information about prospective overseas work prior to obtaining a contract.[5] The seminars, which present information on the "realities" of living and working abroad, are increasingly country- and region-specific.[6] The state has also run versions of these seminars on television and radio shows ("PEOS on air"), featuring guest appearances by POEA officials and migrants. As Guevarra (2010, p. 61) contends, by offering PEOS in schools and popular media, thereby carefully regulating the framing of migration, labour mobility has become "ingrained in the everyday consciousness of Filipinos." The state thus promotes migration by producing a reverie of both migration and the migrant.

Take, for instance, an advertisement described by Guevarra (2014) for an educational upgrading program that was published in the Philippines' most widely circulated newspaper, the *Manila Bulletin*. In it, Gloria Macapagal Arroyo (then president of the Philippines), wearing a superheroine cape, is joined by Mary Joy Buñol, the first graduate of the POEA's migrant worker education program. The two are seen hovering over a group of thirty women, all dressed in maid uniforms. The ad's message is clear: By completing the program, migrant hopefuls will be transformed into supermaids – adept not only at cooking, cleaning, and caring for children, but in fact capable of heroic acts like saving children from fires. They might even get the opportunity to serve a "Royal Family," despite hailing from a "far-flung" (read: "backward" or "underdeveloped") region like Buñol. Indirectly, the ad is promising a new skillset and a new subjectivity that will lead to better jobs and higher wages than those available in the Philippines (Guevarra, 2014, p. 130).

Ads produced or endorsed by the state serve to normalize and celebrate migration while indirectly pointing to the hopelessness of the Philippines. They position migration as *the* route to greener pastures, with more prestigious and higher-paying jobs available overseas. These positive features are contrasted with what is and is not available in the Philippines – a subtle yet effective indoctrination. It stacks the odds in favour of mobility by constantly bombarding citizens with the message that their futures are bleak if they remain in the Philippines.

To appreciate the omnipresence of this message and its effects on the social imaginary, consider how the state promotes migration in the elementary school system. The Philippines instituted changes to elementary school textbooks to include OFWs in the curriculum. Textbook amendments include mentions of notable migrants (such as Flor Contemplacion), depicting them as "heroes of their generation" (Guevarra, 2010, p. 62). While the Department of Education might plausibly include such representations for children whose parents are overseas, the effect is still an early learning, pro-migration indoctrination. Labour migration is presented as a normative step in the Filipino life-course – one that all should emulate.

Beyond the school system, this same messaging is bolstered by pervasive institutional practices that aim to reconfigure migrants as national heroes, or as superheroines in the case of the educational upgrading program for domestic workers. In fact, to offset criticism of the state's labour export policy and temper fears of the dangers of migration, the Philippines has introduced a host of awards and celebrations – including introducing Migrant Heroes Week and declaring December the Month of Overseas Filipinos – elevating both the act of migration and the migrants themselves. There are also ceremonies, awards, and prizes organized by state migration institutions such as the OWWA that accompany a range of celebrations for migrant heroes.

A hero is an exceptional person with outstanding achievements, admired primarily for courageous deeds and selfless acts. By employing hero imagery, the state is promoting an ethos of migration and the notion that being a "good" Filipina/o citizen increasingly requires overseas work through a new state-citizenship relationship of "migrant citizenship" (Rodriguez, 2010). This version of citizenship simultaneously means that one must migrate to be a worthy citizen – even a hero – while those who do not migrate are beyond the normative concern of the state. Indeed, the state increasingly extends economic and welfare rights to migrants and their families while retracting elements of these rights from other segments of the population.

Beyond the state's implicit denigration of the Philippines by popularizing migration across institutional and ideological spaces, labour brokers go one step further by *explicitly* marketing the collective desire to migrate through the implied promises of mobility. Just as recruitment agencies work in concert with state migration institutions to promote the image of the Philippines as "home of the Great Filipino worker" to overseas employers, they likewise collaborate with the state to promote Filipina/os' collective desire to migrate abroad and the notion that their livelihoods rely on their ability to do so successfully. While the state is more subtle in its promotion (relying on guileful discourses of migrants as "modern-day heroes," conditioning citizens for labour migration from a young age, and strategically failing to provide livelihood alternatives), recruitment agencies are freer to market the promises of mobility more directly. Brokers rely on a dual process that involves constructing the receiving context as an idealized space (a dreamland) and, in contrast, depicting the Philippines as a place of hardship. After all, marketing is about generating longings and inadequacies; it is "often designed to make people feel deficient" (Bulloch, 2013, p. 231). The inadequacy projected by recruitment agencies involves the shortcomings of the Philippines as well as individual shortcomings. Aspiring migrants are thus promised a higher status and an upgraded identity if they embark on a self-actualization that they can only obtain through migration.

Take, for instance, a job advertisement I encountered. While in the Philippines conducting field research, I actively sought out job ads for Canada and for fast-food work. I asked labour recruiters if they would share their Canadian job advertisements with me, especially those they used when recruiting food-counter attendants. A few agencies complied with my request and sent me electronic copies, with the caveat I not disseminate or reproduce them. I received one such job from Jason, a recruiter who executes Canadian contracts for a leading global fast-food corporation.

The ad feature four female migrant workers in uniform. The picture appears to have been taken on a bright sunny day in a well-lit venue. The four women are smiling, arm-in-arm, behind the counter of a fast-food restaurant. One might infer that these women are friends. A red and white border with maple leaves frames the picture, suggesting the job is a pathway to Canada. The workers on display are young and conventionally attractive; they have flawless skin, shiny hair, perfect straight white teeth, and relatively light skin. The ad seems to suggest that a fast-food contract in Canada might lead one to become like these women – attractive, happy, and gainfully employed – arguably an "improved" version of the migrant hopeful. The bottom corner of the advertisement lists awards the agency has received from the Philippine Overseas Employment Administration (POEA) for following safe and legal recruitment practices. The awards suggest that applicants have little to fear; they can trust the agency, its recruiters, and the employment awaiting them.

The ad relays the message that migration to Canada through service work is a safe and transformative opportunity that will bring one closer to the women in the ad and that Canada can fulfil one's material and consumptive dreams. The explicit message is that the West affords an improved state – "progress" and greener pastures – including self-actualization. The implicit alternative is that one will *not* benefit from progress or self-actualization if they remain in the Philippines; they will instead be sentenced to a bleak future.

To further illustrate the extent to which government agents and recruiters in the Philippines indirectly disparage the sending context, it is useful to compare the Filipino migration apparatus to the Mexican migration apparatus. When telling me about the benefits of migrating to Canada, Filipino labour brokers and government agents repeatedly cited the desirability of Canada as a destination, how "lucky" Filipina/o OFWs were to be selected for Canada, and that only "the best" are sent to Canada.

Notably absent was concern about the transnational deskilling that accompanied supplying this "best." For instance, when asked about fast-food flows to Canada, a Filipino agent for the POEA responded: "Canada provides a lot of opportunity for Filipinos because ... of our relative [*sic*] high education and skill level ... We can supply good workers." Manuel (the Filipino bureaucrat who worked at the Philippine Consulate General Office in Vancouver, whom we met in chapter 3) similarly noted that Canada "needs immigrants, foreign workers to run the society ... If you close your doors, who's going to clean the toilet? Who's going to wash the cars? Who's going to wheel the disabled and elderly? Who's going to serve the food at the counter?" Both appeared unperturbed that they were intentionally moving highly educated Filipina/os into these entry-level positions.

This willingness to deskill migrants and, in the process, disparage the sending context stands in stark contrast to responses from agents of the Mexican migration apparatus. As mentioned, the practice of deskilling, essential to migration in the Philippines, was not promoted by Mexican agents, who looked for migrants with a maximum high school education (Polanco, 2019). For instance, one Mexican government bureaucrat working in the policy arm of the migration apparatus claimed:

> How you train yourself is how you work ... The objective of a technical school is to train computer technicians to work in that area. Or I want to prepare nurses, physicists, chemists for the job market, that is the objective of our schools. There isn't an objective that I want to prepare my population to emigrate. No ... I train you so that you can work in your area. Not so that you can go.

Indeed, this Mexican agent seemed offended that I might be suggesting that they could send higher-status migrants to Canada to work as entry-level food-counter attendants.

Mexican agents working in the operation divisions of the migration apparatus displayed a similar tendency: Their work was informed by a desire to match workers with the skill designation of the job in question, not to supply "the best," who could boast a high education and skill level. As one such Mexican agent said, "If I send university graduates, those university graduates would have a different perspective on life. And they weren't going to be able to stand work as food-counter attendants. They [Tim Hortons] were worried that the [Mexican] university graduate who arrived for food counter attendant work … would leave [the position]."

Interestingly, there was no similar worry when it came to Filipina/o migrants – college-educated subjects presumably happy to accept this "low-skilled" work. Considered comparatively, one might conclude there is a fundamental difference in the governance of migration between Mexico and the Philippines when recruiting for the *same* occupation, sector, and employer. The Philippines is readily willing to deskill its citizenry in pursuit of remittances, and it has managed to cast such migration as a highly desirable opportunity. As the case of Mexico shows, though, embracing deskilling as a policy is not a universal tendency. Rather, it is endemic (though perhaps not exclusive) to the Philippines – and it relies on institutionally indoctrinating the polity with an idea of the hopelessness of the Philippines.

The Diaspora and the Consumable "Push Forces" of Migration

We cannot consider the social imaginary of migration in the Philippines without acknowledging the importance of the diaspora and remittances in reinforcing national dreams and migrant desires. The diaspora reinforces a sense of the limits of the Philippines. Take these five photographs as examples.

These are pictures of jeepneys I took while on the streets of Metro Manila. Jeepneys are a popular method of transportation in the Philippines. For many, owning a jeepney is an income-generating opportunity in a national labour market characterized by low wages and high unemployment. Many jeepneys are decorated with flags and symbols of foreign countries, paying homage to the OFWs who, through their labour overseas, fund their purchase and operation (Rodriguez, 2010, p. 1). Figure 4.1 shows a jeepney decorated with a flag of Canada; figure 4.2 shows one with a flag of Australia; figure 4.3, with a US flag; and figure 4.4 is adorned with the Japanese comic style of manga as a symbol for Japan. These flags and symbols tell a story of (labour) migration and its economic benefits; they are a quotidian signalling that one's

Figure 4.1. Jeepney – Canada, Metro Manila, Philippines, 26 June 2011. Photo by author.

Figure 4.2. Jeepney – Australia, Metro Manila, Philippines, 25 June 2011. Photo by author.

Figure 4.3. Jeepney – USA, Metro Manila, Philippines, 25 June 2011. Photo by author.

Figure 4.4. Jeepney – Japan, Metro Manila, Philippines, 26 June 2011. Photo by author.

Figure 4.5. Jeepney – Singapore, Metro Manila, Philippines, 26 June 2011. Photo by author.

economic survival and well-being lie overseas. Sometimes jeepneys are symbolic of more than just where the funds to purchase the vehicle were accrued. Figure 4.5 resembles the lion on Singapore's flag. The boat and plane suggest that the resources used to buy this jeepney may have come from both a land-based and sea-based OFW. The building might represent a construction worksite. Overall, the literal circulation of these national symbols through the streets (re)produces in the Filipino consciousness the message that "progress" lies overseas and is obtainable through migration.

While jeepneys offer a tangible instance of how the benefits of migration circulate in the Philippines, less tangible examples also circulate widely and are omnipresent. Remittances – the lifeblood of the Filipino national economy and of so many domestic livelihoods – function as objects of social differentiation, fuelling the social imaginary around the benefits of migration and costs of staying. As Small (2012, p. 160) puts it, remittances "raise awareness of the fact that contemporary possibilities of accumulation are not equally distributed across geographic, political and economic terrains." While remittances highlight the material possibilities that exist overseas, they also underscore the limits of one's local reality (Small, 2012, p. 175), positioning the place of residence as a place of comparative deficiency. This deficiency is an important part of how remittances and the social imaginary shape notions of progress and push people culturally to migrate.

Literature has documented this phenomenon in countries with significant labour migration and remittances.[7] Remittances bestow status to migrants by converting their economic capital to symbolic capital while influencing perceptions of host and home contexts. Nieswand (2014) documented the impact of remittances in shaping Ghanaian migrants' social imaginaries of host destinations. By tracing the lives of "Burgers" (global migrants who achieve middle-class status in Ghana by performing working-class jobs in Western Europe and North America), Nieswand (2014: 410) shows that when migrants perform status-related activities transnationally or during visits "home," such as building houses, remitting money, and engaging in conspicuous consumption, they "convert money … into recognition and social status in Ghana." They gain the admiration of local residents and become a "role model for many of those who see few chances to achieve upward social mobility in Ghana by conventional means" (Nieswand, 2014, p. 408). This in turn stimulates a desire to migrate among those left behind by corroborating the view that bleak futures comparatively characterize the home context.

Small (2012) reports similar findings on the imaginative impact that remittances have on Vietnamese society and how consumable items can stimulate desires to migrate due to (inadvertent) processes of devaluating the place of residence. Those who receive gifts during return trips "home" imagine that in "core capitalist countries" money is "accumulative rather than scarce," and they view migration as a pathway to social mobility (Small, 2012, p. 160). The place of residence is reinscribed as a place devoid of opportunities. Importantly, the impact of remittances on the imagination is felt not only by those receiving the gifts but also by those who observe and bear witness to such transactions.

The promise of material abundance abroad and increased status at home stimulates desire for labour mobility and informs people's imagination of an idealized overseas landscape: the national dreams that vary across countries but promise some form of upward mobility and the ever-coveted greener pastures (the cultural pull-force of migration).Mahler (1995, p. 53) notes that even though many immigrants' lives in the United States "are miserable, even worse than those left behind," their gifts and material display of affection produce a different story – one that supports the American Dream and incites further migration. Through their economic behaviour at home (either when returned, or in the form of transnational gifts and remittances), migrants send messages to non-migrants displaying the benefits of (labour) migration: "The gifts serve as symbols of their success and foster an American dream vision among other community members" (Mahler, 1995, p. 53).

Thai (2014) and Kent (2010) describe how remittances and gifts produce and reinforce the American Dream in the Vietnamese and Salvadoran contexts, respectively. Migration comes to be interpreted as the principal means to obtain these dreams. The implicit message is that the "good life" (greener pastures) lies overseas and is obtainable for those industrious enough to migrate. Those who are *not* industrious enough to attempt this mobility, in contrast, will be excluded from the benefits of migration, triggering the desire to flee a life of (material) hopelessness (the cultural push-force).

The cultural pull and push forces of migration, then, are two sides of the same coin – the social imaginary – and how it operates concurrently to shape perceptions of host and sending milieus. The silencing of hardships experienced by migrants abroad becomes essential to promoting and sustaining these national dreams (a theme I take up in greater detail in chapter 6).

As a transnational social practice, remittances have far-reaching consequences that bleed into the sociocultural and subjective domains. They structure local hierarchies between those with and without ties to migrants overseas (especially in the West), and in so doing, they help perpetuate the colonial mentality. As Bulloch (2017) explains, because symbols of the West continue to structure local hierarchies, the colonial mentality is sustained in the postcolonial context. These symbols, which include remitted items such as household goods, imported foods, houses, clothes, and the like, become part of the symbolic landscape of social distinction; they gesture at the limits of the local. They engender longings that concurrently devalue the place of residence and culturally propel migration. This may be an unintentional consequence of remittances from the diaspora, but it is forcefully felt on a micro and quotidian scale. While state migration institutions and labour brokers spearhead the institutional production of the colonial mentality, the diaspora sustains national dreams abroad and the social imaginary of the "hopelessness" of the Philippines.

Resisting the Pervasiveness of the Colonial Mentality

During my field research in the Philippines, I was invited by organizers from the migrant worker organization Migrante International to accompany them to what they referred to as a "migrant-sending community" – a region where a large proportion of the working-age population lives and works abroad. Migrante International is a leading advocate for Filipina/o OFWs globally, operating as an international alliance of OFWs and their allies and families. The five-hour bus ride to the migrant-sending community provided ample opportunity to learn about the work the organization and organizers were doing and about the local and global challenges faced by labour migrants and their families. Our conversations flowed from the organizing to the personal and the plight of Filipina/o nationals in the face of the state's labour-export policy. I absorbed a great deal over the course of our travel, and I considered myself lucky to be in the company of such knowledgeable organizers. As we neared our destination, however, I became both amused and perplexed by one of the organizers warnings about what our stay in the community would look like. He wanted to ensure that I did not undermine the work they were doing in the community. He commented on the fact that I often compliment people on their objects and surroundings, and he asked me if this was a typical Canadian trait or if I would attribute it more to my Salvadoran origin. I was confused by both the essence and direction of the question. He then instructed me not to do this with the families we were about to meet, including with respect to their houses. "It's nice you want people to feel good," he sympathized. "But please don't compliment people on their houses, especially the big ones."

For years I pondered the significance of this interaction and the logic informing his instructions. It was not until I began to seriously consider how remittances operate as forces of social differentiation that I started to grasp what he meant. In retrospect, I believe he did not want me unintentionally celebrating the benefits of migration or unknowingly promoting the belief that the path to a "good life" only exists abroad. He feared that I might inadvertently promote the notion that development and progress exist overseas and that, by celebrating the products of remittances, such as big homes, I would be idealizing the West. He recognized that consumable items take on significance not only for their material value but for their symbolic value and, importantly, for how they gesture at local limits. That is, they manufacture desires and dreams while simultaneously denigrating the local context, and this denigration operates as a cultural push-force of migration.

Much of what I cover in this chapter has been explored in the literature, including how migrant dreams propel mobility, the national hierarchies that extol the West, the role of colonization and development metanarratives that prescribe ideals for progress, how these metanarratives bleed into individual and collective aspirations and identities, and how these forces culminate in the creation of temporary labour schemes to propel migrants onto the migratory stream. What has been comparatively overlooked is how, under temporary-labour schemes, state migration institutions and recruitment agencies, aided by the diaspora, actively promote the colonial mentality that stimulates this migration. This governance is especially relevant for qualified segments of the polity in sending contexts that are deskilled through these programs.

Migrants must be enticed onto global circuits of labour, and how they interpret, desire, and make sense of potential destinations and employment opportunities vis-à-vis the home context – that is, cognitive migration – is central to how temporary-labour schemes operate. Migrant dreams and favourable assessments of this cognitive migration are produced by a host of social actors and institutions to propel mobility. It is the governance of these comparisons and dreams under TMWPs that I theorize here. These social imaginaries do not arise organically; they are actively manufactured by state migration institutions and recruitment agencies. The diaspora, too, is implicated in the production of these social imaginaries through the remittance practices that shape daily life and Filipina/o livelihoods. Remittances incite aspirations for mobility not only for their promise of greener pastures but also for what they say about the relative "hopelessness" of the Philippines – the "nothing" that Rosamie wanted to leave behind.

The Philippines may be unique in the degree to which it denigrates the local context, conditioning desires even among those with higher status and better livelihood options to leave the Philippines for low-waged occupations. Through its governance of the social imaginary, the Philippines is willing to supply the "best" – subjects like Rosamie who are skilled, well-educated, young, and English-speaking – despite the deskilling and labour-market segmentation this migration entails. This readiness to deskill transnational migrants then reinforces the same disparaging message, suggesting that greener pastures lie overseas even for those of a higher social location. Interestingly, not every country appears to have chosen this path to "development"; thus, it is likely that not all citizens of the Global South have this same orientation, as my Mexican case study appears to suggest. This finding points to a new line of inquiry: To what extent do other developing countries disparage their local context and promote a colonial mentality, stimulating migrant flows of qualified subjects to develop their economies?

The colonial mentality and the social imaginary of national dreams are indeed powerful and pervasive forces, produced and reinforced by wide-ranging institutional and cultural practices. But we should not lose sight of the counter-hegemonic social imaginaries promoted by other segments of the population. The Migrante International organizer was intent on upholding a different metanarrative: a refusal to celebrate the fruits of migration given the costs to individuals, families, communities, and the nation. The social imaginary *can* be employed to stimulate a different vision of the future – one beyond a labour-export policy and the ideological conditioning this policy entails. Yet unlearning the colonial mentality and resisting the institutional imposition of its ideals will involve reinscribing the moral economy of key institutions, including the neoliberal values the Philippines upholds in the domains of migration, work, and the economy. Organizing at the scale of the social imaginary will surely be an uphill battle.

Chapter 5

Harnessing Dreams to Manufacture Consent

In 2006, Maria saw a job posting in the classified section of a Filipino newspaper for a "service crew, Alberta, Canada." She explained, "I don't know about Alberta, but I *know* about Canada! 'Oh, I love it! I like it! I've read enough, yes!'" For Maria, Canada was a desirable destination, so the job was worth pursuing. Confirming she met the requirements detailed in the advertisement (including her age and a college degree), she travelled to the agency to apply. She was disappointed to learn there were fifteen positions, but hundreds of solicitations had already been made. But Maria remained hopeful that she had a chance. Sheepishly, she recounted that one of the recruiters had looked her over approvingly. Her reading was correct. Maria was offered and accepted a position in an Alberta-based Tim Hortons. She was convinced she had secured the golden ticket to a "better life."

Given the costs associated with this migration – including her transnational deskilling – I asked her to reflect on her motivation. After talking about the status and wages she expected to earn through service work in Canada, Maria surmised:

> But my first motivation was [*pause*] I was dreaming that after two years I'll be a permanent resident, and I can get my loved ones. My parents, my siblings … I can get that dream, and I will be happy … They [the employer and managers] treat you bad but it's part of the work … it is okay because I am motivated … [I used to think] maybe I will be nominated [for permanent residency] this year.

For a while, we sat quietly as I tried to think of a gentle way to state the obvious: Maria had sacrificed a lot in pursuit of permanent residency (including acquiescing to poor working conditions and a precarious employment contract), yet there we sat in a coffee shop in the

Philippines. Finally, I pivoted and inquired about her plans. Maria responded:

> I was in Tim Hortons, but when I saw that was not going to happen [permanent residency under the Provincial Nominee Program, or PNP], I transferred to the hotel. And then, after that, it is no good. So, I transferred again. I am here, but I will keep trying. I'll keep searching how to be immigrant there. I am looking right now, looking for a contract … I still have my dream.

Maria's experience illuminates how aspirations fuel migration and how aspirations are then mediated through the infrastructures of migrant worker programs. How Canada's temporary migration schemes (such as the Low-Skilled Stream, LSS) are implemented in practice stands in stark contrast with many migrants' expectations and experiences of labour migration. Maria yearned for the benefits she associates with the Canadian Dream (including permanent residency and the opportunity to sponsor the immigration of her family), and she considered a temporary work contract at Tim Hortons (or a hotel) as a path toward meeting this end. She even felt it was "okay" to be treated poorly by her managers and employers in exchange for the benefits she associated with this dream.

However, Maria's presence in the Philippines illustrates the inaccuracy of this belief. She was denied a viable pathway to citizenship because of her employers' reluctance to advance a nomination. What is surprising about Maria's account, then, is the power of the Canadian Dream to draw in qualified individuals despite conclusive evidence to the contrary: that achieving the dream often involves insurmountable barriers. Her failure to achieve permanent residency status should thus shield her from the desire to remigrate; she knows intimately the contradiction between dream and reality. Nevertheless, she is "looking for a contract" and, if given the opportunity, will (this time) knowingly gamble in pursuit of the Canadian Dream.

The belief that labour migration is a pathway to formal citizenship propels Filipino migration to Canada, where migrants are then subjected to their bosses' whims if they want to stay. Worksites such as fast-food restaurants that take on temporary migrant workers thus take on heightened importance: As sites of encounter, they become transnational nodes that have their own histories; they become places where desires are pursued and filtered through unequal power relations (Faier, 2009, p. 41). Studying these sites allows us to examine how desires are negotiated during the intimacies of the everyday and vis-à-vis the infrastructures that shape and enable them. By examining fast-food restaurants as sites of encounter, I show how a new "precarious labour migration regime" has emerged in Canada: one that avails aspirations for the Canadian Dream yet largely limits realization via the infrastructures that regulate it. It marks a new level of precarity in the possibility of belonging in Canada, one that exploits the social imaginary and vulnerability associated with migrant noncitizenship status.

The Infrastructures of Subjectivities and Dreams

Appadurai's (1996) work on the imagination is foundational to the study of the relationship between desires, dreams, and migration (e.g., Bal, 2014; Collins, 2018a, 2018b; Wang, 2013), particularly how the social imaginary operates as a powerful social force through which desires and subjectivities are formed. While his work was pioneering, opening new lines of inquiry at the nexus of culture and globalization, it overlooked the role of political economy. Research has since shown how structures of mobility and capital accumulation shape subjectivities and migration practice (e.g., Ong, 2006; Bal, 2014; Paul, 2017). And migration itself is now viewed as a site and process of subjection because "subjects cannot be removed from the external forces that constitute the meanings of their existence" (Parreñas, 2001, p. 24). There is a regulatory component to desires and dreams; subjectivities are constrained by markets, institutions, and other structural dimensions.

Desires emerge through material relations, and dreams are the compilation of "figures of desire"; they are the host of desires in their entirety (Faier, 2009). For example, the Canadian Dream is shaped by figures of desire that include a yearning for permanent residency status, access to generous social services, and the ability to sponsor the migration of family members (to name a few). Depending on the immigration stream and the subject in question, different figures of desire are associated with Canada. Employers exercise different strategies to manage workers as the quality of the workforce shifts, and this bleeds into the labour process and management techniques for disciplining and enacting labour consent.

The surge in temporary migrant workers introduced a new workforce to Canada's fast-food sector. Employers responded by implementing new management strategies via the Canadian Dream to establish discipline and consent among this new workforce, a facade not available to employers when they deal with domestic recruits.

Labour process theory examines how capital maximizes the extraction of surplus value in worksites, including their physical organization and systems of discipline and control. It examines how capital incentivizes workers to align their goals with organizations and the subject's role in struggles over labour control (Burawoy, 1979; Lee, 1998; Rosenthal, 2004; Sewell & Wilkins, 1992). Scholars who have studied the role of immigration controls on consent among noncitizen workers argue that states impose different legal categories on workers (such as "illegal" or "temporary migrant worker") and that these categories shape work and employment relations, by granting employers additional mechanisms to establish control (e.g., Anderson, 2010; Preibisch, 2010; Rogaly, 2008).

This chapter highlights how systems of labour control, in concert with immigration controls, spawn new management regimes for enacting labour consent. Through the LSS, low-waged employers leverage migrant dreams to secure a desired workforce and resolve human resource challenges that have plagued the sector.

Discipline, Consent, and Resistance

The fast-food sector faces a host of human resource challenges, but turnover and optimal customer-service delivery are the most pressing. The sector's management thus prioritizes the physical features of the work and strategies for socializing energetic and eager subjects.

The quick-service restaurant industry is a labour-intensive niche in which human-resource costs constitute a significant proportion of business operations. Accordingly, management strategies focus on minimizing labour costs through the physical organization of worksites and systems of control (Royle & Towers, 2002, p. 192). The industry applies principles of scientific management to the organization of the labour process.[1] Employees enter a production system where tasks, pace, and productivity are centrally controlled, alongside the disciplining power exerted by customers through service interactions (Leidner, 1993). Surplus value is maximized using "low-skilled," low-paid, and (purportedly) easily replaceable labour (Royle & Towers, 2002).

Prior to the LSS, fast-food employers in Western Canada were discontent with their staffing options. Domestic workers consisted primarily of "nonpreferred" workers, including youth, part-time staff, single mothers, aging workers, women, and immigrants (of colour) (Leidner, 1993; Reiter, 2001). Their perceived shortcomings were specific to the labour segment but included limited motivation (read: customer service) and commitment (read: turnover) and the inability to keep up with the demanding pace of work.

Youth are widely viewed as uncommitted and unreliable, as simply working for extra spending cash (Tannock, 2001). In the words of a Tim Hortons franchise owner: "Student and part-time workers are not working to pay the rent, and you're not working for groceries. You're working for spending money and the motivation, so reliability isn't quite the same." Given the fast pace of work in the quick-service restaurant industry, older staff are viewed as too slow. In the words of a Canadian labour consultant, fast-food workers "have to be able to do things in a reasonably methodical time manner ... There's a lot of people out there [*pause*] older people and handicapped that are not capable." Lack of English skills among immigrant workers (real or perceived) was also lamented by fast-food employers, labour consultants, and recruiters (Polanco & Zell, 2017).

Although the goals of efficient, fast, and pleasant service cut across many service sector occupations, they are especially pronounced in fast food, which is emblematic of poor working conditions, low-status, and negligible remuneration. A chronic challenge faced by management is, therefore, low worker morale and high rates of attrition, as noted in the literature (e.g., Reiter, 1996, 2001; Talwar, 2002) and detailed above.[2] In Western Canada, a franchise owner I interviewed bemoaned that his Tim Hortons franchises had reached turnover rates of over 125 per cent in 2008; two other franchisees reduced their operating hours because of high turnover. Industry associations widely lament high turnover rates, and it informs hospitality lobbying efforts.

A report produced by a multistakeholder committee in preparation for the 2010 Vancouver Winter Olympic Games identified high turnover rates as a driving force behind the tourism and hospitably sectors' lobby for access to migrant workers: "The tourism sector [in British Columbia] has a significant 'retention' issue in keeping and developing entry-level employees" (HRPC, 2003, pp. 3, 17). The report also warned that "declining customer satisfaction" will result in a "decline in repeat visitors." Fast-food employees often reject their poor working conditions by either quitting or resisting pressure to interact pleasantly with customers. Thus, fostering positive orientations toward the work while resisting improvements to the employment contract are leading management objectives.

To offset high turnover rates and low worker morale, fast-food corporations rely on socialization practices and (nonmonetary) incentives, including training programs for "thinking about the work" alongside parallel strategies to "indoctrinate the worker into a 'corporate culture'" (Ritzer, 1996, p. 84).[3] These strategies have dimensions of coercion and accountability, as workers are instructed on how to be loyal and disciplined subjects (Sherman, 2007, p. 77). Considerable management research has been devoted to developing acquiescent workers while resisting improvements to the employment contract.

Employers also try to hire staff from the outset presumed to possess preferred qualities and orientations. After all, in the service sector, workers are both the inventory and the producer (Macdonald & Sirianni, 1996, p. 12). How well they perform the service delivery determines surplus value (Constani & Gibbs, 2005). Recognizing this, employers attempt to control other features of the labour process. Managers engage techniques to discipline workers' bodies, and they hire based on personality, selecting candidates deemed most likely to "fit in" and deliver the desired experience (Seymour, 2000). Since the product delivered includes the customer's emotional state, managers try to enlist workers to perform emotional labour at the point of interaction (Hochschild, 1979). Service work has physical and interactive elements, and both inform labour management strategies.

Ching Kwan Lee's (1998, p. 12) research into two manufacturing worksites shows that managerial disciplining techniques are explicitly linked to the workforce in question. In one field site, management relied on a coercive disciplinary regime that exploited workers through their local networks. In another, management established control through familial responsibilities and the construction of women as domineering veterans. In comparing these two worksites, Lee concludes that management relies on different strategies for achieving labour consent depending on the characteristics of the workforce in question.

Managing Workers via the Canadian Dream

In transnational recruitment, fast-food management applies new strategies for disciplining global staff by exploiting the infrastructures of migrant worker programs. Employers leverage immigration controls to secure a compliant workforce and generate profits (Anderson, 2010; Rogaly, 2008). While lower wages are identified as a benefit employers enjoy when contracting migrant workers, "cheapness" is more aptly tied to the role of vulnerability in promoting compliance and accumulating capital. Migrant workers are regarded as having a stronger "work ethic" compared to domestic recruits. They are more willing to work overtime and on weekends (Preibisch & Binford, 2007), and they are less likely to demand overtime pay and compensation for unpaid work (Oxman-Martinez et al., 2004). Their vulnerability means they will often withstand abuse and other difficult conditions (Parreñas et al., 2021). The fear of being fired and repatriated (their "disposability") is a structural feature of temporary labour programs that promotes compliance, irrespective of conditions (Sharma, 2006). These and other shortcomings are systemic vulnerabilities faced by workers of less than full citizenship status (Goldring & Landolt, 2013).

As described in chapter 3, Filipina/o migrants go through a series of socialization processes in the Philippines geared toward producing eager and compliant workers who believe labour migration will lead to membership in the Canadian polity. Unbeknown to many, however, permanent residency via the LSS requires employers to support the nomination of a candidate under a PNP. But under PNPs, employers have no obligation to support a nomination, and as we will see, most food-counter attendants are not nominated.

In 2011, I attended a Pre-Departure Orientation Seminar (PDOS) for Canada-bound workers, hosted by the Overseas Workers Welfare Administration (OWWA). Several institutional actors presented at the session, and the disciplining function of the PDOS permeated their addresses. The facilitator, an agent of OWWA, emphasized the need for Filipina/os to be "grateful" to the Canadian government for giving them "permission to work for these Canadian employers" (despite deskilling). A Catholic nun encouraged participants to be resilient and morally upright while abroad: "You will have to overcome challenges ... like the Israelites of the chosen people. You must make sure while you are abroad that you stay resilient." Of the seventeen seminar participants, ten had been contracted as "food-counter attendants," eight of them for Tim Hortons. The remainder were recruited as hotel cleaners and skilled tradespeople in the oil and gas sector.

The third presenter was Carlo Bautista from the recruitment agency Mercan. Trained to discipline recruits into being energetic and "superior" workers, Carlo embellished employment scenarios specific to Tim Hortons: "You will need to be able to make 300,000 sandwiches per shift and pour even more coffees, double-doubles, than that."[4] His presentation intimated that migrants can serve as an innovation in labour control – a form of intensification to maximize surplus value (Rogaly, 2008).

The seminar was infused with the figures of desire associated with Canada. The OWWA facilitator presented the country in a highly favourable light – a society of polite individuals boasting generous social services and multicultural policies, implying that audience members, too, could belong to an idyllic version of Canada. Indeed, when the facilitator asked, "Who plans to pursue citizenship?" seventeen hands shot in the air. Contrary to the "bottom of the heap" status of fast-food work in North America (Schlosser, 2002, p. 75), at the PDOS, a nun, a recruiter, and a government bureaucrat – representing three important Filipino institutions, the Church, the recruitment sector, and the migration arm of the state – reminded workers they were lucky to be going overseas. The intent was to socialize eager workers.

Yet migrants desire the destination, not necessarily the work, indicating Canada's favourable position along a hierarchy. Indeed, when they detailed the process of securing a guest worker contract, research participants said they applied for "Canada," rarely citing Tim Hortons or fast food. As one participant described it, "Canada is a dreamland … More money, and the [social welfare] benefits! I saw Canada, and I applied." Another worker explained, "I worked as a university instructor … for two years before applying to Canada."

The people I spoke to had lavish ideas regarding the benefits of migration, indicating the power of the social imaginary to propel migration. One worker stated, "You work in Canada, you get everything. Your kid gets sick, it's free. Your kid wants to go to school, you can send them. Do you know what it costs to send your kid to college here [in the Philippines]? But in Canada, all these services are free." Another worker explained, "I really want to work in Canada because I want to get my kids to study in Canada and my mom and husband to live there. My mom because the medical and everything. The benefits are free! It's so good. That's why I work for two years there." According to another migrant hopeful, "I've never been to Canada, but I feel that there's no discrimination. That's what I love about it. Everybody is equal. You will not feel out of place. Health and education are free … That is what I love about Canada."

As noted throughout this book, the primary goal driving migration is permanent residency status. A Tim Hortons worker explained, "I have this idea that when you go to Canada, after some time, you could apply as an immigrant. The reason for most Filipinos to go to Canada [is] because we can be Canadian citizens." In a similar vein, a male Tim Hortons worker explained, "It is an opportunity. I can bring my kids over with my wife, and we will be immigrants … While working, I will go through the immigration process." Another Tim Hortons worker stated, "I am not after the money, I am just after to get my family to live there, because I really want my family to live there." Similarly, "I went because I wanted to immigrate, and my employer actually promised me. He said, 'Okay, go get the LMO [labour market opinion], and we will put up your papers so you can apply for a PR [permanent residency].' But they didn't … I was hoping and praying that they were going to work [on] my papers, but they didn't." Migrants had overly generous ideas regarding Canada, including the benefits of the welfare state and the openness of the immigration system. They had faith in the Canadian Dream and the figures of desire associated with this social imaginary.

Thus, motivated by these imagined values and norms, aspiring Filipina/o migrants spend years trying to accumulate the necessary education and work experience to be deployed to Canada through the Philippines' highly regulated migration apparatus.[5] Requirements include a college degree, a friendly demeanour, relevant work experience (often in managerial positions), and strong language skills. Some subjects even engage in "step-wise international migration," migrating their way up "a hierarchy of destination countries" and accumulating "sufficient migrant capital" to gain "legal entry into their preferred destinations" (Paul, 2011, p. 184; see also Paul, 2017). They are therefore committed to the work.

Neil, for instance, studied hospitality business in college and then, in his mid-twenties, worked consecutive contracts in the Middle East (including in Saudi Arabia and the United Arab Emirates) in chains such as Dunkin' Donuts, in upscale hotels, and a Starbucks before eventually landing his "dream" opportunity in a Tim Hortons. The years and effort (in Neil's case, over ten years) invested in securing a fast food or other (low-waged) contract in "preferred destinations" makes the employee's investment in the employment high. Migrants assess their contracts not only in financial and personal development terms but also with the (misinformed) expectation that they will attain formal citizenship. They esteem these low-waged contracts more than domestic recruits.

Migrants view their transnational work through a dual (read: transnational) lens – through the (often) impoverished socio-economic context they leave behind, and through the privileged material spaces they enter. *Interior conditioning* refers to the effects of limited options in home countries and the "amorphous socio-economic forces" that propel south-north mobility. *Exterior conditioning* refers to shop-floor disciplining mechanisms such as the extreme routinization of the (fast-food) labour process (Binford, 2009, p. 514). The workers I spoke with showed widespread interior conditioning at the scale of the worksite. Even a Filipino recruiter with contracts for a fast-food corporation observed that "'these' people will do as they are told primarily because they want to stay. That's how it works … [Employers are] making a profit out of these people's desire to leave [the] Philippines to look for greener pastures." Ironically, absent from his surprising critique are the benefits that recruitment agencies and sending states gain from internal conditioning forces and global inequalities.

Migrants are thus managed via the Canadian Dream, including the figures of desire associated with Canada. Indeed, as agentic actors, the Filipina/o migrant workers in my study consistently expressed a willingness to withstand unfavourable working conditions to secure an employer PNP nomination. They are thus at the mercy of their bosses, who become significantly empowered, if the worker wants to stay. One worker explained, "Sometimes it is not perfect. They [management or employers] will treat you bad … But after that, everything will be okay … I am motivated … to attain citizenship this year." Neil explained:

> I want to bring my family here, so I am going to work really hard. First point of the first day, I am working hard … We were all. We were even extending hours … for them. For free! Because that is what Filipinos are. We work hard because we are motivated … Because everybody was saying, I want to be nominated. I want the company to nominate me, help me bring my family over.

The Canadian Dream operates as a disciplinary force on migrant workers willing to withstand violations to the employment contract and poor working conditions. The goal of permanent residency shapes an eager and compliant workforce and promotes competition for a nomination, a scenario that empowers managers with a disciplining technique that is unavailable to them when dealing with local recruits. Neil noted that TMWs even perform tasks to impress their employers (like shovelling snow and cleaning walls). But employers eventually come to expect this extra effort from their migrant workforce.

Fast-Food PNPs and Regulating Migrant Incorporation

Provincial nominee programs consist of multiple evolving streams with rules and regulations for different occupations and sectors. (See appendix 1 for an Infrastructures of Migration Map that details relevant PNPs and offers a broader Filipino Canadian fast-food migration map). At the time of my field research, in Alberta and British Columbia, food-counter attendants could be nominated for permanent residency status under a PNP.[6] Each stream specifies the minimum criteria for nomination and other regulations, including human and language capital and the percentage of migrants per worksite. In Alberta's PNP for fast food at the time, the Foodservices Industry Pilot Project, employers were eligible for only one allocation per restaurant. (Between 13 September and 28 November 2013, however, food service employers were allowed to nominate up to 20 per cent of their migrant workforce as part of the Foodservices Industry Pilot Project–Additional Allocations.) In April 2023, Alberta announced a new tourism and hospitality immigration stream, promising a faster and dedicated sector-specific program. The provinces/territories are allotted a total number of PNP nominations; Alberta was allotted 6,000 nominations for 2019. If the candidate is successful at the provincial level, they are forwarded to the federal level, where Immigration, Refugees and Citizenship Canada (IRCC) makes the final decision over permanent residency. Thus, even if employers were inclined to nominate their entire migrant workforce (my research suggests they are not), there are institutional barriers and a broader political context that would limit their ability to do so.

LSS and PNP regulations are critical infrastructures that enable and constrain migrant dreams. Not well known by migrants prior to migration, they spark fierce competition among workers once they arrive within a zone of encounter. They give employers access to workers whose goals have been aligned with that of the corporation, something the sector has been unable to meaningfully accomplish with local recruits. Thus, there is no need for store-level competitions, training programs, or rewards such as free meals and company-sponsored outings.

The Canadian Dream exerts a strong disciplinary force on workers, enforcing migrants "ideal," ready-made standing (chapter 3). After describing the status and wages she could attain, one worker stated: "But my first motivation was [*pause*] I was dreaming that after two years I'll be a permanent resident … I can get that dream, and I will be happy." Some workers even expressed a willingness to withstand (verbal) abuse from managers and employers:

> Those White people [Canadians], they do not [take abuse] because they can just quit. I can find a new one [job]. But a foreign worker, they have to stay. Like no "You cannot talk to me like that, you owe me my overtime!" No. Treat you bad … You cannot say that 'cause you are foreign worker. Work really hard. Do everything … I say [it's] okay … I want to be nominated.

Immigration controls "help produce 'precarious workers' over whom employers and labour users have particular mechanisms of control" (Anderson, 2010, p. 300). Global recruitment gives employers access to a "labour force whose appreciation of the opportunity to earn relatively higher wages reflect[s] heavily in their on-the-job performance and acceptance of substandard working … conditions" (Preibisch, 2010, p. 414).

It also shapes turnover and retention. Because dismissal can be tantamount to deportation, the mere threat of repatriation operates as an effective labour control tool. Most managed migration schemes, including the LSS, set limits on mobility in the receiving labour market.[7] Migrants are tied to, or dependent on, their employers for the right to live and work legally in Canada (Faraday, 2012; Sharma, 2006). The result is decreased employee turnover. Ironically, employers attain a relatively permanent workforce by hiring TMWs, resolving one of the most pressing human resource challenges facing the sector:

> You can't quit. You're under contract. Even if you really don't like the job, your owner treats you bad. We cannot quit 'cause we want to stay ... That's why the management love us, all the people there, all the Filipinos. 'Cause we don't complain. We just always say, "Yes, I will do that, sir. Yes, I will do." We don't complain. We want to bring our families. Even if we really want to complain, we cannot do that. 'Cause we are under contract.

While some might argue that this, in the end, is a mutually beneficial arrangement for employers and workers, the problem with the Canadian Dream is that few migrants attain it.

The Facade of the Canadian Dream

Unlike domestic caregiver streams in which workers initiate the immigration process after meeting a set of criteria, streams covering workers with a job offer give employers the power to decide *if* they want to support a nomination. Between 2002 and 2019, most fast-food migrant workers in Western Canada did not secure permanent residency through a PNP stream while labouring under the LSS or while on a temporary work visa under the International Mobility Program (IMP).[8]

From 2002 to 2019, Alberta had a total of 36,210 visa holders: 35,080 under the LSS and 1,130 under the IMP. Of this total, only 1,521 transitioned to permanent residency status (24 per cent of visa permit holders working under NOC 6711, "food-counter attendant"). Breaking these figures down by nationality, 81 per cent of the 546 under the LSS and 85 per cent of the 975 under the IMP were Filipina/o. That such a high proportion transitioned to permanent residency status under the IMP suggests that many were likely PNP nominees under the LSS with expired visas, so they were working under the IMP as they awaited a decision on their permanent residency applications. Only 24 per cent of fast-food TMW permit holders in Alberta transitioned from temporary to permanent status, but 84 per cent were Filipina/o.[9]

Similarly, in British Columbia, a total of 17,455 food-counter attendant worker visas were granted from 2002 to 2019: 14,645 under the LSS and 2,810 under the IMP. Only 2,778 transitioned from temporary to permanent status (16 per cent of temporary migrant permit holders working under NOC 6711, "food-counter attendant"). Breaking these figures down by nationality, 45 per cent were Filipina/o while 24 per cent were Indian nationals. As in Alberta, a high proportion – 81 per cent – of permit holders working under the IMP transitioned to permanent status.[10]

If my speculation about workers in the IMP is incorrect, the proportion of LSS workers that transitioned from temporary to permanent status under the LSS may actually be *lower* than 24 per cent and 16 per cent in Alberta and British Columbia, given the high rates of IMP workers transitioning to permanent status. Comparatively and cumulatively, the data suggests that the proportion of food-counter attendants that achieved permanent residency status through labour migration was low, but that Filipina/o nationals outpaced other citizenry groups.

A Precarious Labour Migration Regime

The LSS introduced a new labour regime in Canada for disciplining workers in low-waged worksites. In concert with PNPs, it marks a new level of precarity when it comes to incorporation. It introduces workers such as Maria and Neil at the point of production and leverages immigration controls to enact their consent.

Under Canada's long-standing Seasonal Agricultural Worker Program (SAWP), migrants are explicitly denied permanent residency status through their transnational work, whereas under the LCP, the Caregiver Program and its later configurations, there is a "two-step" institutionalized path toward permanent residency (Hennebry, 2010): Workers apply/applied for permanent status after meeting a set of criteria, including twenty-four months of continuous employment.[11] While the reconfigured caregiver pilot programs have put pauses and caps on the number of applicants to be selected for permanent residency per year, with a lack of clarity on the criteria for selecting applicants, TMWs still crucially control(led) the initial application. In contrast, the LSS neither excludes opportunities for permanent settlement (like the SAWP) nor offers a direct path toward attaining permanent residency (like the domestic caregiving streams). Instead, the LSS (in concert with Alberta's and British Columbia's PNP immigration schemes) offers migrants the opportunity to secure a permanent residency nomination through temporary employment in a low-waged occupation. It offers migrants few if any opportunities to solely initiate the transition from temporary to permanent residency status, rendering worksites into spaces where migrants compete for employer nominations. In practice, low-waged employers are granted access to a new set of management tools that operate as a highly effective workplace regime, accomplishing what fast-food employers have long sought to accomplish through incentive and socialization programs: "to increase employees' commitment to corporate goals and to personal excellence in work performance" (Leidner, 1993).

This new labour and migration infrastructure in Canada can best be described as a "precarious labour migration regime" (PLMR), one that neither directly denies *nor* facilitates access to legal incorporation. It converts the worksite into a zone of encounter in which migrants are solicited to compete for employer-nominated citizenship. As a transnational employment practice, PLMRs empower employers with a figurative carrot (permanent residency) and persuade workers to sign a precarious employment contract and accept poor working conditions. Aided by labour exporting regimes and the structurally shaped precariousness that typifies life in the Philippines, employers gain access to subjects pre-incentivized to align their goals with their corporations, counting on subjects to retain their motivation because of the ambiguity and competitive nature of employer-nominated citizenship. There is no guarantee of citizenship, but the potential remains, so TMWs perform. It is the productivity of hope, then, that employers enjoy through the PLMR. Hope resolves long-standing challenges in the sector by granting employers access to a new workforce from which to organize consent.

With the LSS, employers can be highly selective and recruit along a range of attributes and social qualities well-suited to fast-food work, circumventing vulnerable segments of local labour markets (Polanco, 2017). This includes a "workforce more willing to accept the industry's working and living conditions and one less able to contest them" (Preibisch, 2010, p. 413). A Canadian labour consultant clarified in an interview:

> Here come these bright university graduate foreign workers that are delighted to be here, are happy for what you are paying them. They are not whining about their salary all the time or expecting you to pay them double because they are charming … [Employers] put up with a lot. They really do. A lot. And when they get these foreign workers, it's a treat … It makes a big difference. Maybe the labour shortage may not be as bad as employers make it out because they want those people. And if

they can find them in the [local] labour market they will hire them right away ... But those people in the Canadian labour market aren't looking for those jobs.

While this description is biased and open to debate, what the consultant's account implies is that, with a shift to transnational employment practices, interior conditioning alters the landscape of available workers and shop-floor dynamics (Binford, 2009). Moreover, contrary to Salzinger's (2003) assertion that subjects are produced (or resist being formed) on shop floors across the world, under managed migration schemes, "migrants are 'made' even before they have actually left their respective countries" (Rodriguez & Schwenken, 2013). In concert with the Filipino migration apparatus, TMWs resolve the sector's longstanding challenges of high turnover and the delivery of exceptional customer service. Global tropes regarding Canada encourage subjects to pursue the Canadian Dream while the infrastructures of migration and (global) labour market dynamics govern whether it is attained.

Notwithstanding the disappointments associated with labour migration, the power of the Canadian Dream is exceedingly robust. Indeed, despite being passed over for permanent residency while employed at a Tim Hortons, Maria was still looking for a temporary work contract. This raises the question: How does the Canadian Dream thrive despite evidence to the contrary?

Chapter 6

The Institutional Resilience of National Dreams

In 2015, I met Dalaya in Alberta. At the time, she was facing the prospect of a forced return to the Philippines. The "four-in, four-out rule" was in effect. The policy dictated that many low-wage migrants' maximum stay in Canada would be limited to four years, at which point they would have to leave the country for a minimum of four years to be re-eligible to return as temporary migrant workers (TMWs).[1] This policy (retracted in December 2016) instigated chaos and turmoil for many (Filipina/o) migrants who longed to remain in Canada. Over coffee, Dalaya and I discussed what the prospect of returning to the Philippines would mean to her if she was unsuccessful in securing permanent residency status.

Dalaya's dream of immigrating to Canada began when an acquaintance migrated to Canada to be a gas station attendant and later pivoted to food-counter-attendant work, reportedly because it appeared a surer path to legal incorporation. As a graduate of hospitality management, Dalaya felt she, too, could be an ideal candidate for global work. Through her acquaintance, she solicited a position as a food-counter attendant, a job she coveted for its prospects, and she successfully obtained one at Tim Hortons. During her tenure, she did everything she could to achieve an employer nomination, including "going the extra mile" in her work tasks and enduring the practice of wage theft. She believed her efforts – and suffering – paid off; her employer insinuated that plans were in the works to support her nomination. But months passed to no avail. She thought, perhaps it's not going to happen.

When I asked her what returning to the Philippines meant to her, her eyes welled with tears: "I don't have good future in the Philippines. That's why I stay here ... But I guess I have to go." She explained, "Right now, it's like half of my body is buried, like we don't know what's your future. If you're going back, if you can get that security ... You have a nervousness ... I will start from zero." Dalaya's primary goal had been to secure permanent residency status, but as the days passed, she was haunted by the prospect of failure. Her metaphor of being half in the grave captures the hopelessness and despair she associated with the Philippines, and her unwavering belief that success resides in the West (chapter 4).

In the summer of 2011, when I met Neil in the Philippines (see chapter 5), he was one of a handful of migrants I connected with who had returned to the Philippines following global work in Canada. After working in an Alberta-based Tim Hortons for three years, he returned to the Philippines indefinitely. At the time of our meeting, he had been back for only a few months. Unlike Dalaya, he had had years of experience with overseas work. When he was in his mid-twenties, he accepted his first contract in a Dubai-based coffee shop. For the next decade, he worked consecutive contracts, primarily in the Middle East in food service establishments, and he worked his way into management. But his long-term goal was migration to North America.

While overseas employment gave him the migrant capital required to eventually enter Canada, he lamented the toll of transnational work. He was tired of being separated from his wife and two sons (sometimes for years on end), and he longed for more stability. He also worried about his sons' long-term prospects. He was convinced he had "won the golden ticket" – a chance for a better life – when, after a drawn-out process, he received confirmation that he had been "chosen for Canada." Neil and his family celebrated what they "knew" to be a better future. One final separation would culminate in their immigration to Canada.

Once in Canada, however, Neil had a rude awakening. While he liked Canada (especially compared to the Middle East), he was shocked to discover that, unlike "the nannies," he could not initiate the process of becoming a permanent resident. In response, he tried to secure a better life for himself and his family through his job performance. Neil believed his efforts paid off. Shortly before the termination of his second contract (this time, a one-year visa), the store owner decided to "support his nomination." Later that day, Neil had a videoconference with his wife, and they both cried tears of relief and joy. Almost fifteen years of being a global worker and a transnational family had finally paid off: They would be reunited and have all the perks of first-world citizenship.

Neil's employer advised Neil to go home to the Philippines, get his affairs in order, and prepare to emigrate. It would happen once his papers were in order. In anticipation, Neil purchased a car and other necessities he felt his family would need in Alberta. Clearly, he never doubted his emigration was imminent. But his employer ghosted him. He could not be reached, even at the restaurant. Reluctantly, Neil realized his employer had misled him: There was no permanent residency (or better life) awaiting him and his family. When I asked about his plans, he said he was looking for another contract. His dream had almost been realized; maybe next time he would have better luck. Despite everything that had transpired – his emigration precarity and his employer's traumatic betrayal – he still believed Western citizenship was within reach. The Canadian Dream remained alive and well.

As the experiences of Dalaya and Neil reveal, the Canadian Dream is exceedingly resilient, even after events reveal it to be a facade. Bryan and Barber (2021) have documented a similar finding. From 2010 to 2019, they conducted interviews with sixty Filipina/o Tim Hortons workers at different stages of labour migration to Canada.[2] Although their participants were aware of the evolving and uneven opportunity structures in the Canadian immigrant system, including people being unable to achieve permanent residency status, most (like Dalaya and Neil) remained hopeful that they would one day achieve incorporation.[3] In a parallel study, Paul (2017) documented that Canada was a "dream destination" for Filipina domestic workers. They believed they could achieve permanent residency status despite barriers and immigration controls that promoted their exclusion. According to Paul (2017, p. 170), "In many respects, what these migrants described was the Canadian version of the mythical American dream – a chance at a comfortable life, a social safety net, family reunification, and guaranteed upward socioeconomic mobility – and just as difficult to achieve."

In this chapter, I consider the persistence and resilience of national dreams in the face of sustained evidence to the contrary, and I argue that their durability rests on four pillars: (1) the diaspora, (2) state migration institutions, (3) recruitment agencies, and (4) employers.

Transnational Social Optics and the Elasticity of National Dreams

The research on national dreams and their relationship to migratory flows provides an entry point for explaining why migrants like Dalaya and Neil (alongside their social networks) continue to have faith in the Canadian Dream despite evidence to the contrary. One reason, related to the diaspora, involves status performances.

As previously detailed in chapter 4, overseas migrants often send remittances to loved ones back home. These monetary and material objects operate as symbols of status and upward mobility. They distinguish the sender and receiver and act as symbolic capital, whether by intent or effect, by sending a message that socio-economic mobility can be attained through (labour) migration (e.g., Kent, 2010, Faier, 2013; Lopez, 2010; Thai, 2014, p. 74). To offset what is often a loss of status when living and working overseas, migrants engage in a host of status-accumulative activities, including building "dream homes" in countries of origin and other acts of conspicuous consumption (Nieswand, 2014, pp. 409–413). The sending context is viewed as a place of hardship, while the West is where dreams are achieved (Small, 2012, p. 167). Critically, sustaining this dream requires concealing the hardships associated with life and employment overseas.

The ability to (wilfully) hide or conceal the truth about transnational (labour) migration depends on managing transnational information flows. Research shows that many migrants either conceal, unintentionally mislead, or wilfully misrepresent their situation to their loved ones, resulting in the continued circulation of national dreams. In some cases, migrants may continue sending money home to keep their loved ones from suspecting the truth of their dire financial situation (e.g., Sana, 2005, p. 239). In other cases, relaying the virtues of migration may be unintentional. Because remittances signal success (not the hardships associated with accruing capital), they maintain and perpetuate the trope of the national dream (chapter 4). Concealment ensures a disconnect between the symbolic capital accrued through giving and the realities of attaining economic capital.

The structural inequalities that characterize the global North and South allow these fantasies to reign. Migrants such as Dalaya and Neil who engage in south-north migration often live in two distinct worlds and make sense of their lives and material well-being through a transnational optic (e.g., Thai, 2014) or dual frame of reference (e.g., Louie, 2012). The first frame is marked by the "stark inequality and economic instability in countries of origin" (Louie, 2012: 35), while the second is characterized by relative wealth and opportunities for material consumption. Because their social fields are transnational, and because "their lives are lived simultaneously within two or more nation-states" (Basch et al., 1994, p. 28), migrants who have strong transnational ties interpret their lives through a "third world" and "first world" optic. They may conclude that their lives in the West are successful even if they "earn salaries that classify them among the working poor" (Mahler, 1995, p. 91). In fact, research has shown that "immigrants breathe new life into the American dream" (Mahler, 1995, p. 233) and that those who do not have a transnational optic to draw from have a harder time believing in it (e.g., Hochschild, 1995; Louie, 2012; Clark, 2003). The

American (or Canadian) Dream is more plausible for some immigrants *because* the third world is their frame of reference, a comparator not available to other populations, such as American-born African Americans (Hochschild, 1995, p. xviii).

Because success in national dreams is envisaged as a range, national dreams are resilient. Hochschild (1995) documents this quality, arguing that success can include absolute, relative, and or competitive success. Thus, the American Dream is highly fluid, encompassing a range of potential scenarios and outcomes. Mahler (1995, p. 232) observes this tendency in the case of Salvadoran migrants to the United States: "They can point at some accomplishments ... Even among what might be an 'unsuccessful' immigrant group ... there is some socio-economic mobility ... This helps keep the American dream alive, however unintentionally." National dreams are impressive social imaginaries, then, in part because of their ambiguity and broad applicability. They "provide a unifying vision but allow infinite variations within that vision" (Hochschild, 1995, p. 250). A variety of contexts and outcomes – including transnational deskilling and temporary employment in the bottom rungs of the Canadian service economy – can be read as absolute, relative, or competitive successes.

Aside from the elasticity and ambiguity of national dreams, another feature is their highly individualized nature. Achievement is deemed the product of hard work and individual merit, obscuring the role that structures and policies play in shaping opportunities and outcomes. The result is that migrants have many (unwarranted) hopes for success but no viable explanations for "failure" (Hochshild, 1995, p. 37). They may internalize these perceived inadequacies as individual shortcomings (e.g., Thai, 2014, p. 136; Nieswand, 2014, p. 416). When migrants rather than structural inequalities and barriers are blamed for their defeat, or when they attribute failure to their own performance, "the idea can be maintained that migration normally would bear fruits of success" (Nieswand, 2014, p. 416). The national dream is legitimized. In turn, those who "fail" try to become invisible, silencing counter-narratives that might otherwise challenge the status quo.

Tim Hortons and the Diaspora's Role in Sustaining the Canadian Dream

Many of the participants in my study sent money back to support loved ones and engaged in "status performances" during return visits home. These practices conferred messages about the migrants' economic success. Remittances took a variety of forms: monetary circulations, supporting relatives' educational endeavours, modest improvements to homes, and material exchanges through popular balikbayan boxes.[4]

Remittances were usually described as acts of love, though the pressure to remit appeared to be a motivating factor. About half the participants reported being (highly) motivated to remit to their family and other loved ones, sometimes in what appeared to be difficult situations. As one participant explained: "My father, he has been paralyzed for twenty-one years ... My mother [*pauses*] she worked hard for [the] five of us. I wanted her to stay at the house [and not work anymore], because she deserves it. That's why my motivation to make money is very high." As Jacinto explained, "My brother is the only family that I've got, and I really want to help him, and since he was separated [from his wife] ... I want to help him, [and] my niece and nephew ... I really, really work hard to help them. But it's hard because I don't make a lot."

To afford remittances on a fast-food salary, migrants made sacrifices in their daily lives, often unbeknownst to their families. They lived in adverse housing arrangements, spent sparingly, and took on extra work despite (physical) exhaustion and (sometimes) noncompliance with visa requirements. As Neil recalled, to remit money to his wife and children, he lived frugally. He had more roommates than was congenial, spent sparingly on living costs (including groceries and entertainment), and walked an hour to and from work (sometimes in inclement weather) to save on transportation costs.

Ligaya likewise lived in unfavourable housing conditions to maximize savings:

> I lived in the housing provided by my employer. Fourteen ladies, Filipina/o workers, lived in a seven-bedroom house ... The store is twenty-four hours operational, so every eight hours ... a few workers come in and out, you know. It's like the house never sleeps ... It is noisy all the time in that house ... Every eight hours people are getting ready for work.

She remained in the house even though she had minimal privacy and found it difficult to rest because she was scared to express her discontent to the store owner, and the rent, at $450 a month, was "pretty reasonable." Migrants endured these hardships to help their loved ones. As one participant explained:

> I work hard, not because I'm enjoying doing it ... But it is like, you know, I have to consider the financial stuff ... I can save some money for them. That's what I worry ... if I really want to save money for my kids and my family back home, I need more hours. 'Cause I don't know what will happen in the future.

Maximizing work hours (beyond a full-time schedule, or outside of the restaurant) was a common practice that sent out a message of economic success. Neil was eager to take on extra work to maximize what he could remit to his family. He felt exhausted but thought the benefits were worth the costs. Jessica similarly took on extra work, in her case for cash outside of the restaurant: "I pick up extra work when I can [cleaning houses and restaurants under the table], even when I'm really tired … I'm scared … I'm scared I'll get found out, but the money is good." When I asked them whether their loved ones knew about these money-saving strategies and related conditions, they said they withheld information, because they did not want to worry their loved ones. As Neil explained, "No … no, I can't. It was hard for them with being far [away]. I didn't want them to worry."

Conspicuous consumption during return visits home likewise projected an image of success in the West, even when subjects did not want to engage in status performances. Jessica was reluctant to return home to the Philippines after a recent visit and swore not to return until she secured permanent residency status. She felt pressure to provide gifts and outings, which (by her account) her family had come to expect. She lamented that they did not understand the reality of living in Canada, namely, the high cost of living and taxation. Indeed, she acknowledged her lack of knowledge: "When we were in the Philippines looking at how much I would be earning, we [my husband and I] thought it would be, like, huge, because, at that point, we didn't realize that we were actually basing it according to the Philippines … We didn't realize we were also spending dollars in Canada."

She recalled a Sunday afternoon when her siblings and their families were visiting her parents, and they all decided to dine at a local restaurant. Once there, she realized they expected her to pay. She reluctantly did so. While the outing did not cause financial harm, repeated scenarios pushed the boundaries of what she was giving out of "love." Uncomfortable, she explained that she was motivated to share with her family (especially her daughter) the returns of her migration, but they did not fully grasp the limits of her gains.

Most concealed critical aspects of life and employment in Canada, including the high cost of living, work and employment violations, maltreatment by employers, and discrimination. In cases where they were unsuccessful in securing permanent residency status, concealing and carefully guarding this information caused a great deal of turmoil. According to Rebecca:

You feel like you failed, and you cannot, you [*long pause*] can't face your family. They're supposed to be [*crying, long pause*] my daughter is saying to me, "Oh mom. Where – where am I going to Canada? When can I see snow?" 'Cause I told her that, after a few years, you can go. You can go, you can go here with me, with your dad. You can study here. You can live here. But [*pause*] I go back. I feel like I failed for two years. I feel like for two years I have done nothing.

Failure emerged as a repeated theme, especially among migrants passed over for permanent residency status – the majority.[5] When questioned about whether she'd disclosed the reality of her status in Canada, Janelle responded:

Only my family knows it. Yeah, because, I didn't, I didn't tell it to [*pause*] because it is hard to explain, you know, because if you are going to [*pause*] tell them the situation, they don't understand ... They don't understand. How come? It is, like, instilled in their mind that after two years ... Same with me. Before I went [to Canada, I thought] after two years, you'll be an immigrant. So they say, "Oh, Janelle, you stayed there for four years so, you can bring your family now to there" ... Oh, I just told them, "Not for me." That's all they get from me because it is hard to explain to them ... It is stressful for me.

She lamented, "I'm a failure."

Janelle's social networks believed she should have the ability to "bring your family now there" because, under the Live-in Caregiver Program, caregivers could apply for permanent residency and then sponsor the migration of their family (albeit after meeting a set of criteria, including two years of employment as a live-in caregiver), a scenario that does not apply to the Low-Skilled Stream (LSS).

But the history of migration between the Philippines and Canada and the longer history of permanent migration and family reunification informs what Filipina/os believe about Canada and the perceived rights afforded to labour migrants. These beliefs are also the product of Canada's reputation and perceptions about what the country has to offer (its figures of desire): permanent residency, the ability to sponsor family migration, and a brighter future premised on belonging to a multicultural society governed by a state that takes care of its people.

As Dalaya explained, "For people in the Philippines ... it is a big thing if you reach Canada. You can bring your family ... the health and education ... Maybe not rich like other places [which she later qualified as the United States] ... But life is good in Canada." Another participant explained, "I've heard that it's worse [*pause*] people who work in those areas, Middle East and Hong Kong, it is worse than what you have in Canada … People [Filipina/os back home] think you have got greener pastures if you go to Canada." Another participant explained, "Canada is a dreamland … More money, and the [social welfare] benefits! I saw Canada, and I applied."

Bryan and Barber (2021) found that aspiring Tim Hortons workers were aware of the uneven and evolving opportunity structures associated with Canada's immigration program, yet they still vied for the opportunity to migrate as fast-food workers. They argue that these migrants are asserting their agency by knowingly taking a risk on permanent residency; they were not merely being duped by government agents, recruiters, and other actors. While this argument is credible, I contend that they may not have fully grasped the information they received. Mahler (1995, p. 53) argues that when relatives in the developing country learn about hardships, they can "believe so fully in this new 'El Dorado' that they refuse to hear the downside of migration or they underestimate it." In other words, although Filipina/os *may* be increasingly aware of policy barriers to integration, the values and faith they associate with the Canadian Dream are more powerful than the "bald truth" (Mahler, 1995, p. 84). This causes them to underestimate or ignore the barriers associated with transitioning from temporary to permanent status (see also Paul, 2017, pp. 168–170). The literature on cognitive migration echoes this tendency. Migrants tend to imagine a future that is "much more optimistic about reaching our goals, less constrained by reality checks and tend to neglect many contextual details of future realities" (Koikkalainen & Kyle, 2016, pp. 764–765), even when privy to contravening information.

Returning to Rebecca's and Janelle's assertions that they were failures for being passed over for permanent residency, what this sentiment reflects is the highly individualized nature of national dreams. Indeed, despite knowing the regulatory limits of the LSS, they still blamed themselves for not transitioning to permanent residency status. Rebecca, Janelle, Neil, and others did not fail to secure permanent residency status because of a lack of individual merit. Indeed, by all accounts, they were excellent and dedicated workers. Rather, the policy framework of the LSS, in concert with relevant provincial nominee programs (PNP) in Western Canada at the time of their residence, ensured that, in most instances, legal incorporation was denied. Indeed, as I demonstrate in chapter 5, "failure" is the probable outcome. Yet by individualizing the dream, the role of structures and policies in shaping opportunities and outcomes is obscured. In turn, this sustains the legitimacy of the Canadian Dream by individualizing "failures" as exceptions, especially given the reluctance of migrants to share the exclusionary forces and policy barriers mediating their incorporation.

One governance factor that determines formal belonging (and that has nothing to do with individual merit) is the PNP streams administered by each province and the criteria they use to assess applications. As noted in chapter 5, each province makes decisions about potential streams and occupations based on regional labour market pressures. And both the provincial and federal governments establish the criteria applicants must meet. For example, an applicant must be able to provide for themselves and their dependants at their occupation's prevailing wage in the region in question and demonstrate other competencies (such as education and language skills). If a migrant goes to a province where food-counter attendants are no longer a potential occupation for nomination under a PNP, even the "best" food-counter attendant will not stand a chance for incorporation. Fast-food wages are generally low, so whether an applicant lives in an expensive city or whether they are married and have dependants will impact their prospects.

These factors have nothing to do with an applicant's job performance or individual merit. Instead, the state – through its immigration policies – mediates whether they stand a chance at formal membership. This leaves open the possibility (however implausible) that the dream is attainable for some. Indeed, between 2002 and 2019, Alberta received 3,387 PNP applications (i.e., nominations) for food-counter attendants, and the province approved 1,754 (Government of Alberta Department of Labour and Immigration, 2019).[6] Many participants were well aware of these immigration controls (particularly pertaining to occupations and wages relative to the cost of living) and sought to migrate to other regions or provinces where they might stand a better chance (such as from British Columbia to Saskatchewan) or lamented their marital status and dependants for making them ineligible.

One woman explained:

> I am married. So, when I got to Canada, I'm married, and I only have this salary [of] $10 per hour. So, the question, the Canada government question, "How can you feed your family if you only have this salary?" But if you are single, that salary is enough for you to stay and live in [name of city]. So, all the single people in our agency, all the single people who worked in that company, they get their PR [permanent residency]. Me? I am married so no PR.

What is especially distressing about these policies is that subjects spend years planning for these migrations with the goal of Canadian citizenship. Federal and provincial migration institutions, however, change labour programs and immigration streams repeatedly, opening and closing opportunities for incorporation and belonging in real time, while migrants retain the hope (however implausible) that they will achieve permanent residency status.

The Canadian Dream continues to be a productive force for drawing migrants because there *are* "lucky ones" who achieve it. This includes Eleanor, who, after two years' employment in an Alberta-based Tim Hortons restaurant, was successfully nominated under Alberta's PNP. In 2023, she was living in Winnipeg with her husband and daughter and awaiting the arrival of her mother, whose migration she sponsored. Lynette likewise secured Canadian citizenship through Alberta's PNP and is now married, has a Canadian-born son, and is gainfully employed in the social services sector.

Between 2002 and 2019, the number of food-counter attendant visa holders who received permanent residency in Alberta was 1,521; in British Columbia, 2,778; and in Saskatchewan, 3,153 (IRCC, 2020). These figures cover only food-counter attendants. The LSP has facilitated the recruitment (and prospective incorporation) of low-waged workers in other occupations. Even though the prospect of obtaining citizenship through the program is precarious, some do achieve permanent residency status.

Institutional Management of Migrant Dreams

The diaspora and the receiving state are among multiple actors who sustain national dreams. Other institutional actors (including sending-state migration institutions, recruitment agencies, and employers) likewise contribute to its robustness. I began with the diaspora for two reasons. The first was to highlight individual migrants' practices, discourses, and agency in pursuing their dreams despite the infrastructures and governance that enable and constrain them. The second was to offset the notion that the regulation of national dreams is a concerted, calculated agenda.

Institutional actors have divergent interests in regulating national dreams, and how they operate to meet their ends is the interplay of these agendas and practices, as I detail in chapter 7. For example, Filipina/o migrants have little incentive to uphold the Canadian Dream, yet through their practices and discourses (including silences), they contribute to its maintenance. The Canadian state maintains the dream through the implied (yet often undelivered) promises associated with legal incorporation, while employers, recruitment agencies, and immigration consultants support the dream by raising hope.

Recruitment agencies offer immigration services to migrants in Canada. Migrant workers are vulnerable in reception contexts because of immigration controls that regulate their employment and residence. Migrants often solicit immigration advice from their social networks to chart a path forward, especially under ambiguous and precarious immigration programs such as the LSS. Before the end of her four-year maximum term, for instance, Dalaya got advice from compatriots regarding her options for staying in Canada. On their recommendation, she sought employment in Saskatchewan, a region deemed more likely to grant permanent residency status. But Dalaya lacked the networks to see this strategy through to fruition.

When migrants fail to resolve immigration or employment challenges, they often solicit immigration advice from consultants and other for-profit intermediaries, including recruiters that connect migrants to employers. There are widespread abuses in this sector, however, and the very existence of these intermediaries can operate to sustain the national dream.

Some participants connected with intermediaries in Canada to extend their visas or find new employers. Sometimes, they approached agencies that marketed their services online and in ethnic newspapers. These agencies promised to resolve their immigration woes for a fee. This was how Dalaya ended up spending upwards of Can$3,000 for advice from an immigration consultant and a recruitment agency. The consultant made her (wrongly) believe she had viable options for staying, while the agency was unsuccessful in securing an alternative employer or labour market impact assessment (LMIA).

The usefulness of these intermediaries is questionable, particularly in contexts where migrants are desperate to alter their precarity. As Larios and colleagues (2020) document, agencies will often charge exorbitant fees to process paperwork or provide (poor) immigration advice that can increase immigration precarity. They manipulate the hopes of Filipina/o migrants to achieve the Canadian Dream by circulating messages that promise integration while often failing to deliver. This tendency is exacerbated by the fact that these agencies are ineffectively monitored (Faraday 2014).

Paul's (2017) research on stepping-stone destinations reveals how recruitment agencies outside the Philippines institutionally contribute to sustaining the Canadian Dream. These agencies encourage migrants to pursue better destinations by regulating the social imaginary. Placement agencies build a desire for "greener pastures" by promising better working conditions and a brighter future to migrants willing to journey up a hierarchy of destinations. As with recruitment agencies in the Philippines (chapter 4), they use advertisements and "success stories." One ad in a bilingual newspaper in Taiwan featured a story about Filipina/o domestic workers who had "succeeded" in Canada. The story outlined the case of a caregiver who secured permanent residency status, got a job at a technology company, joined the Canadian Armed Forces, and received a Canadian government grant to start her own small business. For migrants, success stories such as these expand their notion of "what is achievable if they too move to Canada" (Paul, 2017, p. 234).

The print ad also featured pictures of overseas workers deployed by the agency. Migrants are pictured laughing and picnicking in Canadian parks alongside pictures of passports that display their Canadian visas. The implied message is that while Taiwan and Hong Kong may offer limited gains, Canada has greener pastures. A brighter future awaits if they continue to other destinations.

The practice of step-wise international labour migration is especially relevant given that Tim Hortons now has 230 stores across the Gulf Cooperation Council. The company also signed a memorandum of understanding in 2021 to open its Middle Eastern headquarters in Riyadh, Saudi. Arabia. Given regional patterns of recruitment, it is likely Filipina/os will largely staff these worksites. This may lead to more recruitment agencies advertising in the region, promising greener pastures for fast-food workers willing to move on to better destinations such as Canada.

The lower status associated with non-Western destinations and the privileged (imaginative) position of Canada in the global hierarchy help sustain the Canadian Dream. In McKay's (2012) research on global Filipina/os, she recounts the case of Luis, a migrant worker recruited to Western Canada. Like others in her study, Luis desired migration and incorporation into Canada given its implied promises, including permanent residency status. He believed in a "rose-tinted picture of middle-class Canadian encounters with the 1980s welfare state. [But] by the time Luis got to Canada, the state had receded" (McKay, 2012, p. 185). In its place, Luis encountered a neoliberal, market-driven state (chapter 2). He felt betrayed by the country's failure to deliver on central elements of the Canadian Dream.

Canada was recently ranked the top aspirational labour destination for Filipina/o nationals (Social Weather Survey, 2022). In her analysis of the uneven global market for migrant domestic labour, Paul (2017, pp. 87, 93) likewise found that Canada was often listed at the top of Filipina/o workers' rankings of global destinations: "Canada is one of only a handful of destination countries that offers even the possibility [however unlikely] of permanent residence and eventual citizenship ... which means it will continue to feature in many migrants' destination dreams." Given that Tim Hortons now boasts stores in the Philippines and stepping-stone destinations across the Gulf Cooperation Council, new migration routes will probably emerge in the pursuit of the Canadian Dream.

Like intermediaries, employers contribute to the robustness of the Canadian Dream. They lure migrants with the promise of permanent residency. They wield power through the possibility that they *might* support a migrant nomination. In Dalaya's case, her employer intimated they would support her nomination, but she was eventually passed over. Neil had a more traumatic experience when his employer pledged a nomination that never materialized.[7] Some employers appear to go out of their way to support migrants by exhausting their possibilities for incorporation. This was the case with a franchise owner in Alberta who was intent on helping Jesus (a Mexican migrant worker) secure permanent residency through his work as a food-counter attendant. Although the employer nominated Jesus, he did not meet the provincially mandated human or language capital requirements. His application was denied. Outraged, the employer reported that they would look for another way to help Jesus return to Canada. Given the outsourcing of the border associated with temporary migrant worker programs, Jesus believed the franchise owner could help him. What this suggests is that employers, intentionally or not, are central actors in sustaining the Canadian Dream because of governance structures that dictate their participation.

The Filipino Canadian Dream

National dreams are powerful, but they are not monolithic. In her research on the American Dream, Park (1997) notes that the Korean version is based on a Korean rendition of the colonial mentality – "American fever." Rather than a quest for economic advancement or mass consumption, American fever involves "a cultural complex of longing for political, economic, social and cultural well-being" (Park, 1997, p. 29). From the Korean example, Park concludes that distinct national versions of the American Dream run alongside its core elements. To get at the heart of a dream, we must move beyond the overarching dream toward its more nuanced, hyphenated or rather, dual character. Like Park (1997), I echo the need to theorize the localized and ethnic variants of the national dream.

This need was not apparent to me until I did comparative, global field research on Mexican, fast-food labour migration and observed similarities and dissimilarities between the Mexican Canadian and Filipino Canadian Dreams. Mexican migrants had fewer specific ideas about Canada (including the expectation of legal incorporation) than Filipina/o migrants. They reported being drawn by the prospect of higher wages and economic advancement through "legal" migration. Moreover, they saw Canada as an extension of "el Norte," with the added benefit of legal migration. Canada had qualities often attributed to the American Dream, such as opportunities to make economic gains and engage in mass consumption. While many Mexican migrants had the same desires associated with the Filipino Canadian Dream (namely, transitioning from temporary to permanent status), the United States at first played a bigger role in their vision of the Canadian Dream.

In other words, the imaginative forces propelling their mobility had a distinct origin, pointing to the need to interrogate the *specific* formation of national dreams, including how "social actors and the institutionalized thought-systems and discourse of a given society" shape these social imaginaries (Park, 1997, p. 2). This includes how dreams and institutions are governed and connected to each other, ultimately shaping how labour chains operate.

Recognizing the specific national flavour of the Filipino Canadian Dream, the infrastructures that enable it, and the relationship of institutional actors to the formation of this social imaginary, the above raises questions about other dual versions of the Canadian Dream, and how (transnational) institutional actors – such as state migration institutions, employers, and labour brokers – govern alternative versions of it. Indeed, a central contention of this book is that to understand how temporary labour programs operate, we need to consider how the institutional actors that underlie labour chains work and how they relate to each other (chapter 7).

Social Imaginaries and a Landscape of Broken Dreams

Canada is moving toward more exclusionary immigration programs and ambiguous systems for transitioning migrants from temporary to permanent status. These policy shifts raise important questions regarding the future of the Canadian Dream. Will the power of the Canadian Dream remain vibrant in its various hyphenated forms? Or will its ability to draw migrants to Canada become compromised? If fractures in the Canadian Dream come to the fore on a global scale, will Canada lose its global appeal, or will (highly qualified) migrants continue to give it an esteemed place in the global hierarchy?

These are empirical questions worthy of examination. My hunch is that despite exclusionary immigration trends and policies, the Canadian Dream (in its varied, dual forms) will continue circulating because a few migrants will achieve the dream, and the rest will continue to engage in status performances and conceal their hardships; because of transnational social optics; because of Canada's highly celebrated reputation as a champion of multicultural and human rights; and because transnational migration industries and apparatuses will continue to shine an ideational light on Canada.

Migrants such as Dalaya and Neil – and their social networks – may well come to know of the hardships associated with labour migration to Canada, yet they will remain highly optimistic about achieving the Filipino Canadian Dream. Two questions remain unanswered: Who benefits from the circulation of the Canadian Dream? How do relations *between* migration institutions that govern mobility shape these desires, social imaginaries, and migration practices? In the following chapter, I consider how dreams, imaginaries, and institutions are connected to one another, and how migration institutions interactively operate to uphold dominant moral economies.

Chapter 7

A Global Infrastructure of Migrant Dreams

Skilled Filipina/o migrants such as Maya and Rosamie told me they viewed food-counter-attendant work in Canada as an opportunity, despite de-skilling. Before coming to Canada, Maya was a masters-level business professional with trade and consular experience. Rosamie was an accounting professional working for a business processing outsourcing company (BPO) in Makati. I also spoke with a college instructor, a medical representative for a global pharmaceutical company, and a manager for a popular international foundation. Their resolve to pursue the Canadian Dream was steadfast. Indeed, Maria was so sold on the figures of desire associated with the Canadian Dream that despite being passed over for permanent residency by her employers at Tim Hortons and the hotel, she was actively searching from the Philippines for a contract in Canada. These migrants' accounts raise pertinent questions left partially unanswered in previous chapters, namely: Who are the benefactors of the Canadian Dream? And what is the relationship between dreams, social imaginaries, and institutions? In this chapter, I take a panoramic view to show that these dynamics are often the incidental interplay of a host of interests, values, and operations.

Filipina/o migrants go through a series of institutional processes in both Canada and the Philippines to pursue the Canadian Dream via the Low-Skilled Stream (see the appendix for an infrastructure of migration map). A host of institutional actors – in isolation and in tandem – govern their mobility, including drawing from and contributing to the social imaginary. In this book, we have homed in on the workings of corporations, employers, recruiters, and states. We have done so, however, by focusing on their workings in isolation. By considering these situated processes across stakeholders, the complex relationship between dreams, social imaginaries, and institutions is illuminated alongside the moral economies that underlie them. Institutions are, after all, not siloed bureaucratic islands but interactive compilations of the values and norms that govern their operation.

Migrant Governance and Institutional Interactions

The growth of temporary labour schemes and the commodification of migration has engendered new migration infrastructures and dynamics, including the birth of profit-driven intermediaries. These consultants, immigration lawyers, and labour recruiters handle a range of services for corporations and employers, from overseeing applications to vetting workers and delivering them to global employers. They have benefited from the growth of migrant worker programs. As an industry, their success reflects the commodification of migration in Canada and the shift toward market-driven policies. It also reflects the state's acceptance at multiple scales (provincial and federal) that capital *should* have a crucial say in determining flows to Canada, engendering a demand for their services. It marks the devolution of nation-building to the private sector, a trend that is only increasing.

In recent years, the ease by which employers can recruit temporary foreign workers (TFWs) has resulted in a surge in the number recruited to Canada, alongside the loosening of federal restrictions to prevent abuse of the Temporary Foreign Worker Program (TFWP). In 2022, the federal government relaxed restrictions introduced in 2014 to address employers' abuse of the TFWP, including the sidelining of local workers (Alsharif, 2023a). It granted employers the ability to employ up to 20 per cent of their workforce under the LSS, previously capped at 10 per cent. But employers in accommodation and food services were granted the right to hire up to 30 per cent of their workforce under the LSS (ESDC, 2023). The change led to a surge in Labour Market Impact Assessment (LMIA) requests and approvals (Alsharif, 2023b), marking the growth of hospitality labour migration to Canada. It also conveys the growing demand for the services of intermediaries.

Whether governments are winners or losers in this arrangement is debatable, but given a state's mandate to govern the welfare of its citizenry currently in the face of neoliberal norms, it is purposeful that the state is opting to expand those considered beyond its purview through facilitating the recruitment of non-citizen workers. In so doing, it satisfies employer demands for access to low-waged labour, while refraining from extending these workers corresponding citizenship rights. Intermediaries do the exclusionary work within the confines of weak regulatory structures specified by the state, while the state maintains its good standing.

The Canadian state is consigning governance responsibilities from the public to the private sector, following neoliberal principles and directed by market forces. It has lost (partial) control of the border to profit-driven actors (employers and recruiters) and spends more time creating (weak) legislation to protect migrants and defend its moral standing. This is why the Canadian government implemented a moratorium on food services migration in 2014, including caps on the percentage of temporary foreign workers per site and more stringent requirements for advertising job vacancies. At that time, its legitimacy and priorities were under question, especially given the sidelining of domestic workers. Once the crisis of legitimacy was gone (or at least forgotten), the federal government, through Employment and Social Development Canada (ESDC), again waived restrictions in the face of purported labour shortages, loosening federal barriers that led to a surge in LMIA approvals. However, in 2024 its legitimacy was once again under question when a widely cited UN report concluded that Canada's TFWP is a "breeding ground for contemporary forms of slavery" (Hussan, 2024). Again, the state has turned to (weak) legislative changes to publicly defend its moral standing.

Because Canada's multicultural identity is important to the state but fragile, its varied institutions and actors oscillate between inclusive and neoliberal values and practices. When need be, it villainizes profit-driven agents as a functional tactic to maintain its moral standing. For instance, in 2022, amendments to the Immigration and Refugee Protection Act (IRPA) included state authority to inspect and penalize employers suspected of or found guilty of noncompliance. When accounts of unscrupulous employers or recruiters come out, the state blames and punishes these "bad apples" by publishing names, addresses, and details about the violations on the Immigration, Refugees and Citizenship Canada (IRCC) website.

But even on defined social issues, state programming is inconsistent. The IRPR is meant to increase protections for temporary foreign workers, and IRCC purportedly publicizes and punishes violations, but ESDC policies have primarily loosened restrictions and made it easier for employers to recruit and (in turn) hire flexible labour. By distancing itself from the recruitment process while maintaining neoliberal agendas, the labour and migration arms of the Canadian government uphold neoliberal programming while presenting a righteous, multicultural facade.

The recruitment sector in the Philippines likewise serves a similar ideological purpose. It allows the state to claim a caring and protective identity in the face of colonial and neoliberal mandates. The Philippine

Overseas Employment Administration (POEA) is highly focused on regulating the private sector when it comes to recruitment; it believes close oversight will advance the welfare of migrant hopefuls. The POEA conducts performance evaluations of recruitment agencies every four years, evaluating dimensions such as the volume of deployments, their record of violations, and migrant welfare. Successful agencies are bestowed and awarded a Top Performer Award, an Award of Excellence, or a Presidential Award. Through vetting and award systems, employers are led to specific agencies. Receiving an award from the POEA gives recruitment agencies benefits, including recognition, referrals, and invitations to participate in recruitment and (international) job fairs sponsored by the state.

Recall, for instance, that in chapter 1, Maya's Aunt Jane met Felix, a Filipino-based recruiter in Alberta competing to become an agency for the Alberta Hotel and Lodging Association's affiliated hospitality employers. All the recruiters I met in the Philippines with contracts to Canada had a POEA award. Through these government seals of approval, employers, corporations, or their third-party intermediaries are (presumably) reassured that they are working with reputable agencies.

Ideally, the state acts in an oversight capacity while agencies engage in recruitment at the behest of employers. But the system is fraught with tension. The relationship between the recruitment sector and the state is volatile. Guevarra (2010, p. 89) suggests that the Philippine state "sees them both as partners and enemies." The state imposes stringent recruitment rules (including licensing fees and penalties for violations), which makes recruiting workers a more involved and, according to recruiters, difficult and bureaucratic process. Indeed, agencies can be scapegoated (e.g., for the abuse of prospective migrants), allowing the state to assume the role of a caring, protective actor while agencies are framed as ruthless, uncaring, and profit obsessed.

But this dichotomy is misleading. The POEA, the Department of Labor and Employment (DOLE), and the International Labor Affairs Bureau (ILAB) (through consular and Philippine Overseas Labour Offices) likewise hold market fairs and other activities geared toward streaming workers into international labour markets. DOLE and the POEA rely on agencies to vet, prepare, and deploy migrants and engage in market development. The POEA operates as a gatekeeper for agencies, determining whether they will be invited to job fairs or referred for contracts. But who will be blamed when violations come to light? In their current rendition, the POEA and other migration arms of the state have donned the mantle of a responsible and caring identity in a moral economy that deflects neoliberal values onto recruitment agencies. This portrayal is, of course, unwarranted since the state's migration apparatus needs the recruitment sector to operate and in fact performs 5 per cent of overseas-foreign-workers recruitment itself (Guevarra, 2010, p. 105).

The above institutional arrangement implies that recruiters are at the helm of the recruitment process while employers and the state operate as clients and overseers respectively, but employers are highly influential in guiding recruitment selections transnationally. Moreover, recruiters want to deliver desired candidates, and gathering information is pertinent to this objective. This arrangement serves the mandate of the market and resolves underlying tensions regarding Canada's moral economy.

From a market perspective, agencies seek to uphold their reputation and secure maximum job orders; a satisfied employer or corporation is central to this goal. By offloading selection transnationally onto recruiters and agencies, employers and corporations can distance themselves from any discriminatory practices common in sending states (e.g., specifying age or gender requirements). But whereas employers seek to distance themselves from these processes, recruiters want employer and corporate input into migrant selection. Thus, recruiters often report the roundabout ways they will solicit this information from Canadian employers and corporations and appear rather amused by how uncomfortable employers are with these solicitations but pleased with their selection.

Ultimately, Canadian stakeholders (employers and state actors), in absolving themselves of any responsibility for discriminatory practices in transnational spaces, come across as either oblivious or as playing jurisdictional *futbol* (soccer) in the face of violations (Hennebry, 2010). Employers and corporations maintain the facade that they are, indeed, moral, non-discriminatory, and proper multicultural Canadian subjects while retaining access to flexible (read: exploitable) migrant labour. The Canadian state retains an inclusive and welcoming identity. Recruiters and agencies are thus the ideal scapegoats. In practice, neoliberal mandates trump caring or multicultural values.

Within this institutional landscape, prospective workers must compete to be selected for oversees work. Migrants interface primarily with recruitment agencies, but employers and corporations shape recruitment requirements and often weigh in on selection. Workers are often excited about the prospect of Canada (especially compared to other regions) given Canada's favourable position on a global hierarchy. What pulls and pushes them through the application process, then, are previously discussed aspirational and structural factors, which position the work as a coveted opportunity, especially in contrast to the hopelessness that purportedly characterizes life and employment in the Philippines.

A host of actors inform these sentiments: the Canadian state, through its multicultural marketing and policies; various arms of the Filipino labour and migration apparatus, through their failure to create jobs domestically while intimating that greener pastures lie overseas; and recruitment agencies, which more explicitly relay the message of greener pastures elsewhere. Moreover, while the recruitment process may appear to be but one in a triadic process that involves migrants, agencies, and employers, there are many other actors, institutions, social imaginaries, histories, geopolitical relations, and forces at play. Even the diaspora encourages applications by conferring status and, through remittances, by boldly declaring that a brighter future exists abroad. Migrants' mobility is thus shaped by and reliant on a host of institutional actors.

Within this structural and ideational landscape, employers can be hyper-choosy about their desired global workforce, rendering them (and the intermediaries working on their behalf) clear winners inundated by qualified applicants, as shown in chapters 3 and 5. Given Canada's favourable position in a hierarchy of potential destinations and the potential earnings and figures of desire associated with the West, recruitment agencies are thrilled to receive job orders from Canada.

Although a host of profit-driven actors have emerged to connect employers with workers, the receiving state does not fully relinquish control over governing flows. The embassy's evaluation complicates the narrative that employers (or recruiters working on their behalf) control the social dimensions of global flows in temporary labour programs. Instead, the applicant must satisfy embassy agents, following guidelines provided by IRCC. The values and preferences of the host state therefore influence the social constitution of flows. For instance, as we have seen, recruiters at first did not require applicants to have a college degree but amended this requirement when the Canadian embassy began denying work permits on this ground. Thus, recruiters (at the employer's behest) select the workers they perceive to be ideal, but there are mediating judgments and forces that shape the selection process, with higher levels of human capital being an esteemed value upheld by Canada transnationally. Mobility can also be terminated at any moment – for example, by a recruiter, an employer, a POEA agent, a Canadian consular official in Manila, or a Canadian Border Services agent.

Beyond the requirements of the labour-receiving state, applicants must also successfully meet the requirements of the Filipino migration apparatus.[1] The Philippines has a highly coordinated transnational mechanism for systematizing mobility that focuses on ensuring workers meet the requirements to enter foreign destinations and promoting a certifiably "ideal" worker subject for export (through pre-departure orientation seminars and Technical Education and Skills and Development Authority, or TESDA, courses), as detailed in chapter 3. The highly systematized Philippine migration apparatus demonstrates the state's faith in exporting labour to mitigate domestic economic challenges, even though, officially, it claims to be responding to – rather than encouraging – labour migration.

Governments such as Canada's rely on and entrust labour-sending states such as the Philippines to prove that the migrants they are sending meet minimum requirements for the job in question.[2] If this vetting process is deemed unsuccessful and migrants "unworthy" of entrance – for failing to be morally "upright," physically sound, or temporary – there will be fewer prospects for other Filipina/o nationals (Rodriguez, 2010). Thus, the Philippines is invested in governing the activities of its migration institutions and recruitment agencies and projecting the image of a trustworthy state; its ability to compete with other labour-sending states in a saturated market depends on its good standing.

This does not mean that government bureaucrats or institutions are indifferent to the plight of their nationals or monolithic in their goals. Different agencies have distinct interests and mandates that can undermine state objectives (Voorn et al., 2019). Indeed, some agencies (such as the Philippine Department of Health) work to retain medical staff in the face of critical shortages and, thus, are not mobilizing to promote emigration. During my research, some agents working on behalf of the POEA and Overseas Workers Welfare Association (OWWA) also appeared to be genuinely concerned for the welfare of their compatriots and were critical of state endeavours to shift responsibility to workers in the face of perilous journeys.

One OWWA agent expressed his frustration with the difficulties some workers face, a sentiment he struggled to express given his role as a state agent involved in the institutional process of exporting labour. The main contradiction he found was between the mandate to empower workers to exercise their rights substantively while also encouraging them to be ambassadors for the country and professional in their comportment. NGO staff assigned to facilitate PDOSs (especially an ex-migrant advocate working as a PDOS facilitator for an NGO with workers primarily en route to the Middle East) faced similar challenges. Although caring sentiments and even criticisms may circulate among relevant actors and institutions marking a counter-normative, moral subjectivity, the dominant moral economy guiding the state's overseas labour program is insistently neoliberal and dominates relations and practices on the ground.

Moral Economies Regulating Flows

While Canada and the Philippines are distinctly positioned in my study as labour-receiving and -sending states, their moral economies are akin, reflecting the exclusionary and neoliberal logics at the heart of their nations, institutions, and policies.

In the case of Canada, its exclusionary and neoliberal logics are evident when considering the mere expansion of the TFWP. As a program that resides at the intersection of labour and immigration policy, the LSS functions to recruit flexible labour to Canada; workers formally denied many substantive rights associated with citizenship due to their "temporary foreign worker" (read: non-citizenship) status. These workers are managed under immigration controls that produce spaces of exception where migrants are channelled into the bottom tiers of the labour market and governed by policies that generate their vulnerability. These workers are insecure not only with regards to the precarity that characterizes their work and employment relations, but also their long-term prospects for becoming members of the polity. Regulated by PNPs, which give the provinces and territories increased control over regional migration patterns, these programs are highly insecure when it comes to prospects for incorporation. They neither deny nor directly facilitate legal incorporation, marking the downloading of risk and insecurity from the state onto (racialized) migrant subjects. This stands in contrast to Canada's welcoming, multicultural reputation.

In the case of the Philippines, the state's labour export policy and related commodification of the Filipino citizenry is likewise informed through exclusionary and neoliberal logics. What initially began as a stop-gap policy has been transformed into a highly institutionalized migration apparatus rendering the Philippines the premier labour exporting state globally. Working in concert with labour recruiters and other profit-driven intermediaries that perform what might arguably be state functions, the commercialization of the state and the goal of developing the economy through remittances means the Philippines must betray its citizenry in pursuit of this goal. Moreover, it has pursued a particular line of development that includes inserting the Philippines into the global economy in a flexible, neoliberal fashion, rendering the state's ability to advocate for the rights of its citizenry frail at best.

The Philippine state markets its citizens to global employers along lines favourable to capital accumulation and aims to deliver commodified, responsibilized, economically competitive, and disciplined workers; in other words, neoliberal subjects. These policies rely on a manipulation of the social imaginary and a corresponding reformulation of belonging that Rodriguez (2010) defines as migrant citizenship. Governed by a host of actors, the Filipino state through its migration institutions, the recruitment sector, and, incidentally, by the diaspora circulates ideas about the promises of host destinations and the purported shortcomings associated with the Philippines. By denigrating the Philippines (intentionally and incidentally), a host of actors encourage workers to desire overseas work while the state vehemently resists taking responsibility for its role in these dynamics; the state argues it is merely managing a "natural" inclination among Filipinos to migrate overseas. The disconnect between stated policy and reality allows relevant state institutions to portray themselves in a caring and favourable light.

Like the Philippines, Canada is similarly invested in portraying the Canadian nation in a positive light despite evidence to the contrary. While Canada has a long history of discriminating against newcomers along lines of race, nationality, and class, it boasts a multicultural reputation that encompasses being socially just. Canadians have come to identify themselves as belonging to a welcoming, open country that celebrates and upholds difference. Yet as I document in chapter 2, the state has long patrolled the borders of the nation along temporally relevant lines, currently marked by a neoliberal and exclusionary moral economy that masquerades as a knowledge-based economy. This knowledge-based economy relies on a racialized capitalist system; even when citizens of the Global South have higher levels of human capital, they can still be segmented to the bottom tiers of the labour market and marginalized to the peripheries of the nation. Moreover, while Canada is deeply invested in thinking of itself as inclusive and socially just, the values and affects that underpin its (and the Philippines') immigration policies are racialized neoliberal values.

Migrants, however, are the ones who must live the realities of these policies, including the management of their desires and dreams for the benefit of capital. They are the ones at the centre of these forces.

Chapter 8

Reimagining a World beyond Labour Migration

Enter a Tim Hortons restaurant and you'll experience a clean, comfortable environment with an array of product offerings at bargain prices. Like other fast-food corporations, Tim Hortons competes for consumer dollars, an increasingly difficult endeavour given the proliferation and aggressive expansion of many fast-food corporations. Despite this saturated market, Tim Hortons is the leading quick-service restaurant chain in Canada, boasting the most stores and largest share of the consumer market. A host of forces have contributed to its success, including Tim Hortons' special place in Canada's social imaginary.

To brand itself with an appealing identity, Tim Hortons has long exploited a romanticized version of Canada's values and norms. Clichéd symbols – beaming with national pride and flattery – are meant to represent the social fabric of the nation, an ideal Tim Hortons has long claimed for itself and promoted in its marketing. This imagery, in turn, has shaped Canada's identity, operating as a force that draws migrants to Canada. Yet much like the idealized versions of small towns and quotidian moments, Tim Hortons' reputation and Canada's national identity conceal more discriminatory profiles. It is this disconnect between imaginary and reality that harms migrants.

Migrants and the Canadian Dream

From the perspective of workers, Canada's favourable reputation and location in the global hierarchy is problematic. In contrast to other nations, Canada is imagined as a welcoming, open country that celebrates difference and has viable prospects for belonging. Migrants are, thus, disarmed by Canada's reputation. They do not expect to face violations at work or hardships in the broader society; they believe Canada champions human (and thus labour) rights domestically and globally.

When they experience hardships (including being passed over for permanent residency), their experience stands in stark contrast with their institutionally mediated expectations of incorporation. This view is bolstered by the value and esteem the Filipino state, recruitment agencies, and the polity place on migration (especially to the West) and the role of the colonial mentality (as a form of autoracism) that make forsaking professional jobs commonsensical.

Within this ideological landscape, it is difficult for migrants who are passed over for permanent residency to make sense of or reconcile their stalled trajectory. As we saw, most internalize their "failed" migrations; they blame themselves for being denied the figures of desire associated with incorporation rather than blaming the structures that shaped their rejection. This precarity contrasts with both the social imaginary of Canada and the orderly ideals widely imposed onto regulated migration.

International organizations such as the International Labour Organization and the Global Commission on International Migration champion temporary worker programs as safe, orderly, and dignified vehicles for migration. In the face of irregular flows and perilous journeys, these programs appear to be viable solutions, especially in the context of fortified borders and limited pathways to incorporation. Thus, discourses of dignified migration and orderly flows circulate widely. But what is meant by *dignity*? And orderly for whom?

Given the conditions attached to most low-waged temporary migrant worker schemes (including tied contracts), migrant vulnerability benefits employers and intermediaries. Receiving states and employers can access qualified workers while withholding substantive citizenship and labour rights to meet "market demands," causing chaos and feelings of failure among workers. Since the worst jobs are reserved for temporary migrant workers, and because more countries want to send labour than receive it, the recruitment sector and the migration arms of the Filipino state must motivate qualified migrants to engage in overseas work and transnational deskilling. Indeed, because labour and immigration policies are meant to align with the market, the need for flexibility is embodied principally by temporary migrant workers.

As a nation dependent on the remittances of its citizens by design – at a tune of US\$38.34 billion sent back to the Philippines by Overseas Foreign Workers in 2024 alone (Fintech News Philippines, 2025) – the Philippines thus promotes colonial and neoliberal values, contributing to the racialization of precarity and low-waged migration. Critical scholars rightly argue that workers are disenfranchised in this arrangement, but whether they are winners or losers is largely subjective and dependent on the outcomes of governance. Some migrants may interpret fast-food work as a coveted opportunity and appreciate the chance to migrate and belong in Canada. Others may lament leaving their families behind for entry-level hospitality jobs, for forsaking professional training and identities for a mere *chance* at Canadian citizenship. Across space and time, migrants likely oscillate between these two sentiments, depending on the outcome.

The question of whether it was worth it, then, appears to be a longitudinal query, one that must be assessed systematically, both before, during, and following employment under the Low-Skilled Stream. What is clear is that within this governance structure, there *are* clear winners: corporations, employers, and for-profit intermediaries who leverage the social imaginary to meet profit-driven ends. Receiving states likewise gain access to workers without having to contribute to the costs of their reproduction. It is migrants like Maya and Maria who are left to pursue their desires and dreams within these infrastructures – institutions and policies that uphold neoliberal values.

Moral Economies and the Future of Migrant Dreams

This book described a new landscape of labour migration from the Philippines to Canada under conditions of neoliberal globalization. Through shifts in labour and immigration policies, Canada encourages qualified people to gamble at improbable odds for permanent residency and belonging under employer-sponsored nomination programs. This landscape reflects new conditions of competition, risk, and social exclusion, features increasingly common in a precarious world, features that increasingly reflect Canada's neoliberal moral economy. The LSS, as a manifestation of this moral economy, is narrowing the traditional pathway for middle-class people to enter and settle in Canada with viable prospects of incorporation. This raises the questions: Is the Low-Skilled Stream the end of the Canadian Dream? Does it reflect a broader diminishment of the middle class?

The move toward market-driven citizenship has become the Canadian norm, evidenced by sustained shifts in immigration programming. Canada has seen a notable growth in temporary migrant workers for low-wage occupations, as well as territorial and provincial nominee programs that grant provincial and territorial governments the authority to make recommendations and initial nominations regarding prospective migration and incorporation to Canada. These programs are geared at the economic development of regions and sectors, with industry stakeholders often having a leading hand at influencing decision making regarding the occupations and sectors that will be covered by Provincial Nominee Programs (PNPs). In the words of the immigration arm of the federal government, "the government also works closely with … economic development partners, and industry to attract and retain economic immigrants and ensure that all areas of the country benefit from immigration" through PNP programs (IRCC, 2020). Indeed, the PNP is now the "second largest economic immigration program" in Canada, with the bulk of PNP admissions – 85 per cent – being for higher-skilled occupations in 2019 (IRCC, 2017a, p. 2, 2020). In contrast, only 8 per cent of successful PNP nominees in 2018 were for intermediate and lower-skilled classifications (IRCC, 2020).

Working alongside other immigration programs meant to attract the "best and brightest" and retain them by providing viable pathways for incorporation, the PNP reflects both the classed nature of potential belonging in Canada and the inherent risks of migration to the country. Indeed, legal belonging is rendered more direct and feasible for those regarded as desirable based on levels of economic and human capital (such as through investment class programs such as the Start-Up Visa Program, the Federal Skilled Worker Program, and a combination of the Post-Graduation Work Permit Program and Canadian Experience Class). In contrast, while there appears to be a need for workers in lower segments of the labour market, Canada has embraced a host of strategies (such as the LSS) to access this labour while denying workers corresponding citizenship rights. This speaks poorly for the future of work and migrant conditions in Canada.

What is interesting about PNPs beyond their market-driven orientation is that there is both an inherent precarity to these programs (an application for permanent residency can result in failure) and – as my study shows – many applicants classified as "lower-skilled" are in fact qualified subjects. In the case of inherent precarity, Canada wants to expedite migration to address purported labour market needs while withholding rights and entitlements formally associated with migration to and membership in Canada. That migrants are looking to enter Canada on temporary work visas for a shot at formal belonging (and the Canadian Dream) points to the existence of a new neoliberal terrain in which subjects are called upon – sometimes unknowingly – to engage in precarious migration. This precarity is consistent with core neoliberal principles wherein the state narrows and contracts its obligations and responsibilities while enlisting individuals to take on more risks.

Beyond the risky, competitive, and employer-driven nature of TMWPs and, specifically, the LSS, the cultural logics informing immigration policy also raise troubling questions regarding power, the outsourcing of migrant selection to the private sector, and the increasingly exclusionary nature of Canadian immigration policy and its longer-term consequences. Take the need for workers in Canada as an example. Many Canadian employers and government officials bemoan labour shortages (especially in Western Canada). The policy response has been to implement and institutionalize a labour program that facilitates recruitment of low-waged, temporary-status migrants. In so doing, labour-market regulation in the bottom tiers of the Canadian labour market now relies on a host of profit-driven and transnational actors to evaluate and select those judged suitable for entry, with limited accountability. Once in Canada, these migrants compete for permanent residency within the worksite, a practice that encourages violations and lower work and employment standards. Those few who do manage to settle in Canada have to contend with the long-term, negative economic consequences of entering the country with a precarious legal status (Goldring & Landolt, 2012, 2013). Will new hierarchies (along lines such as nationality, race, and immigrant status) result from these new labour programs? Can alternatives to this bleak future be imagined?

Reimagining a Future beyond Labour Export

In chapter 4, I recount travelling to a migrant sending community with organizers of Migrante International. During the journey, I was reminded by organizers of various dos and don'ts, such as not complimenting residents on their possessions or homes, especially if they had been purchased with remittances. At one point, I asked an organizer whether he discouraged (prospective) migrants from going overseas. He said no. Although Migrante publicizes the perils of overseas work, it likewise understands the structural and material conditions that propel migrants into global circuits of labour. He did, however, emphasize the need to remind his compatriots of the costs of migration and encourage them to desire a "simpler" life. I understood *simpler* to mean free from acquisitive fantasies for consumable items and the idea that labour migration is the sole (or at least most viable) means to attain these ends. On more than one occasion, organizers of Migrante International credited the desire for mobility and consumptive patterns as products of a colonial mentality.

The effects of colonization are pervasive features of many developing societies; they bleed into and inform individual and collective desires. While this certainly holds true for the Philippines, the Philippine government also seeks to leverage social imaginaries that celebrates the American Dream (Guevarra, 2010), or Canadian Dream, to encourage migration through a highly institutionalized system of labour brokerage (Rodriguez, 2010). Going one step further, to get migrants past the point of ambivalence, overseas work is presented as preferable to life and employment in the sending context. That other actors, such as members of the diaspora, (unintentionally) contribute to this social imaginary, marks the pervasiveness and power of these social imaginaries.

Imagining a future beyond labour export appears to require, then, a clear-eyed assessment, even a rejection, of national dreams (such as the Canadian Dream) and the social denigration of the sending context. But desires and dreams are iteratively manufactured as workers navigate through institutional mazes in response to the implied and stated benefits of different nations. We thus need more empirical research on national dreams, including the actors and institutions involved in their governance. National dreams are also dual and context-specific, raising the question of whether the Canadian Filipino Dream is applicable beyond my case study. If so, along what lines does it convene and converge?

We are only beginning to understand the role of the social imaginary, state migration institutions, employers, and labour brokers in the regulation of migration flows. Research into other sectors, labour chains, and migration corridors will advance knowledge in this area. Such knowledge, in the right hands, will provide the empirical context for resisting the range of social imaginaries that disenfranchise migrants and render labour migration both commonsensical and desirable.

Appendix: The Infrastructure
of Migration Map

Stage 1: Obtain Relevant Credentials and Work Experience

For workers, the first stage of the migration cycle involves obtaining relevant work experience and credentials. Because Canadian recruiters often require a college degree for workers as food-counter attendants, most attend a postsecondary institution. The breadth of majors and specialties varies. In some instances, migrant hopefuls opt to study hospitality, while others also complement this work experience with training in private facilities (such as training courses put on by the Technical Education and Skills Development Authority, or TESDA) and fast-food chains, domestic or global. Since Tim Hortons now has restaurants in Manila and the Middle East, workers may opt to pursue employment there as a pathway to Canada. Some agencies prefer experience in specific chains (such as Jollibee), while others require experience in supervisory roles, despite recruiting for entry-level positions.

Stage 2: Labour Market Impact Assessment

For employers, the initial step in the supply chain involves applying to Employment and Social Development Canada (ESDC) for a Labour Market Impact Assessment (LMIA). Employers often hire a consultant, labour recruiter, or immigration lawyer, or they use an in-house or corporate human resource person to oversee the LMIA application. In the case of Tim Hortons, the corporation is increasingly taking over the LMIA process for its franchisees.

Federally, the Immigration and Refugee Protection Act governs the activities of Canadian-based labour consultants and recruiters, and lawyers and consultants are often self-regulated or overseen by their professional bodies. Service Canada officers evaluate whether there is a

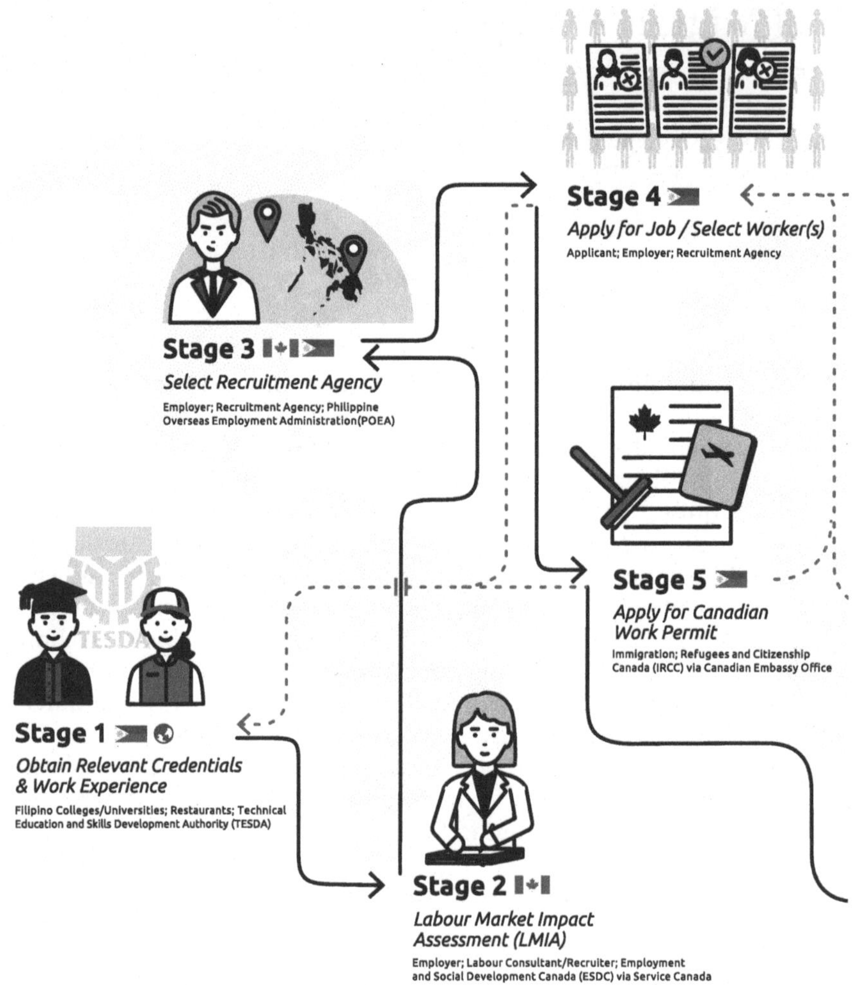

Figure A.1. Filipino Labour Migration Map (Low-Skilled Stream)

Source: Design by Broadbent Studio; Flags and Map: Commons.Wikimedia.org

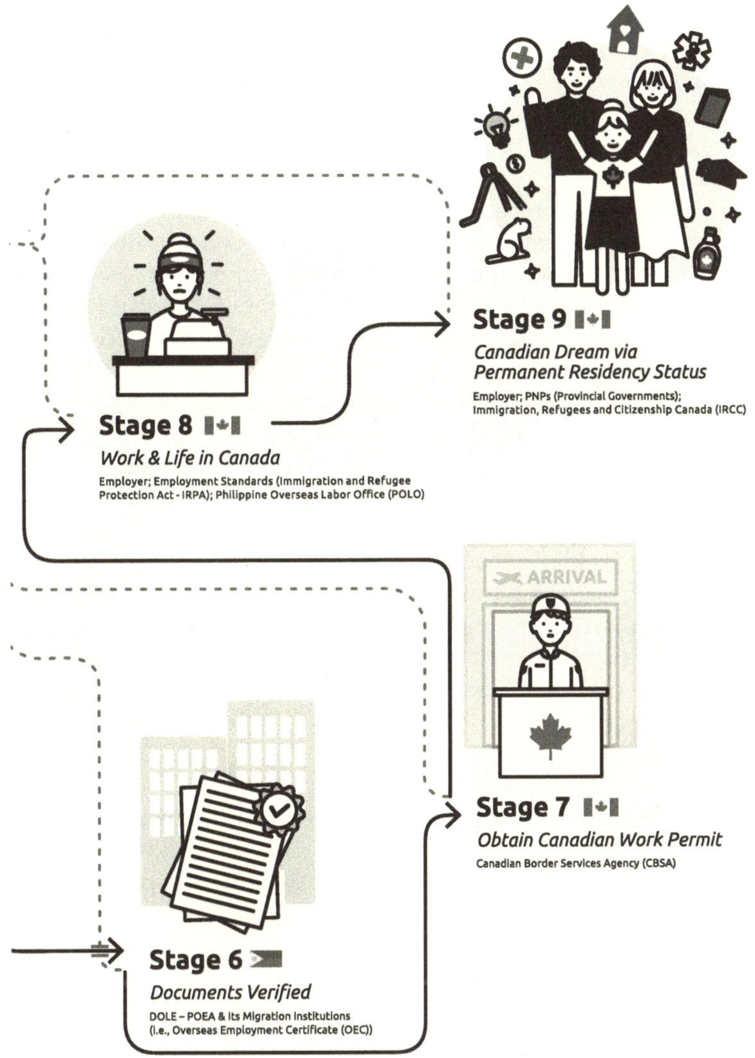
Stage 9
Canadian Dream via
Permanent Residency Status
Employer; PNPs (Provincial Governments);
Immigration, Refugees and Citizenship Canada (IRCC)

Stage 8
Work & Life in Canada
Employer; Employment Standards (Immigration and Refugee
Protection Act - IRPA); Philippine Overseas Labor Office (POLO)

Stage 7
Obtain Canadian Work Permit
Canadian Border Services Agency (CBSA)

Stage 6
Documents Verified
DOLE – POEA & Its Migration Institutions
(i.e., Overseas Employment Certificate (OEC))

ARRIVAL

need for a foreign worker and whether domestic workers will be negatively impacted by their recruitment. Employers can either "name" the worker in the application or submit an "Unnamed LMIA," indicating that the candidate(s) will be selected later. If the LMIA is approved, however, the employer must name the worker on the official positive LMIA letter.

During the LMIA process, only the projected impact on the labour market is under consideration, not the source country or candidate. They also vet the genuineness of the employment offer via factors listed in subsection 200(5) of the Immigration and Refugee Protection Regulations (IRPR). These factors include but are not limited to (1) the employer being actively engaged in the activities for which the offer is made; (2) past compliance with federal and provincial laws regulating employment and recruitment of temporary foreign workers, and (3) proof that the employer can fulfil the terms of the contract (Dixon-Perera, 2020, p. 12). Provincially, employers must comply with provincial recruitment legislation. Both Alberta and British Columbia have legislation that regulates the recruitment of workers to their provinces.

Research suggests employers and recruiters have developed sophisticated techniques to pass the LMIA (Zell, 2018 p. 130). Thus, despite the above safeguards, there are widespread accounts of abuses, including domestic workers being sidelined in favour of foreign workers.

Stage 3: Select Recruitment Agency

Once an LMIA is secured, the employer begins the recruitment process by (1) contracting a recruitment agency directly in the Philippines, (2) hiring a consultant or recruiter in Canada who will partner with a recruitment agency in the Philippines, (3) or hiring a recruitment agency in Canada that has offices in both Canada and the Philippines to act as an intermediary. Employers or corporations must partner with a local agency for recruitment purposes. This institutional requirement by the Philippine Overseas Employment Administration (POEA) is intended to protect Filipina/os from unscrupulous agents since the POEA, under the direction of the Department of Labor and Employment (DOLE), regulates the workings of recruitment agencies.

In Alberta, the Consumer Protection Act and its Employment Agency Business Licensing Regulation oversee national and international employment agencies, which must be licensed. In British Columbia, starting in 2019, Employment Standards (under the Ministry of Labour) regulates recruitment under the Temporary Foreign Worker Protection Act (TFWPA). The TFWPA oversees the licensing of recruiters and the registering of employers (Dixon-Perera, 2020, p. 26).[1] Together, provincial and federal regulatory bodies try to promote fair recruitment practices, including no recruitment fees, freedom from deception and coercion, and grievance processes.

When employers (or corporations) hire an agency in Canada with ties to the Philippines, the agency must undergo a "rigorous prequalification certification from the Philippine Overseas Labor Office [or Filipino consulate office] before they can officially partner with the Philippine based agencies" (Guevarra, 2010, p. 67). This POEA requirement (administered through the Department of Foreign Affairs, the institutional body that oversees consulate offices) is meant to provide the Filipino state with an opportunity to vet the foreign agency and its workings, presumably to ensure the well-being of Filipina/o migrants' during recruitment.

When employers, corporations, or their third-party intermediaries (such as labour consultants and recruiters) look to hire a recruitment agency in the Philippines, they commonly solicit recommendations from the POEA. Tim Hortons is increasingly spearheading this portion of the process on behalf of its franchisees since, according to POEA agents, human resource personnel travel to the Philippines multiples times to meet and follow up with agencies referred to it by the POEA. Tim Hortons thus not only relies on transnational relations in the selection and recruitment of flows; Tim Hortons itself has become a transnational agent to support the recruitment process.

The POEA is highly focused on regulating the private sector when it comes to recruitment; it believes close oversight will advance the welfare of migrant hopefuls. To this end, the POEA conducts performance evaluations of recruitment agencies every four years, evaluating factors such as the volume of deployments, their record of violations, and migrant welfare. Successful agencies are bestowed one of three awards: a Top Performer Award, an Award of Excellence, or a Presidential Award. Through these vetting and award systems, employers are led to specific agencies.

Stage 4: Apply for Job/Select Workers

Jobs are increasingly advertised online, and workers either email or upload their applications through an agency's portal. While travelling directly to the agency is reportedly less common (though not unheard of), it still occurs, especially to other regions. If migrant hopefuls are shortlisted for a job, they must navigate the recruitment process. The process may include supplying additional information, attending individual or group interviews, and participating in video interviews with employers or corporate human resource personnel. Employers often weigh in on the recruitment process and usually have the final say over desired candidates.

Stage 5: Apply for Canadian Work Permit

Once selected, the candidate must apply for a work permit. The employer provides the migrant (or the intermediary) a copy of the LMIA to submit with an application to IRCC via the Canadian embassy office in Manila. Most of the people I spoke with said recruitment agencies completed and submitted the paperwork to the embassy on their behalf. Embassy staff then assess the suitability of the applicant. The assessment might include a criminal record check, an evaluation of past work experience in the occupation, and an assessment of things such as adequate language skills, human capital, and recent ties to the Philippines (the latter to ensure that workers do not go "TNT," the label applied to Filipina/os who overstay their visas or work permits in foreign countries and become undocumented residents).

Stage 6: Documents Verified

Migrant hopefuls must also successfully meet the requirements of the Filipino migration apparatus, including documentation. The Filipino state will screen the following: (1) the applicant's "good character," with police clearances from the National Bureau of Investigation, (2) their identity, verified through the issuance of a passport from the Filipino Department of Foreign Affairs, (3) and their health, which is assessed through a medical examination. In the case of Canada, the immigration medical exam is performed in Manila by a "panel physician," a doctor approved by IRCC as part of a network to perform medical screening of prospective migrants to Canada. Documentation also includes attending a Pre-Departure Orientation Seminar (PDOS), run by the Overseas Workers Welfare Administration (OWWA),[2] the Commission on Filipinos Overseas (CFO), NGOs, and private agencies approved by the POEA. Documents are evaluated for their conformity to the host's requirements; if they are incorrect or incomplete, migrants are instructed on how to meet the requirements (Rodriguez, 2010, p. 39). The verification of documentation also involves the overseas foreign worker (OFW) registering with the POEA to receive an Overseas Employment Certificate (OEC), which certifies that the worker is a legal migrant, that their documents are in order, that they have attended a

Pre-departure Orientation Seminar, that they are registered with the POEA, and that they are thus cleared for deployment.

Stage 7: Obtain Canadian Work Permit

When Filipina/o migrants arrive in Canada, they have not yet received their work permit. The Canada Border Services Agency (CBSA) is responsible for ensuring the migrant still meets the four genuineness factors before issuing them the permit at the port of entry (the airport). Indeed, CBSA agents, operating as border enforcers, have the final authority to deny entry, even if a work permit has been obtained (see Zell, 2018).

Stage 8: Work and Life in Canada

Assuming everything has gone smoothly, the migrant officially earns the title of temporary foreign worker (TFW). They must now navigate life and employment in Canada. Franchise owners or their designated recruiters often meet workers at the airport to start the (temporary) settlement process, including administrative and practical steps. On the administrative side, there is a waiting period between arrival and permission to access publicly funded medical care in the provinces and territories. Employers are thus required to secure and pay for private health insurance to cover emergency medical care during this holding period. For low-waged workers, employers are also required to ensure adequate, affordable housing.

Failures or abuses often occur at this stage. Sometimes employers will purchase homes and rent them out to their foreign staff at exorbitant rates or fail to do their due diligence, as described in chapter 2. Because workers can't navigate the rental market on their own, they are at the mercy of their employers' judgment or goodwill.[3] Since housing is a monthly and permanent expense, not finding adequate, affordable housing has real consequences.

Before the worker's first day, an employer must provide them with a signed copy of their employment agreement, presumably to ensure consistency between the original offer and real wages and working conditions. Once migrants sign this agreement and start their job, their working conditions are governed by employment standards. As shown earlier, abuses are common and facilitated by immigration controls that render migrants vulnerable because of their precarious legal status. In these cases, TMWs will often solicit support from relevant institutions (e.g., NGOs, migrant support centres, churches, unions, volunteer-run agencies, or publicly funded support systems). These agencies can operate as a lifeline, offering knowledge about rights or practical support, though workers often refrain from resisting too much out of fear of reprisal or repatriation.

In some cases, workers seek the advice of immigration consultants or lawyers to learn their immigration options, governed under the Immigration and Refugee Protection Act. However, profit-driven actors can charge substantial fees for their services and often exploit workers' hopes and vulnerabilities (e.g., Larios et al., 2020). Workers may sometimes seek institutional support through their country's consular or Philippine Overseas Labor Office. However, consular agents are often interested in protecting their nation's market prospects and will often pressure migrants to acquiesce to their employers. Thus, while TFWs in theory enjoy the same labour and employment rights as Canadians, many regulatory shortcomings make them vulnerable in practice.

Stage 9: Canadian Dream via Permanent Residency Status

Permanent residency is the driving force propelling Filipino migration to Canada. At this stage, if a relevant Provincial Nominee Program (PNP) is available and a worker has succeeded in satisfying minimum requirements, they may pursue permanent residency status. A host of intermediaries are involved in vetting candidates, and IRCC has the final say. Although employers do not initiate the nomination process under current Alberta and British Columbia PNPs (as was the case during the time of my study and under the Foodservices Industry Pilot Project and its Additional Allocations, described in chapter 5), they are required to support them. Workers are completely dependent on their employers for a chance to access belonging in Canada.

Alberta and British Columbia operate PNPs for hospitality occupations. In British Columbia, the program is administered by the province's Immigration Programs Branch. Food-counter attendants pursue formal belonging through the Entry Level and Semi-Skilled (ELSS) Stream (2023). Under the ELSS, workers must meet a set of criteria that includes the following: nine consecutive months of work with the same employer; a Canadian Language Benchmark (CLB) Level 4 in listening, speaking, reading, and writing;[4] a valid work permit; a high school diploma; and a minimum family income to support the number of dependants listed in the application.[5] Employers must support the candidate's nomination and provide a full-time, signed job offer, a recommendation letter, a detailed job description, company information, a copy of the certificate of incorporation, and a copy of the municipal business licence.

The employer must also have a minimum number of years in operation, a minimum number of employees in British Columbia (region dependent), and be in good standing concerning the laws and regulations governing temporary migrant workers. They must also provide evidence, and sign an affidavit, demonstrating their effort to recruit from the domestic labour market. A candidate's application may be refused if the employer is discovered to be in violation. If both the worker and employer meet program requirements, and the employer agrees to support the nomination, the worker can apply. The application is then assessed by the province along a series of qualifiers.[6] If the applicant is assessed favourably by the PNP, the applicant can then apply to IRCC for a chance to become a permanent resident (Government of British Columbia, 2025).

The Alberta Immigration Nominee Program (AINP) is administered by the Ministry of Immigration and Multiculturalism. It consists of four streams, from which food-counter attendants can be newly nominated under the Tourism and Hospitality Stream (since March 1, 2024), previously nominated under the Alberta Opportunity Stream. As in British Columbia, a host of criteria are required for nomination: a high school diploma; a valid work permit; a Canadian Language Benchmark (CLB) Level 5 in reading, writing, speaking, and listening; relevant minimum work experience; and a job in an eligible occupation in the province. Employers in Alberta must also support a candidate's nomination, produce a signed job offer for continuous full-time employment, be registered or incorporated, provide evidence of their effort to recruit workers locally, and be in good standing with regard to the laws and regulations governing temporary migrant workers. If the nomination is successful, the applicant has six months to apply for permanent residency to IRCC, which also assesses whether they meet its minimal requirements for educational attainment, income, and language skill.

If the employer refuses to support the nomination, migrants can renew the work permit (assuming the employer is willing) or search for another contract, which involves attaining a new LMIA. In the latter case, the worker is again at the mercy of an employer and ESDC. At this stage, they often rely on their networks for information about prospective employers and occupations and regions more likely to lead to permanent residency status. Once the work permit has expired, workers will either receive their permanent residency from IRCC or work under the International Mobility Program as they wait for their papers to be processed (and hopefully approved).

If permanent residency is not forthcoming or the migrant has not secured their employer's support for a nomination or another LMIA, they will either return to the Philippines (be repatriated) or go TNT ("underground"). Those who return home can either attempt to reintegrate fully or reintegrate with the goal of looking for another contract. If the latter, they will re-enter this migration circuit, arguably better positioned than before since they have secured relevant Canadian work experience and social networks.

The market-driven nature of the Low-Skilled Stream and employer-dependent incorporation programs continue to characterize governance dynamics in the sector. In April 2023, Alberta announced plans for a new tourism and hospitality immigration stream under the Alberta Immigration Nominee Program. It promised a faster and more dedicated sector-specific program for tourism and hospitality. According to the announcement, Alberta was working out the design and implementation, expected to align with existing priority areas (including food-counter attendants). The Tourism and Hospitality Stream came into effect on March 1, 2024, as noted above. This new program demonstrates the tourism and hospitality sector's ongoing success in advancing its interests through market-driven policies and the relevance of PNPs in driving Filipino migration flows to Canada.

Notes

1. The Institutions and Governance of Labour Migration

1　All persons in this study, including the migrant workers and applicants I interviewed, were assigned a pseudonym to protect their identity.

2　This is not to suggest that values and affects circulating within a society are fixed and invariable; in fact, in chapter 2, I describe how shifts in dominant ideas about immigration to Canada have been informed by changes in dominant values and objectives. Fassin is also not suggesting that states promote a coherent project or master plan (in fact, different institutions may defend different ideas and interests within a given state), though there is often a longevity and broad moral cohesion to these practices. Instead, the moral frameworks (the values and emotions) that guide policies and actions (the moral universe of institutions) alongside the genealogies by which these rationalities have shifted over time offer insights for comprehending the moral dimensions of a given state. They also provide insight into the broader society, given that societies are produced and reproduced through the workings of institutions (Fassin, 2015, p. 7).

3　Flor Contemplacion was a Filipina domestic worker executed in Singapore in 1995 for the alleged murder of another Filipina domestic worker (Delia Mamaril Maga) and the boy in Maga's charge (Nicholas Huang). The incident sparked outrage throughout the Philippines regarding the treatment of migrants and the state's failure to accord them protections and rights while overseas. Activists, journalists, and the citizenry demanded amendments to state policies that eventually resulted in "profound changes within the governance of migration" and "a new kind of extraterritorial and cultural citizenship" (in McKay, 2012, p. 60). The new governance regime that unfolded following Contemplacion's execution is covered in more detail in chapters 3 and 4.

4 A prime example of social memory assets are Tim Hortons' wildly popular "True Stories" advertisements. These ads are generated by customers and store owners and feature unpretentious, down-to-earth customers. The ads often unfold in small Canadian towns, sometimes in the past, among subjects who embody celebrated Canadian values (like endurance and ruggedness) and overcome clichéd and relatable hardships (like inter-family conflicts between first- and second-generation immigrants). These advertisements inevitably end with the comfort of rituals like drinking Tim Hortons coffee. Tim Hortons thus appropriates quotidian moments of Canadian enjoyment and casts them as mundane acts that signal that Tim Hortons is an "organic, and natural social site to articulate versions of Canadianness" (Cormack, 2008, p. 382). It does this so successfully that Tim Hortons has transformed itself "into something approaching a national institution" and "an essential part of a project of nation-building" (Foster et al., 2011, p. 113).

5 In 2004, for instance, Foreign Affairs Minister Peter MacKay took U.S. Secretary of State Condoleezza Rice to a Tim Hortons restaurant for a cup of coffee, inviting her to an "authentic" Canadian experience. Similarly, in 2009, then Prime Minister Stephen Harper regularly used Tim Hortons restaurants as the site for public announcements, expropriating the cultural value that the brand invokes. As Delacourt (2013) explains, "in the space of a couple of minutes … Harper managed to link this doughnut store [as well as himself] to many great things about Canada: hockey, family and even Pierre Berton, chronicler of Canada's nation-building efforts." In 2004, the Canadian military also selected Tim Hortons as the sole distributor of the Royal Canadian Mint's Remembrance Day poppy coin.

6 Many historically colonized groups experience the colonial mentality, including (but not limited to) African American and Latino populations (see: Jackson & Cothran, 2003; Miranda, 2011; Padilla, 1999; Traore, 2004).

7 Following a series of reviews and amendments to Canada's caregiver streams, the current program operates as two pilot projects: the Home Childcare Provider and the Home Support Worker. These streams and their features are explored in chapter 2.

8 "Food counter attendant" is the official title given to entry-level fast-food workers in Canada.

9 Rather than one field site for a longer period, which is more common in ethnographic case studies.

10 Migrant communities are regions where a considerable proportion of the working-age population has left in pursuit of (global) work.

2. Tim Hortons and the Low-Skilled Stream

1 Agricultural workers have been streamed through the Seasonal Agricultural Workers Program (SAWP) since 1966; domestic caregivers through employment visas and other labour programs such as the Caribbean Domestics Scheme (1955), the Live-in Caregiver Program (1992), the Caregiver Program (2014), and more recently the Home Child Care Provider Pilot and Home Support Worker Pilot (2019) programs.

2 TEER stands for training, education, experience, and responsibilities.

3 Citizenship is not confined within national borders, as scholars of transnational and post-national citizenship assert (e.g., Bauböck, 1994; Soysal, 1994). Indeed, in an age of porous borders and increased flows, the citizenship of transmigrants (like Filipina/o migrant workers) offers an important line of inquiry for considering what rights, membership, and belonging mean and look like across borders in an age of hyper-globalization.

4 Labels such as "foreign worker," or more generally, "noncitizen," position people vis-à-vis the nation-state and determine their corresponding access to social, political, and legal rights. This bleeds into their position within global capitalism and experiences at work, given that "the accumulation of capital continues to take place through the social and legal differentiation of labour" (Sharma, 2006, p. 29).

5 While the points system is not explicitly racist, critical scholars have documented its gendered and racialized qualities and outcomes (Ng, 1992; Thobani, 2000; Sharma, 2002).

6 The standard employment relationship implies "the worker has one employer, works full-time, year-round on the employer's premises, enjoys extensive statutory benefits and entitlements, and expects to be employed indefinitely" (Cranford et al., 2003, p. 7).

7 The case of the McDonald's franchise owner sidelining Canadians in favour of migrant workers, which led to the moratorium, suggests that, in practice, LMIAs may not be as successful as intended in meeting this objective.

8 In the case of the Philippines, employers or their designated third-party representatives are required to partner with a recruiter on the ground in the Philippines. An exception is made in the case of direct hires, though this practice appears to be less common.

3. Beguiling and Brokering the "Great Filipino Worker"

1 The POEA works under the Department of Labor and Employment, whose mandate is to promote opportunities and formulate policies and programs

related to labour and employment, including global work. ILAB provides policy and program recommendations to DOLE regarding global labour market opportunities and strategies for protecting Filipina/o nationals while abroad.

2　There are also many tensions that underlie relations between the recruitment sector and the Philippine migration apparatus. These are taken up in detail in chapter 7.

3　These marketing materials are often (though not solely) produced by DOLE and secondarily by the POEA. Recruiters produce their own material for their marketing missions, and other migration institutions also produce relevant material.

4　Through documentation and TESDA training courses, the Philippines generates significant revenues from the mandatory processing of migrant worker documents.

5　Interestingly, the skill level of workers and occupations in the Philippines is partly determined by the status of the host country. Canada is not seen as a country that receives "low-skilled" workers, even for occupations like fast food. This theme is explored in further detail in chapter 4.

6　This marks the neoliberal offloading of funding services onto citizens previously under the purview of the state.

7　LMIAs are not required for TMWs recruited under Canada's International Mobility Program (IMP), an important exception noted in chapter 2 and taken up in detail in chapter 5.

8　Nationality was not specified for 8 per cent of workers granted positive LMIAs.

9　Note that this figure refers to the actual number of food-counter attendant visas, meaning that the LMIA came back either positive or neutral, *and* that IRCC approved the worker visa.

10　In the data provided by ESDC, the gender of the worker was unspecified for some years but not most. In this minority of cases, the percentages were calculated by omitting the unspecified gender designations from the total for that year. This practice was deemed appropriate since "gender unspecified" accounted for a minority of cases.

4. Migrant Dreams and the Colonial Mentality

1　Nititham (2011, p. 185) views this tendency as the product of being "doubly" inscribed inferior by the Spanish and US colonial powers and a resultant colonial mentality that generates a longing for "greener pastures" through labour migration; what she argues becomes a strategy for accruing cultural capital.

2　See David (2013) and his colonial mentality scale.

3 A notable exception was among those with family members in Canada,
for whom Canada was an equally (if not sometimes a more) desirable
destination.

4 This is consistent with Bulloch's (2017) research, wherein she argues that
"*Amerika* is a fairly loose concept synonymous with what we might call the
'West'" (224).

5 PEOS are now mandatory workshops delivered asynchronously, organized
around eight modules delivered through slide presentations and video
recordings.

6 Themes include health and security risks, wages, impacts on relationships,
warnings about illegal recruitment, and the migrants' "responsibility" to
their nation and families while abroad.

7 While scholarship has also documented the role of social remittances in
shaping transnational social fields through a "migrant-driven form of
cultural diffusion" (Levitt, 1998, p. 926), in this chapter I am concerned
primarily with how consumables shape desires and propel migration.

5. Harnessing Dreams to Manufacture Consent

1 Indeed, Ray Kroc, the man responsible for building McDonald's into
an empire, often boasted of "putting the hamburger on the assembly
line" (Penfold, 2008, p. 113). Other strategies included applying time-
and-motion studies to simplify tasks, which renders them repetitive
and deskilled, and technological innovations to monitor and speed
up work.

2 In Leidner's (1993) research on McDonald's restaurants in Chicago, she
found staff turnover levels of over 200 per cent in 1985. Schlosser suggests
that annual turnover in American fast food is 300 per cent to 400 per cent
(Schlosser, 2002, pp. 51, 73).

3 Store owners and corporations will sponsor events such as picnics,
holiday parties, and baseball games to foster loyalty, team spirit, and
competitiveness (Leidner, 1993; Schlosser, 2002). They also introduce
intra- and inter-store competitions (for top sales or delivery times) to
increase productivity. Rewards range from free meals, cash, and coupons
to company-sponsored outings and "the pride of being the best" (Tannock,
2001, p. 52).

4 A *double-double* is the term used in Tim Hortons to describe a coffee with
two creams and two sugars.

5 When workers are recruited transnationally, employers can be significantly
choosier and require qualifications that they could never require
domestically because of low wages and lack of available workers (see
Preibisch, 2010). The increased specialization associated with global

recruitment, moreover, is an important feature of managed migration programs.

6 The practice fluctuates. Alberta removed food-counter attendants from its PNP list in 2018. During the same period in British Columbia, food-counter attendants could only be nominated under the Entry Level and Semi-Skilled PNP in the province's Northeast Development Region. By 2023, however, food-counter attendants were back on the list. Other provinces (such as Saskatchewan) have continuously included them. The list of covered occupations is constantly evolving. In 2023, Alberta announced a new PNP specifically designed for the hospitality sector, which came into effect in 2024.

7 In 2019, the Canadian government proposed amending the TFWP to allow occupation-specific (rather than employer-specific) permits to offset the vulnerabilities associated with tied work contracts. Specifically, "foreign workers in the low-wage and primary agriculture streams would be allowed to move between jobs, as long as it is in the same occupation classification" (Pinto, 2019). Employers and industry associations have organized against this amendment. Nevertheless, the norm in Canada is employer-specific contracts, which has implications for manager-worker relations in the organization of labour consent.

8 As previously mentioned in chapter 2, the IMP is a labour program that allows an employer to hire a TMW without a Labour Market Impact Assessment (LMIA), which is required under the LSS. This includes (but is not limited to) TMWs waiting decisions on permanent residency applications, postgraduate work permits, spouses/common-law partners of skilled workers, and those in Canada on humanitarian grounds (e.g., refugees). The IMP also covers exchange programs like International Experience Canada that permit youth from specified countries to live and work in Canada for a maximum of two years (otherwise colloquially known as "working holidays"). Contract workers labouring under the IMP are technically TMWs, although this stream covers subjects distinct from those I have explored in this monograph.

9 Recognizing that, in the words of an official with Immigration, Refugees and Citizenship Canada, "Custom transition data based on prior temporary residency is unavailable" (personal correspondence, 22 November 2019), the data presented here is the best possible documentation of fast-food transitions from temporary to permanent status. With that said, it is important to note that IMP visa holders constituted a relative minority of fast-food TMWs in Western Canada: 3 per cent and 16 per cent of all fast-food TMWs in Alberta and British Columbia, respectively.

10 Future research on fast-food visa workers labouring under the IMP would add depth to my theorization, including insight into how the distinct

subsets (and social locations) of IMP workers translates into prospects
for incorporation. My speculation that they were initially LSS workers
awaiting a decision on permanent residency under a PNP aligns with the
work of Goldring and Landolt (2012), who theorize migrant incorporation
as a long-term, multilevel complex process – the "chutes and ladders" of
incorporation. Goldring and Landolt note that formal incorporation (if it
ever happens) can take a long time under Canada's current immigration
system, which involves migrants shifting from different status
categories (and sometimes into "illegality") in their path toward formal
incorporation. This indeterminacy is the product of policy changes that
have resulted in a more precarious immigration program. That contract
workers under the LSS can find themselves working under an IMP or
under another occupation under the LSS (Maria, for instance, worked
initially as a food-counter attendant and later in a hotel) is an example of
this complex process. I take up this theme again in the conclusion of
this book.

11 Not all workers manage to obtain permanent residency through the LCP.
See, for example, Oxman-Martinez et al. (2004). However, while some are
denied on questionable grounds, there is nevertheless an institutionalized
pathway. Workers may also initiate the process after meeting a set of
criteria.

6. The Institutional Resilience of National Dreams

1 This cumulative-duration policy (colloquially known as the four-in, four-
out rule) was introduced in April 2011.

2 The different stages of the migration process included those seeking
employment at Tim Hortons, those who had secured a contract but were
waiting to be deployed, those who were working at a Tim Hortons, and
those who had returned post-contract.

3 Bryan and Barber (2021, p. 81) cite upgrading, seeking out specific
Canadian provinces more favourable to their desired outcomes ("ideal
immigrant slots"), and cultural prescriptions about faith and the value of
hard work as partial rationales for continued faith in their prospects for
permanent residency. They also attribute this faith to "ideational factors
inspired by cultural prescriptions about faith and the value of hard work."

4 Balikbayan boxes are care packages sent home, either by freight or air, by
Filipina/o migrants in the form of boxes. They contain items the sender
believes the recipients may like, such as clothes, toys, electronic items,
toiletries, and nonperishable food products.

5 Interestingly, Bryan and Barber (2021) reported that Bryan's ten Tim
Hortons migrant participants in Manitoba all secured permanent residency

status. This speaks to the unevenness of Provincial Nominee Programs (PNP) across Canada, and that Manitoba-based employers and the province have leveraged the PNP as a de facto immigration program, which is uncommon when compared with other regions in Canada.

6 This data is distinct from the IRCC data (2020) cited in chapter 5, which tracks the number of food-counter attendants that transitioned from temporary to permanent status from 2002 to 2019. The data documents the number of applications provincial governments received and approved under PNP streams. These approved nominated applicants are then forwarded to IRCC for final selection.

7 Neil later learned that his employer's wife became terminally ill shortly following his return to the Philippines. While this explains his apparent betrayal, it also demonstrates the precarity and dependency migrants endure under the LSS/PNP.

7. A Global Infrastructure of Migrant Dreams

1 This includes, but is not limited to, documentation (see appendix 1, stage 6).

2 The Overseas Employment Certificate promises this and fosters the impression that the workers in question have received ample training, support, and preparation.

Appendix: The Infrastructure of Migration Map

1 Employers, family members, educational institutions, and governments are exempt from this licensing requirement.

2 OWWA became an attached agency of the Department of Migrant Workers founded in 2022, tasked with promoting the rights and welfare of overseas Filipino workers and their families.

3 It is very challenging to find housing without a credit report, Canadian employment history, or housing references.

4 The evaluation must be conducted via an Accepted Language Proficiency Test (like CELPIP General).

5 The amount is based on annual wages in British Columbia, the area of residence in British Columbia, and (if applicable) a spouse or common-law partner's regular gross annual wage in British Columbia.

6 Other qualifiers include human capital, hourly wage, years of relevant work experience, and region, for a total of 200 possible points.

References

Alberta, Employment, Immigration & Industry. (2007). *A Workforce Strategy for Alberta's Tourism and Hospitality Industry*. Government of Alberta.

Alsharif, G. (2023a, June 2). Yoga giant Lululemon wins exemption to immigration rules that limit hiring foreign workers. *Toronto Star*.

Alsharif, G. (2023b, July 19). Canada's Temporary Foreign Worker program is ballooning to fill the labour gap, but workers say they're abused and poorly paid. Is that the solution we want? *Toronto Star*.

Alsharif, G. (2024a, August 28). Ottawa to cut number of temporary foreign workers, could limit permanent resident admissions. *Toronto Star*.

Alsharif, G. (2024b, August 10). "A new kind of slavery": Skyrocketing use of temporary foreign workers in restaurants and fast-food chains has advocates concerned. *Toronto Star*.

Anderson, B. (2010). Migration, immigration controls and the fashioning of precarious workers. *Work, Employment & Society, 24*, 300–17. https://doi.org/10.1177/0950017010362141

Anderson, B., Gibney, M., & Paoletti, E. (2011). Citizenship, deportation and the boundaries of belonging. *Citizenship Studies, 15*(5), 547–63. https://doi.org/10.1080/13621025.2011.583787

Appadurai, A. (1996). *Modernity at large: Cultural dimensions of globalization*. University of Minnesota Press.

Bal, E. (2014). Yearning for faraway places: The construction of migration desires among young and educated Bangladeshis in Dhaka. *Identities: Global Studies in Culture and Power, 21*(3), 275–89. https://doi.org/10.1080/1070289X.2013.833512

Bandelj, N. (2020). "Relational Work in the Economy." *Annual Review of Sociology, 46*, 251–72. https://doi.org/10.1146/annurev-soc-121919-054719

Barber, P. (2008a). The ideal immigrant? Gendered class subjects in Philippine-Canada migration. *Third World Quarterly, 29*(7), 1265–85. https://doi.org/10.1080/01436590802386385

Barber, P. (2008b). Cell phones, complicity, and class politics in the Philippine labor diaspora. *Focaal – European Journal of Anthropology, 51*, 28–42. https://doi.org/10.3167/fcl.2008.510104

Barber, P. (2013). "Grateful" subjects: Class and capital at the border in Philippine-Canada migration. *Dialectical Anthropology, 37*, 383–400. https://doi.org/10.1007/s10624-013-9321-2

Basch, L., Glick Schiller, N., & Szanton Blanc, C. (1994). *Nations unbound: Transnational projects, postcolonial predicaments, and deterritorialized nation-states*. Gordon and Breach.

Bauböck, R. (1994). *Transnational citizenship: Membership and rights in international migration*. Edward Elgar Publishing.

BC Tourism HRD Task Force. (2003). *Recruit, retain and train: Developing a super, natural tourism workforce in British Columbia*. British Columbia Tourism Human Resources Development Task Force Action Plan.

BC Tourism Labour Market Strategy. (2012). *BC Tourism labour market strategy (2012–2016)*. (Funded in whole or in part by the Canada-British Columbia Labour Market Development Agreement). go2. https://www.go2hr.ca/resource/bc-tourism-labour-market-strategy-2012-2016.

Binford, L. (2009). From fields of power to fields of sweat: The dual process of constructing temporary migrant labour in Mexico and Canada. *Third World Quarterly, 30*(3), 503–17. https://doi.org/10.1080/01436590902742297

Bloemraad, I., Korteweg, A., & Yurdakul, G. (2008). Citizenship and immigration: Multiculturalism, assimilation, and challenges to the nation-state. *The Annual Review of Sociology, 34*, 153–79. https://doi.org/10.1146/annurev.soc.34.040507.134608

Bonifacio, G. (2014). *Pinay on the prairies: Filipino women and transnational identities*. UBC Press. https://doi.org/10.59962/9780774825818

Borjas, G. (1990). *Friends of strangers: The impacts of immigrants on the U.S. economy*. Basic Books.

Bosniak, L. (2006). *The citizen and the alien: Dilemmas of contemporary membership*. Princeton University Press. https://doi.org/10.1515/9781400827510

Boyd, M., & Vickers, M. (2000). *100 years of immigration in Canada*. Statistics Canada – Canadian Social Trends, Catalogue No. 11–008: 1 – 13.

Bryan, C., & Barber, P.G. (2021). Parsing the mobilities of capital and labour: The case of Tim Hortons and internationally mobile Filipino workers. *International Migration, 59*(2), 72–86. https://doi.org/10.1111/imig.12826

Buist, R. (2003). *Tales from under the rim: The marketing of Tim Hortons*. Goose Lane.

Bulloch, H. (2013). Concerning constructions of self and other: Auto-racism and imagining *Amerika* in the Christian Philippines. *Anthropological Forum, 23*(3), 221–41. https://doi.org/10.1080/00664677.2013.804400

Bulloch, H. (2017). *In pursuit of progress: Narratives of development on a Philippine Island*. Honolulu University of Hawaii Press. https://doi.org/10.21313 /hawaii/9780824858865.001.0001

Burawoy, M. (1979). *Manufacturing consent: Changes in the labor process under monopoly capitalism*. University of Chicago Press.

Burawoy, M. (2000). *Global ethnography: Forces, connections, and imaginations in a post-modern world*. University of California Press. https://doi.org/10.1525 /9780520924390

Burawoy, M. (2001). Manufacturing the global. *Ethnography*, 2(2), 147–59. https://doi.org/10.1177/1466138101002002001

Canadian Council for Refugees. (2000). *A hundred years of immigration to Canada 1900–1999*. Canadian Council for Refugees. https://ccrweb.ca/en /hundred-years-immigration-canada-1900-1999

Carman, T. (2012). Former Tim Hortons employees from Mexico accuse Dawson Creek franchise owner of abuse. *Vancouver Sun*.

Choy, C. (2003). *Empire of care: Nursing and migration in Filipino American history*. Duke University Press. https://doi.org/10.1215/9780822384410

Clark, W. (2003). *Immigrants and the American dream: Remaking the middle class*. The Guilford Press.

Collins, F. (2018a). Desire as a theory for migration studies: Temporality, assemblage and becoming in the narratives of migrants. *Journal of Ethnic and Migration Studies*, 44(6), 964–80. https://doi.org/10.1080/1369183X.2017.1384147

Collins, F. (2018b). *Global Asian city: Migration, desire, and the politics of encounter in the 21st century Seoul*. Wiley. https://doi.org/10.1002/9781119380030

Constable, N. (2007). *Maid to order in Hong Kong: Stories of migrant workers* (2nd ed.). Cornell University Press.

Constani, P., & Gibbs, P. (2005). Emotional labour and surplus value: The case of holiday 'Reps'. *Service Industries Journal*, 25(1), 103–16. https://doi.org /10.1080/0264206042000302432

Cormack, P. (2012). Double-double: Branding, Tim Hortons, and the public sphere. In A. Marland, T. Giasson, & J. Lees-Marshment (Eds.), *Political marketing in Canada* (pp. 209–23). University of British Columbia Press. https://doi.org/10.59962/9780774822305-016

Cormack, P., & Cosgrave, J. (2013). *Desiring Canada: CBC contests, hockey violence and other stately pleasures*. University of Toronto Press. https://doi .org/10.3138/9781442663299

Cranford, C., Vosko, L., & Zukewich, N. (2003). Precarious employment in the Canadian Labour market: A statistical portrait. *Just Labour*, 3, 6–22. https:// doi.org/10.25071/1705-1436.164

Czaika, M., Bijak, J., & Prike, T. (2021). Migration decision-making and its key dimensions. *The ANNALS of the American Academy of Political and Social Science*, 697(1), 15–31. https://doi.org/10.1177/00027162211052233

David, E.J.R. (2013). *Brown skin, white minds: Filipino-/American postcolonial psychology* (1st ed.). Emerald Publishing.

David, E.J.R., & Nadal, K.L. (2013). The colonial context of Filipino American immigrants' psychological experiences. *Cultural Diversity and Ethnic Minority Psychology, 19*(3), 298–309. https://doi.org/10.1037/a0032903

Dixon-Perera, L. (2020). *Regulatory approaches to international labour recruitment in Canada*. Immigration, Refugees and Citizenship Canada.

DOLE (Department of Labor and Employment, Republic of Philippines). (2009). *World's no. 1*. [CD-ROM]. DOLE Marketing AVP, Version 28 April 2009. Wall City Media.

Employment and Social Development Canada (2022, April 4). Government of Canada Announces Workforce Solutions Road Map – Further Changes to the Temporary Foreign Worker Program to Address Labour Shortages across Canada. Gatineau, Quebec. https://www.canada.ca/en/employment -social-development/news/2022/04/government-of-canada-announces -workforce-solutions-road-map--further-changes-to-the-temporary -foreign-worker-program-to-address-labour-shortages-ac.html

ESDC (Employment and Social Development Canada). (2014). *Special data request* (i.e., Freedom of Information Request). Positive LMIA Requests for NOC 6711 – Food Counter Attendants, Kitchen Helpers and Related Support Occupations (NOC 4 2011) for franchise restaurants (Tim Hortons, McDonald's, and Subway), by province/territory of destination, country of citizenship, gender and year, from 2004–2014.

ESDC (Employment and Social Development Canada). (2022, April 4). *Government of Canada announces Workforce Solutions Road Map – further changes to the Temporary Foreign Worker Program to address labour shortages across Canada.*

Espiritu, Y.L. (1996). Colonial oppression, labour importation, and group formation: Filipinos in the United States. *Ethnic and Racial Studies, 19*(1), 29–48. https://doi.org/10.1080/01419870.1996.9993897

Espiritu, Y.L. (2003). *Home bound: Filipino American lives across cultures, communities and countries*. University of California Press. https://doi.org /10.1525/9780520929265

Faier, L. (2009). *Intimate encounters: Filipina women and the remaking of rural Japan*. University of California Press. https://doi.org/10.1525/9780520944596

Faier, L. (2013). Affective investments in the Manila region: Filipina migrants in rural Japan and transnational urban development in the Philippines. *Transaction of the Institute of British Geographers, 38*, 376–90. https://doi.org /10.1111/j.1475-5661.2012.00533.x

Faraday, F. (2012). *Made in Canada: How the Law Constructs Migrant Workers' Insecurity*. Metcalf Policy Paper. Metcalf Foundation. https:// metcalffoundation.com/publication/made-in-canada-how-the-law -constructs-migrant-workers-insecurity/

Faraday, F. (2014). "Profiting from the Precarious: How Recruitment Practices Exploit Migrant Workers." Summary Report, Toronto Metcalf Foundation, April 2014.

Fassin, D. (2005). Compassion and repression: The moral economy of immigration policies in France. *Cultural Anthropology, 20*(3), 362–87. https://doi.org/10.1525/can.2005.20.3.362

Fassin, D. (2015). Can states be moral? Preface to the English edition. In *At the Heart of the State: The Moral world of Institutions*. Pluto Press.

Findlay, A., McCollum, D., Shubin, S., Apsite, E., & Krisjane, Z. (2013). The role of recruitment agencies in imagining and producing the "good" migrant. *Social & Cultural Geography, 14*(2), 145–67. https://doi.org/10.1080/14649365.2012.737008

Fintech News Philippines. (2025). "OFW Remittances in the Philippines Hit Record USD$38.34 Billion." https://fintechnews.ph/65862/remittance/philippines-ofw-remittances-hit-record-usd-38-34-billion/

Ford, R. (1994). The McDonaldization of society: An investigation into the changing character of contemporary social life. *Clinical Sociology Review, 12*(1), Article 25. http://digitalcommons.wayne.edu/csr/vol12/iss1/25.

Foster, W.M., Suddaby, R., Minkus, A., & Wiebe, E. (2011). History as social memory assets: The example of Tim Hortons. *Management & Organizational History, 6*(1), 101–120. https://doi.org/10.1177/1744935910387027

Francis, D. (1997). *National dreams: Myth, memory, and Canadian history.* Arsenal Pulp Press.

Fudge, J. (2005). After industrial citizenship: Market citizenship or citizenship at work? *Relations Industrielles/Industrial Relations, 60*(4), 631–56. https://doi.org/10.7202/012338ar

Gille, Z., & Ó'Riain, S. (2002). Global ethnography. *Annual Review of Sociology, 28,* 271–95. https://doi.org/10.1146/annurev.soc.28.110601.140945

Goldring, L., & Landolt, P. (2012, October). *The impact of precarious legal status on immigrants' economic outcomes.* IRPP Study No. 35. IRPP.

Goldring, L., & Landolt, P. (Eds.). (2013). *Producing and negotiating non-citizenship: Precarious legal status in Canada.* University of Toronto Press. https://doi.org/10.3138/9781442663862

Gonzalez, J. (1998). *Philippine labour migration: Critical dimensions of public policy.* Institute of Southeast Asian Studies.

Goodman, L.-A. (2014). CFIB wants temporary foreign worker program replaced by special visa. *CBC News – The Canadian Press.*

Government of Alberta Department of Labour and Immigration. (2019). Special Data Request (Freedom of Information): Canada, Admissions of Permanent Residents under NOC 6711 – Food Counter Attendants, Kitchen Helpers and Related Support Occupations by Prior Work Permit Classification, 2002–2019.

Government of British Columbia. (2025). "British Columbia Provincial Nominee Program: Skills Immigration Program Guide." https://www.welcomebc.ca/immigrate-to-b-c/bc-pnp-si-program-guide_jan-7-2025-pdf

Grant, T. (2006). *Discussion paper: Analysis of foreign worker program options to address labour shortages in the tourism industry: Applied to Kootenay region's housekeep labour shortage.* go2 – The Resource People for Tourism.

Green, A., & Green, D. (1995). Canadian immigration policy: The effectiveness of the point system and other instruments. *Canadian Journal of Economics, 28*(4b), 1006–41. https://doi.org/10.2307/136133

Guevarra, A.R. (2010). *Marketing dreams, manufacturing heroes: The transnational labor brokering of Filipino workers* (1st ed.). Rutgers University Press. https://doi.org/10.36019/9780813548296

Guevarra, A. (2014). Supermaids: The racial branding of global Filipino care labour. In B. Anderson & I. Shutes (Eds.), *Migration and care labour: Theory, policy and politics* (pp. 130–50). Palgrave Macmillan. https://doi.org/10.1057/9781137319708_8

Haas, H.D. (2008). *Migration and development: A theoretical perspective.* International Migration Institute (University of Oxford) Working Paper Series. No. 9, Oxford, UK.

Hagen-Zanker, J., Hennessey, G., & Mazzilli, C. (2023). Subjective and intangible factors in migration decision-making: A review of side-lined literature. *Migration Studies, 11*(2), 349–59. https://doi.org/10.1093/migration/mnad003

Hanser, A. (2008). *Service encounters: Class, gender and the market for social distinction.* Stanford University Press.

Healy, K. (2006). *Last best gifts: Altruism and the market for human blood and organs.* University of Chicago Press. https://doi.org/10.7208/chicago/9780226322384.001.0001

Hendry, J. (2003). An ethnographer in the global arena: Globography perhaps? *Global Networks, 3*(4), 497–512. https://doi.org/10.1111/1471-0374.00074

Hennebry, J. (2010, July–August). Who has their eye on the ball? "Jurisdictional Futbol" and Canada's temporary foreign worker program. *Options,* 62–7.

Hennebry, J., & Preibisch, K. (2012). A model for managed migration? Re-examining best practices in Canada's seasonal agricultural workers program. *International Migration, 50*(1), 19–40. https://doi.org/10.1111/j.1468-2435.2009.00598.x

Hochschild, A.R. (1979). Emotion work, feeling rules, and social structure. *American Journal of Sociology, 85*(3), 551–75. https://doi.org/10.1086/227049

Hochschild, J.L. (1995). *Facing up to the American dream: Race, class, and the soul of the nation.* Princeton University Press. https://doi.org/10.1515/9781400821730

HRPC – Human Resources Planning Committee. (2003). *Planning for gold – maximizing 2010-related employment & skills opportunities in British Columbia: Connecting labour market supply & demand?* Final Report for the 2010 Human Resources Planning Committee. Vancouver: Ministry of Labour, Province of British Columbia.

Hsiung, P.-C., & Nichol, K. (2010). Policies on and experiences of foreign domestic workers in Canada. *Sociology Compass, 4*(9), 766–78. https://doi.org/10.1111/j.1751-9020.2010.00320.x

Hussan, S. (2024, August 23). Canada's temporary foreign worker program leads to a new kind of slavery. *Toronto Star.*

IRCC (Immigration, Refugees and Citizenship Canada). (2015). *Facts and figures 2015 immigration overview: Permanent and temporary residents.* IRCC.

IRCC (Immigration, Refugees and Citizenship Canada). (2016). *Facts and figures 2016 immigration overview: Permanent and temporary residents.* IRCC.

IRCC (Immigration, Refugees and Citizenship Canada). (2017a). *Evaluation of the provincial nominee program* (Reference Number: E1–2015). Research and Evaluation Division, IRCC.

IRCC (Immigration, Refugees and Citizenship Canada). (2017b). *Facts and figures 2017 immigration overview: Permanent and temporary residents.* IRCC.

IRCC (Immigration, Refugees and Citizenship Canada). (2020). *Special data request: Canada.* Work Permit Holders under NOC 6711 – Food Counter Attendants, Kitchen Helpers and Related Support Occupations (NOC 4 2011) by work permit classification, province/territory of destination, country of citizenship, gender, and year in which permits became effective, 2002–2019.

Jackson, J., & Cothran, M. (2003). Black versus black: The relationship among African, African American and African Caribbean persons. *Journal of Black Studies, 33*(5), 576–604. https://doi.org/10.1177/0021934703033005003

Joppke, C. (2001). Multicultural citizenship: A critique. *European Journal of Sociology, 42*(2), 431–47. https://doi.org/10.1017/S0003975601001047

Kalleberg, A. (2009). Precarious work, insecure workers: Employment relations in transition. *American Sociological Review, 74*(1), 1–22. https://doi.org/10.1177/000312240907400101

Kent, S. (2010). Symbols of love: Consumption, transnational migration, and the family in San Salvador, El Salvador. *Urban Anthropology and Studies of Cultural Systems and the World Economic Development, 39*(1/2), 73–108.

Koikkalainen, S., & Kyle, D. (2016). Imagining mobility: The prospective cognition question in migration research. *Journal of Ethnic and Migration Studies, 42*(5), 1–18. https://doi.org/10.1080/1369183X.2015.1111133

Kymlicka, W. (2003). Canadian multiculturalism in historical and comparative perspective: Is Canada unique? *Constitutional Forum, 13*(1), 1–8. https://doi.org/10.21991/C9W37Q

Larios, L., Hanley, J., Salamanca Cardona, M., Henaway, M., Dwaikat Share, N., & Ben Soltane, S. (2020). Engaging migrant careworkers: Examining cases of exploitation by recruitment agencies in Quebec, Canada. *International Journal of Migration and Border Studies*, 6(1–2), pp. 138–57. https://doi.org/10.1504/IJMBS.2020.108690

Lea, J. (2013, September). From denizen to citizen and back: Governing the precariat through crime. *Centre for Crime and Justice Studies*, (13), 4–5. https://doi.org/10.1080/09627251.2013.833751

Lee, C.K. (1998). *Gender and the South China miracle: Two worlds of factory women*. University of California Press. https://doi.org/10.1525/9780520920040

Leidner, R. (1993). *Fast food, fast talk: The routinization of everyday life*. University of California Press. https://doi.org/10.1525/9780520914643

Li, P. (1998). *The Chinese in Canada*. Oxford University Press.

Li, P. (2003). *Destination Canada: Immigration debates and issues*. Oxford University Press.

Liang, L.-F. (2011). The making of an "Ideal" live-in migrant care worker: Recruiting, training, matching and disciplining. *Ethnic and Racial Studies*, 34(11), 1815–34. https://doi.org/10.1080/01419870.2011.554571

Lindquist, J. (2010). Labour recruitment, circuits of capital and gendered mobility: Reconceptualizing the Indonesian migration industry. *Pacific Affairs*, 83(1), 115–32. https://doi.org/10.5509/2010831115

Lopez, S.L. (2010). The remittance house: Architecture of migration in rural Mexico. *Building and Landscapes*, 17(2), 33–52. https://doi.org/10.1353/bdl.2010.a402208

Lorente, B.P., Duchêne, A., & Heller, M. (2012). The making of "Workers of the World": Language and the labor brokerage state. In A. Duchene & M. Heller (Eds.), *Language in Late Capitalism* (pp. 183–206). Routledge. https://doi.org/10.4324/9780203155868-9

Lott, J.T. (1976). Migration of a mentality: The Pilipino community. *Families in Society: The Journal of Contemporary Social Services*, 57(3), 165–72. https://doi.org/10.1177/104438947605700307

Louie, V. (2012). *Keeping the immigrant bargain: The costs and rewards of success in America* (1st ed.). Russell Sage Foundation.

Loveband, A. (2004). Positioning the product: Indonesian migrant women workers in Taiwan. *Journal of Contemporary Asia*, 34(3), 336–48. https://doi.org/10.1080/00472330480000141

Macdonald, C., & Sirianni, C. (1996). *Working in the service society*. Temple University Press.

Mahler, S. (1995). *American dreaming: Immigrant life on the margins*. Princeton University Press. https://doi.org/10.1515/9780691225166

Mann, J. (2012). The introduction of multiculturalism in Canada and Australia, 1960s–1970s. *Nations and Nationalism*, 18(3), 483–503. https://doi.org/10.1111/j.1469-8129.2012.00553.x

Marcus, G. (1995). Ethnography in/of the world system: The emergence of multi-sited ethnography. *Annual Review of Anthropology, 24*, 95–117. https://doi.org/10.1146/annurev.an.24.100195.000523

Martin, J., & Lewchuck, W. (2018). *The generation effect: Millennials, employment precarity and the 21st century workplace.* Poverty and Employment Precarity in Southern Ontario (PEPSO), Labour Studies, McMaster University http://hdl.handle.net/11375/30978.

McCollum, D., & Findlay, A. (2018). Oiling the wheels? Flexible labour markets and the migration industry. *Journal of Ethnic and Migration Studies, 44*(2), 1–17. https://doi.org/10.1080/1369183X.2017.1315505

McDowell, L. (2008). Thinking through work: Complex inequalities, constructions of difference and trans-national migrants. *Progress in Human Geography, 32*(4), 491–507. https://doi.org/10.1177/0309132507088116

McKay, D. (2012). *Global Filipinos: Migrants' lives in the virtual village.* Indiana University Press. https://doi.org/10.1355/sj28-21

Miranda, L. (2011). *Internalized colonization and decolonizing Mexican American youth* [Unpublished dissertation, The California School of Professional Psychology, San Francisco Campus, Allianz International University].

Nadal, K. (2011). Colonial mentality of Filipino Americans. In *Filipino American psychology: Handbook of theory, research, and clinical practice* (pp. 89–108). John Wiley & Sons In. https://doi.org/10.1002/9781118094747.ch4

Ng, R. (1992). Managing female immigration: A case of institutional sexism and racism. *Canadian Woman Studies, 12*(3), 20–3 https://cws.journals.yorku.ca/index.php/cws/article/view/10484

Nieswand, B. (2014). The burgers' paradox: Migration and the transnationalization of social inequality in southern Ghana. *Ethnography,15*(4), 403–25. https://doi.org/10.1177/1466138113480575

Nititham, D. (2011). Migration as cultural capital: The ongoing dependence on overseas Filipino workers. *Malaysian Journal of Economic Studies, 48*(2), 185–201.

Ong, A. (2006). *Neoliberalism as exception: Mutations in citizenship and sovereignty.* Duke University Press. https://doi.org/10.1515/9780822387879

Ongley, P., & Pearson, D. (1995). Post-1945 international migration: New Zealand, Australia and Canada compared. *International Migration Review, 29*(3), 76. https://doi.org/10.1177/019791839502900308

Opiniano, J., & Ann, A. (2024, January 3). The Philippines' landmark labor export and development policy enters the next generation. *Migration Information Source.* https://www.migrationpolicy.org/article/philippines-migration-next-generation-ofw

Oxman-Martinez, J., Hanley, J., & Cheung, L. (2004). *Another look at the live-in caregiver program.* Metropolis Publication IM no. 24, Montreal.

Padilla, L. (1999). Social and legal repercussions of Latinos' colonized mentality. *University of Miami Law Review, 53*, 769–85.

Paerregaard, K. (2008). *Peruvian dispersed: A global ethnography of migration.* Lexington Books.

Park, K. (1997). *The Korean American dream: Immigrants and small business in New York City.* Cornell University Press. https://doi.org/10.7591/9781501724558

Parreñas, R. (2001). *Servants of globalization.* Stanford University Press.

Parreñas, R. (2015). *Servants of globalization* (2nd ed.). Stanford University Press. https://doi.org/10.1525/california/9780520294134.003.0004

Parreñas, R. (2021). Discipline and empower: The state governance of migrant domestic workers. *American Sociological Review, 86*(6), 1043–65. https://doi.org/10.1177/00031224211032906

Parreñas, R., Landolt, P., Goldring, L., Golash-Boza, T., & Silvey, R. (2021). Mechanisms of migrant exclusion: Temporary labour, precarious noncitizeship, and technologies of detention. *Population, Space and Place, 27*(5), e2488, 1–6. https://doi.org/10.1002/psp.2488.

Paul, A.M. (2011). Stepwise international migration: A multistage migration pattern for the aspiring migrant. *American Journal of Sociology, 116*(6), 1842–86. https://doi.org/10.1086/659641

Paul, A.M. (2017). *Multinational maids: Stepwise migration in a global labor market.* Cambridge University Press. https://doi.org/10.1525/california/9780520294134.003.0004

Penfold, S. (2008). *The donut: A Canadian history.* University of Toronto Press. https://doi.org/10.3138/9781442687929

Pinto, J. (2019). Federal government looking at partial labour mobility for temporary foreign workers. *CBC News – Windsor.*

Piore, M. (1979). *Birds of passage: Migrant labor in industrial societies.* Cambridge University Press. https://doi.org/10.1017/CBO9780511572210

Polanco, G. (2016). Consent behind the counter: Aspiring citizens and labour control under precarious (im)migration schemes. *Third World Quarterly, 37*(8), 1332–50. https://doi.org/10.1080/01436597.2015.1129892

Polanco, G. (2017). Culturally tailored workers for specialised destinations: Producing Filipino migrant subjects for export. *Identities: Global Studies in Culture and Power, 24*(1), 62–81. https://doi.org/10.1080/1070289X.2015.1091317

Polanco, G. (2019). Competition between labour-sending states and the branding of national workforces. *International Migration, 57*(4), 136–50. https://doi.org/10.1111/imig.12553

Polanco, G., & Zell, S. (2017). English as a border-drawing matter: Language and the regulation of migrant service worker mobility in international labor markets. *Journal of International Migration and Integration, 18,* 267–89. https://doi.org/10.1007/s12134-016-0478-9

Pratt, G. (2004). Between homes: Displacement and belonging for second generation Filipino-Canadian youth. *BC Studies, 140,* 41–68 https://doi.org/10.14288/bcs.v0i140.1689.

Preibisch, K. (2010). Pick your own labor: Migrant workers and flexibility in Canadian agriculture. *International Migration Review, 44,* 404–41. https://doi.org/10.1111/j.1747-7379.2010.00811.x

Preibisch, K., & Binford, L. (2007). Interrogating racialized global labour supply: An exploration of the racial/national replacement of foreign agricultural workers in Canada. *Canadian Review of Sociology, 1,* 5–36. https://doi.org/10.1111/j.1755-618X.2007.tb01146.x

Preibisch, K., & Encalada Grez, E. (2010). The other side of el Otro Lado: Mexican migrant women and labor flexibility in Canadian agriculture. *Signs: Journal of Women in Culture and Society, 35,* 289–316. https://doi.org/10.1086/605483

Premji, S., Shakya, Y., Spasevski, M., Merolli, J., Athar, S., & Immigrant Women & Precarious Employment Core Research Group. (2014, August). Precarious work experiences of racialized immigrant women in Toronto: A community-based study. *Just Labour,22,* 122–43. https://doi.org/10.25071/1705-1436.8

Reiter, E. (1996). *Making fast food: From the frying pan into the fryer.* McGill-Queen's University Press.

Reiter, E. (2001). 3 Fast-food in Canada: Working conditions, labour law and unionization. In T. Royle & B. Towers (Eds.), *Labour relations in the global fast-food industry* (pp. 30–47). Routledge. https://doi.org/10.4324/9780203005774

Reitz, J. (2004). Canada: Immigration and nation-building in the transition to a knowledge economy. In W. Cornelius, P. Martin, J.F. Hollifield, & T. Tsuda (Eds.), *Controlling immigration: A global perspective* (2nd ed., pp. 97–133). Stanford University Press.

Rodriguez, R. (2010). *Migrants for export: How the Philippine state brokers labor to the world.* University of Minnesota Press. https://doi.org/10.5749/minnesota/9780816665273.001.0001

Rodriguez, R., & Schwenken, H. (2013). Becoming a migrant at home: Subjectivation processes in migrant-sending countries prior to departure. *Population, Space and Place, 19,* 375–88. https://doi.org/10.1002/psp.1779

Rofel, L. (2007). *Desiring China: Experiments in neoliberalism, sexuality, and public culture.* Duke University Press. https://doi.org/10.2307/j.ctv11cw96m

Rogaly, B. (2008). Intensification of workplace regimes in British horticulture: The role of migrant workers. *Population, Space and Place, 14*(6), 497–510. https://doi.org/10.1002/psp.502

Rosenthal, P. (2004). Management control as an employee resource: The case of front-line service workers. *Journal of Management Studies, 41*(4), 601–22. https://doi.org/10.1111/j.1467-6486.2004.00446.x

Royle, T., & Towers, B. (2002). *Labour relations in the global fast-food industry.* Routledge https://doi.org/10.4324/9780203005774

Salazar, N. (2020). On imagination and imaginaries, mobility and immobility: Seeing the forest for the trees. *Culture & Psychology, 26*(4), 768–77. https://doi.org/10.1177/1354067X20936927

Salt, J., & Stein, J. (1997). Migration as a business: The case of trafficking. *International Migration,35*(4), 467–94. https://doi.org/10.1111/1468-2435.00023

Salzinger, L. (2003). *Genders in production: Making workers in Mexico's global factories.* University of California Press. https://doi.org/10.1525/9780520929302

Sana, M. (2005). Buying membership in the transnational community: Migrant remittances, social status, and assimilation. *Population Research and Policy Review, 24,* 231–61. https://doi.org/10.1007/s11113-005-4080-7

Sanchez, D., Stoto, I., Capielo Rosario, C., Genao, G., & Serrano, S.D. (2025). Adapting the colonial mentality scale for Mexican-origin emerging adults. *Journal of Counseling Psychology, 72*(2), 172–83. https://doi.org/10.1037/cou0000783

Sassen, S. (1998). *Globalization and its discontents.* New Press.

Schierup, C.-U., & Lund, A. (2011). The end of Swedish exceptionalism? Citizenship, neoliberalism and the politics of exclusion. *Race & Class, 53*(1), 45–64. https://doi.org/10.1177/0306396811406780

Schlosser, E. (2002). *Fast food nation: The dark side of the all-American meal.* Houghton Mifflin.

Schmalzbauer, L. (2005). Transamerican dreamers: The relationship of Honduran transmigrants to the American dream and consumer society. *Berkeley Journal of Sociology, 49,* 3–31.

Sewell, G., & Wilkinson, B. (1992). "Someone to Watch over Me": Surveillance, discipline and the just-in-time labour process. *Sociology, 26*(2), 271–89. https://doi.org/10.1177/0038038592026002009

Seymour, D. (2000). Emotional labour: A comparison between fast food and traditional service work. *International Journal of Hospitality Management, 19*(2), 159–71. https://doi.org/10.1016/S0278-4319(00)00009-8

Shachar, A. (2000). On citizenship and multicultural vulnerability. *Political Theory, 28*(1), 64–89. https://doi.org/10.1177/0090591700028001004

Sharma, N. (2002). Immigrant and migrant workers in Canada: Labour movements, racism and the expansion of globalization. *Canadian Woman Studies, 21/22*(4/1), 18–25.

Sharma, N. (2006). *Home economics: Nationalism and the making of "Migrant Workers" in Canada.* University of Toronto Press. https://doi.org/10.3138/9781442675810

Sherman, R. (2007). *Class acts: Service and inequality in luxury hotels.* University of California Press. https://doi.org/10.1525/9780520939608

Simons, A. (2010). *Immigration and Canada: Global and transnational perspective.* Canadian Scholars Press.

Small, I. (2012). "Over There": Imaginative displacements in Vietnamese remittance gift economies. *Journal of Vietnamese Studies, 7*(3), 157–83. https://doi.org/10.1525/vs.2012.7.3.157

Social Weather Stations (2022). *Fourth quarter 2022 social weather survey.* Quezon City, Philippines. https://www.sws.org.ph/swsmain/artcldisp page/?artcsyscode=ART-20230119062833

Soysal, N.Y. (1994). *Limits of citizenship: Migrants and postnational membership in Europe.* University of Chicago Press.

Spaan, E., & van Naerssen, T. (2018). Migration decision-making and migration industry in the Indonesia-Malaysia corridor. *Journal of Ethnic and Migration Studies, 44*(4), 680–95. https://doi.org/10.1080/1369183X.2017.1315523

Stalker, P. (2000). *Workers without frontiers: The impact of globalization on international migration.* Lynne Rienner Publishers.

Tadiar, N.X.M. (2004). *Fantasy-production: Sexual economies and other Philippine consequences for the new world order.* Hong Kong University Press.

Talwar, J. (2018). *Fast food, fast track: Immigrants, big business and the American dream.* Taylor and Francis. https://doi.org/10.4324/9780429500541

Tannock, S. (2001). *Youth at work: The unionized fast food and grocery workplace.* Temple University Press.

Thai, H.C. (2014). *Insufficient funds: The culture of money in low-wage transnational families.* Stanford University Press.

Thobani, S. (2007). *Exalted subjects: Studies in the making of race and nation in Canada.* University of Toronto Press.

Tomlinson, K. (2014). McDonald's foreign workers call it "Slavery". *CBC News,* Edmonton: Go Public.

Tourism Industry Association of Canada. (2014). *2014 gateway to growth: Travel & tourism labour force report.* TIAC. https://tiac-aitc.ca/_Library/TIAC_Publications/TIAC_Travel_and_Tourism_Labour_Force_Report_FINAL.pdf

Tourism Industry Association of Canada. (2015). *Letter to Bryan May, MP, Chair—Standing Committee on Human Resources, Skills and Social Development and the Status of Persons with Disabilities. Re: Tourism industry submission on the temporary foreign worker program review.* TIAC.

Traore, R. (2004). Colonialism continued: African students in an urban high school in America. *Journal of Black Studies, 34*(3), 348–69. https://doi.org/10.1177/0021934703258986

Tyner, J. (1996a). The gendering of Philippine international labor migration. *The Professional Geographer, 48*(4), 405–16. https://doi.org/10.1111/j.0033-0124.1996.00405.x

Tyner, J. (1996b). Constructions of Filipina migrant entertainers. *Gender, Place & Culture, 3*(1), 77–94. https://doi.org/10.1080/09663699650021954

Tyner, J. (2004). *Made in the Philippines: Gendered discourses and the making of migrants*. Routledge. https://doi.org/10.4324/9780203799895

Voorn, B., Genugten, M., & Thiel, S. (2019). Multiple principals, multiple problems: Implications for effective governance and a research agenda for joint service delivery. *Public Administration, 97*(3), 671–85. https://doi.org/10.1111/padm.12587

Vosko, L. (2000). *Temporary work: The gendered rise of a precarious employment relationship*. University of Toronto Press. https://doi.org/10.3138/9781442680432

Vosko, L. (2008). Temporary work in transnational labour regulation: SER-centrism and the risk of exacerbating gendered precariousness. *Social Indicators Research, 88*(1), 131–45. https://doi.org/10.1007/s11205-007-9206-3

Vosko, L.F. (2009). *Managing the margins: Gender, citizenship and the international regulation of precarious employment.* (1st ed., pp. vii–xvii). Oxford University Press. https://doi.org/10.1093/acprof:oso/9780199574810.001.0001

Wang, C. (2013). Place of desire: Skilled migration from Mainland China to post-colonial Hong Kong. *Asia Pacific Viewpoint, 54*(3), 388–97. https://doi.org/10.1111/apv.12032

Yanagisako, S.J. (2002). *Producing culture and capital: Family firms in Italy.* Princeton University Press. https://doi.org/10.1515/9780691214221

Zell, S. (2018). *Outsourcing the border: Recruiters and sovereign power in labour migration to Canada* [Unpublished dissertation, UBC].

Index